MARSHALL MILES
TEACHES
LOGICAL BRIDGE

By the author of
"How to Win at Duplicate Bridge"
and
"All Fifty-two Cards"

Marshall Miles
TEACHES

LOGICAL BRIDGE

A Novel Approach to
Championship Principles of
Bidding and Playing Your Hand

 An Exposition-Banner Book

EXPOSITION PRESS   NEW YORK

EXPOSITION PRESS INC.

386 Park Avenue South   New York, N.Y. 10016

FIRST EDITION

EP 45735

Contents

Contents

Introduction

THERE seems to be a general impression that it takes a "mathematical mind"—whatever that is—to be a good bridge player. Perhaps one hand out of a hundred requires an elementary knowledge of probabilities or percentages to play to the best advantage. The rest of the time the arithmetic you learned in the second grade will suffice. If a "mathematical mind" means a logical mind, of course the general impression is correct. But the reasoning required at bridge is seldom complex. On most hands even an average player can understand the reasoning process he should have followed—once it is pointed out to him. The fascinating thing about bridge is that there is almost always a clue to the right play, and usually to the right bid, if you interpret correctly all the available information.

Most books for beginners give lots of rules to memorize: this bid shows so many rebid points; that bid shows so many support points; a rebiddable suit must be no weaker than K J x x x; minimum adequate trump support is Q x x unless the suit has been rebid, in which case Q x will be sufficient, and so on. It is necessary to learn some rules, but it seems to me that bridge can be made a terrible chore when the emphasis is on memorizing rules. A person who learns bridge that way is lost when confronted with a situation not covered by a rule, or when common sense should make it obvious that the rule does not apply. Also, it is easy to confuse one rule with another. Consequently in this book the emphasis is on *why* the rules apply.

The usual approach is to start out by telling you how to

count points—how many you need to open and how many to respond. You memorize these rules without understanding the reasons. Even when you look at the two hands with which the author says you belong in four hearts (because there is a combined total of twenty-six points) you don't really know whether four hearts is the right contract because you have no idea how the play should go.

This book reverses the usual order. You are taught how to play the hand first. When you learn to bid, you can see what your objectives are and can figure out anew what the point count requirements must be in case you happen to forget them. I say with confidence, if you really study this book, one chapter at a time, and do all the quizzes, when you finish you will be better than 95 per cent of the bridge players throughout the world.

Now for a word about the form. I thought it would make the book more palatable to have a set of characters and some dialogue, rather than the traditional textbook style; also, it would aid the learning process if the reader would try to answer each question as it is posed before reading on. I still think so despite the comments from some of my friends who criticized the "story" as though it were a novel. Admittedly, there is no climax and there is no plot. Very little time and effort have been spent to make the characters plausible. They merely serve the function of asking questions, making a few mistakes, and answering me so that I do not have to do all the talking.

One of my lady partners thought Barbara was so conceited as to be intolerable, and if I had used her for a model she resented it. Another said that *no one*, absolutely *no one* (looking directly at me), was as bright as Barbara, and it would not be possible for anyone to learn bridge so quickly. As it happens, I think two or three persons I know could have learned that fast, but I agree with my friend that Barbara is hardly a typical beginner; otherwise you might get the impression that you were hopelessly stupid by comparing her with yourself. Anyway, it is not how fast you learn that is important; it is how *well* you learn and how long you can continue to improve. Of course, I may be prejudiced, since I am rather slow at learning new games myself.

This book starts right from the beginning, telling you the ranks of the suits and how to deal. However, it moves along at a pace that will be difficult to keep up with if you are really and truly a beginner. I think you can do it, but you will have to put forth an extra effort.

This book is primarily designed for people who have played party bridge or perhaps duplicate a few times and know the fundamentals of the game. Some of these fundamentals may have been learned incorrectly, or you may not have known the reasons for some of the things you were doing. Consequently everything is explained from the beginning. However, even in my story, Henry and Alice had played before, and Barbara did not learn everything about the play from my lessons alone. She had to "fudge" a bit, and Jerry never did become very proficient in the play or defense. It helps to have someone sitting over your shoulder telling you when you have made a mistake, but the only way I know to become proficient in the play is to get lots of practice.

Now that I have admitted that I am not in competition with Hemingway, I hope you will not let the plot or lack of plot distract you. Study this book just as my fictitious pupils were advised to study. When I tell them to make up hands to illustrate a principle, try to do so yourself. When I ask a question, try to figure out the answer before you read their answer or my comments to it.

Why should you do as I tell you? Because the rewards are great. It is very satisfying to play a good game of bridge—so much so that bridge players often lose their sense of values and neglect other activities of greater importance. I hope you will not do that; in fact, you might be better off if you had never heard of the game. However, if you are going to play it, you might as well learn to play it well. You now have the means at your disposal.

MARSHALL MILES
TEACHES
LOGICAL BRIDGE

CHAPTER 1

How It All Began

My secretary buzzed me, and I picked up the intercom. "A Mr. Henry Harvey just phoned and said something about playing bridge—that his whole family wanted to play. I told him you had clients in your office, and had to leave for court shortly. He left his phone number and asked that you call him later."

"Henry Harvey? I don't know anyone by that name. Well, give me his number and I'll call him this afternoon."

I do not know why, but my curiosity was aroused. It was the part about his family that seemed unusual. Sometimes a stranger passing through town will phone to ask when and where the local duplicate tournaments are held. Perhaps this fellow had his whole family with him. Perhaps he was someone I would recognize at sight—remembering names is not my strong point. There was no purpose in speculating about the reason for his call. I tried to dismiss it from my mind in order to tend to the business at hand.

When I called that afternoon, the answering voice of Mr. Harvey was unfamiliar. After the usual greeting he explained: "I retired a few months ago. My wife and I have just come out from New York City for an extended vacation and visit with our daughter and son-in-law. My wife took a few bridge lessons twenty-five years ago from Ely Culbertson, and I played a little bridge in the Army. However, since it has been so long ago for both of us, we feel that we need to start right from the beginning. Our kids—I mean my daughter and son-in-law—would like to learn with us, and they are truly beginners. I heard that you taught a bridge class a year or so ago, and I wondered if you would be interested in giving us lessons."

"I don't think so," I replied. "I have taught only one class, and it was for advanced players. I hardly know how to teach beginners, and it would require quite a bit of preparation on my part. Besides, the cost would be prohibitive for just four people. My suggestion is that you go into Los Angeles once a week for class lessons. I know an excellent teacher, and if you wish, I'll find out whether he has any beginners' classes in the evening."

"No, we don't want class lessons. One reason is that my son-in-law occasionally has to work evenings, and he would have to miss several lessons if they were given the same evening each week. Besides, it doesn't make sense for four people to spend three hours traveling in order to take a one-hour lesson. Our time is worth more to us than the money we would save.

"What I have in mind," he continued, "would not tie anyone down. Whenever we want a lesson, and if you are free, you can come out to the house for dinner and give us a lesson afterward. My wife and I will be out here about six months and hope to take one lesson a week. I'll pay fifty dollars per lesson and furnish any equipment you need, so that you won't have any overhead. If you don't think fifty dollars is a fair price, I'll pay more. But I think you will find this an interesting challenge and more fun than teaching a large class."

"Okay," I agreed, "I'll try it. Frankly, I have spoken to few people who knew so well what they wanted and why they wanted it. What you propose is quite satisfactory."

We arranged for the first lesson to be the following Thursday evening at the home of Jerry Franklin, Mr. Harvey's son-in-law. After I hung up I wondered what sort of people my pupils would be. Before his retirement Mr. Harvey must have been a businessman, probably an executive, accustomed to ordering others around. Apparently money was no problem with him. He would have paid a hundred dollars per lesson as readily as fifty, but there was something about his frank approach which removed all temptation to take advantage of it.

"Interesting challenge," he had said. How much could I teach four intelligent people about bridge in a six-month period? Should I encourage them to play duplicate between lessons, or should I try to keep them away from any "corrupting" influence so that they would learn only what I told them? I thought of the play *My Fair Lady*, in which a girl selling flowers on the street becomes a polished, sophisticated young lady within an unbelievably short time. With an intensive approach and a receptive attitude miracles could be accomplished in a six-month period. On the other hand, the impression which I received might be entirely false. Even though Mr. Harvey might have the willingness and determination to become a good bridge player, the rest of the family might delay his progress. Further speculation was useless; I had better start deciding what to teach a group of beginners, and how much they could expect to learn in one evening.

The Franklins' home was a lovely modern house in the nicest part of town. As soon as we were introduced Mr. Harvey said, "We are going to see a lot of each other. 'Mr. Harvey' makes me feel as old as the hills. Call me Henry. In fact, let's all use first names."

Henry was the dynamic sort of person I had expected him to be. His wife, Alice, was quiet and retiring. They both conformed to the mental image I had had of them. This was quite unusual, since I am very poor at visualizing what a person will be like from his telephone voice, or what type of woman will marry a certain type of man. The most pleasant surprise was Barbara Franklin. She was an extremely attractive young lady who would have no trouble finding bridge partners regardless of her prowess at bridge. She also appeared bright and enthusiastic, although I have learned to distrust or discount my first impression of an attractive woman.

Only Jerry Franklin was a disappointment to me. He was a nice enough chap, but there was something about his attitude that denoted a lack of alertness or interest—as though he had joined the foursome to be accommodating rather than because of a strong desire to learn to play bridge. But, as both of the

Franklins appeared to be in their mid-twenties, Jerry ought to have something on the ball to have acquired so nice a home at his age. Why should he be enthusiastic about bridge before he knew what it was like? Perhaps his interest would become aroused upon learning to play.

Jerry and Barbara were honest-to-goodness beginners. Barbara had played gin rummy and canasta; Jerry had played pinochle and poker. Neither had ever watched a bridge game before, so it was necessary to explain even the most basic matters.

"Bridge," I explained, "is played with a deck of fifty-two cards, thirteen cards in each suit. The rank of the cards from highest to lowest is ace, king, queen, jack, ten, nine, eight, and so on down to the two. The ace, king, queen, jack and ten are called 'honor cards,' or simply 'honors.' Cards lower than the ten are called 'spot cards.' The rank of the four suits from highest to lowest is spades, hearts, diamonds, clubs. The rank of the suits is important only during the bidding. In the play of the hand the deuce of clubs can win a trick from the ace of spades. Do you have any questions so far?"

"I assume," asked Jerry, "that everyone bids what he thinks he can make before the play begins, just like in pinochle?"

"Frankly, I don't know enough about pinochle to answer your question accurately," I replied. "Bridge is a partnership game, unlike poker or some forms of pinochle. You and your partner try to bid what you can make with your combined assets. I think in pinochle, or at least in many card games, you bid just what you have to in order to take the bid away from the opponents and to choose the trump suit. In contract bridge you frequently bid more than necessary to buy the bid from the opponents. Generally, the more you bid the more you score for making your bid. The rest of you know what I mean by choosing the trump suit. We shall discuss that very shortly, Barbara. First cut for partners and seats, and I'll demonstrate the mechanics of dealing, bidding and playing."

"You said, 'cut for partners,'" Henry interrupted. "In the

Army my buddy and I used to challenge other players. We always played together."

"I was reading about the international match the Italians won," Barbara added. "Didn't the Americans just play with other Americans against the players from other countries?"

"Yes," I replied. "In important tournaments the players choose their partners in advance. In rubber bridge, which is what you are learning to play, you may also choose your partners in advance and keep them all evening if you wish. However, it is customary in a social game to 'cut,' or draw cards, for partners and to change partners several times during the evening. You will note that the cards have been spread out like a fan, face down, on the table. Each of you pick a card."

Alice drew the five of clubs, Henry the king of spades, Barbara the jack of clubs, and Jerry the jack of hearts.

"Henry and Jerry are partners since they drew the two highest cards," I said. "Because Henry drew the highest card, Henry has the choice of seats and will deal the cards. Jerry will sit opposite Henry. You ladies will occupy the two vacant chairs." The players then arranged themselves around the table.

"Why is Jerry's jack higher than mine?" asked Barbara. "I thought you said the rank of the suits only affects the bidding."

"You are right. I did say that, and you were alert to notice and remember. Occasionally I will state a general rule without mentioning minor exceptions to confuse you—but I didn't expect to get caught so soon."

Henry began to shuffle the cards. He then handed them to Alice, on his right, to "cut." She picked up approximately half the deck and placed it beside the original stack. Henry then placed the original stack on top of the half removed.

"Why did you do that?" asked Barbara.

"Someone might have seen the bottom card during the shuffle," answered Henry. "Now no one knows where the card is."

Henry proceeded to deal by handing the cards out, face down, in a clockwise direction, starting with Barbara on his left.

While he was dealing I asked Jerry to shuffle the other deck and to place it on his right, ready for Barbara to deal next time.

"Bridge can be played with one deck of cards," I explained. "However, two decks with different backs are normally used in order to save time. While dealer deals, his partner shuffles. Incidentally, the dealer should deal the last card to himself. If he fails to do so, there has been a misdeal, and he must deal again. The typical reasons for a misdeal are that two cards have stuck together or a card has dropped on the floor. Another possibility is that someone forgot to remove the jokers."

When the deal had been completed, each player picked up his own hand and sorted the cards into suits. The diagram shows what the hands looked like.

"At this stage I shall tell you what you should bid, just so that you will get an idea of the mechanics of the game. Henry, you are the first to bid, as you were the dealer. You should say 'pass,' which means that you make no bid. Barbara should pass also. Jerry should bid one heart and Alice should pass. Henry, what would you have bid with your hand when you were in the Army?"

"One spade."

"That is right. Barbara, you should bid two clubs now. Say 'Two clubs.'"

"Two clubs."

I then explained that Jerry and Alice should pass and Henry should bid two spades. Everyone else would then pass. When three successive players pass, the bidding is over. The bidding always continues until there are three successive passes.

"What did those bids mean?" Barbara asked.

"Each bid was an offer to perform a contract. When Jerry bid one heart, he said in effect, 'If no one else bids, I promise to take one trick in excess of six tricks, with hearts as trumps.' South then offered to take one trick in excess of six tricks with spades as trumps. You offered to take two tricks in excess of six with clubs as trumps, and Henry outbid you with his higher ranking suit by offering to take eight tricks at spades. All bids are offers to take tricks in excess of six tricks. I'll explain what a trick is in just a moment. Henry's offer was accepted by the other players when they passed, and a contract was formed. For fulfilling his contract Henry and his partner will receive a reward. For failure to fulfill the terms of the contract, to take eight tricks, Henry and his partner will suffer a penalty.

"Since the last bid was two spades and Henry was the first

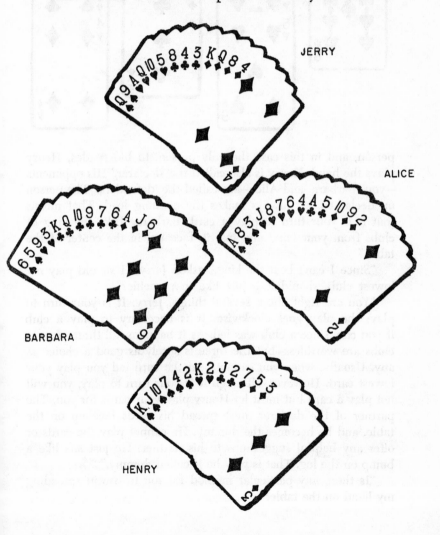

person, and in this case the only person, to bid spades, Henry plays the hand. Henry is also called the 'declarer.' His opponents —you, Barbara, and Alice—are called the 'defenders.' The person on declarer's left always makes the opening lead. That means that it is your turn to play a card, Barbara. Take the king of clubs from your hand and toss it, face up, in the center of the table."

"Since I can't beat the king," asked Jerry, "I should play my lowest club, shouldn't I—just like in pinochle?"

"You are right about several things, Jerry. It is your turn to play; the play goes clockwise. It is necessary to play a club if you can, since a club was led. As it happens, all three of your clubs are worthless—but the three is surely as good a choice as any. Usually, when you cannot beat the card led you play your lowest card. However, although it is your turn to play, you will not play a card but must let Henry play your cards for you. The partner of the declarer must spread his cards face up on the table, and he becomes the dummy. He cannot play the cards or offer any helpful suggestions to his partner. He just sits like a bump on the log. That is why he is called dummy."

"Is there any particular method for me to use in spreading my hand on the table?"

"Yes. The trump suit, in this case spades, must be on the declarer's left. That is, your right. Then you should have a red suit, a black suit, and a red suit. In other words you alternate color of suits. The highest card in each suit should be nearest to you and the cards should be placed in descending order."

The illustration at the top of page 20 shows what the dummy should look like. The hearts and diamonds could be interchanged.

The diagram below is the customary way to show the hands and the bidding. The names of the players have been replaced by compass points, but you will remember that Henry is South, Barbara is West, Jerry is North, and Alice is East.

Henry played the three of clubs from dummy, Alice won with the ace, and Henry played the two. Since Alice played the highest club, she won the "trick," which consists of one card from

♠ Q 9
♡ A Q 10 5
◇ K Q 8 4
♣ 8 4 3

♠ 6 5   ♠ A 8 3
♡ 9 3   **N**   ♡ J 8 7 6 4
◇ A J 6   **W   E** ◇ 10 9 2
♣ K Q 10 9 7 6 **S**   ♣ A 5

♠ K J 10 7 4 2
♡ K 2
◇ 7 5 3
♣ J 2

Bidding:

SOUTH	WEST	NORTH	EAST
P	P	1 ♡	P
1 ♠	2 ♣	P	P
2 ♠	P	P	P

each player. She turned these four cards face down on the table
and stacked them in front of her. It would have been equally
proper for Barbara to gather in the trick. Because Alice won
the trick it was her turn to lead to the second trick. The player
(or dummy) who wins a trick always leads to the next trick.
Alice played the five of clubs.

"I thought Mom had the ace by itself until she led a club
back," Barbara said. "Why did she play her ace, since my king
would have won the trick, and we are partners?"

"Hmm. That is difficult to explain. She did it so that you
could lead the third round of clubs. If she had played low, she
would have won the second trick, but would have no more clubs
to lead. Don't worry about it. I'll explain that type of play to
you later. Apparently your mother still remembers some things
about the game, even if it was twenty-five years ago that she
took lessons."

Barbara led the ten of clubs to the third trick and Alice discarded a heart.

"Doesn't Alice have to play a trump if she has one?" asked
Jerry.

"No," I replied. "A trump does not have to be played unless
a trump is led. In this case Barbara's ten was the highest remaining club, and it would not accomplish anything for Alice to
trump it. She should save her trumps in the hope of putting them
to better use."

"What about Henry? Does he have to take the trick if he
can?"

"No. A player always has the option of refusing to take a
trick. Sometimes by giving away one trick or delaying the winning of a trick it is possible to win two or three additional
tricks. However, in this case Henry has no reason for refusing
the trick. In fact it would be a mistake not to take it. His two
of trumps will beat the ten of clubs. A trump always beats a
card other than a trump. If Henry had played any card except
a trump the ten of clubs would have won the trick. The highest
card of the suit led wins the trick unless one or more trumps are
played, in which case the highest trump played wins the trick."

"If I had played the three or eight of spades, Henry would have overtrumped me," said Alice, "and there was no point in trumping with the ace, since it would always take a trick."

"Henry, how would you play this hand?"

"I would start leading out the trumps."

"Why?"

"So that the opponents couldn't trump my good tricks."

"That is correct. Suppose that Henry starts playing his high hearts. Barbara would trump the third round. Of course, Henry could trump dummy's high heart with a high trump, but in that case he would be wasting his high cards by playing a high card from both hands."

Henry led the four of spades to the queen, won by Alice's ace. She returned a trump. Henry won in his hand with the ten and played the king. That took care of his opponent's trumps. He then played the king of hearts from his hand (low from dummy), followed by a low heart to dummy's ace. On the good queen of hearts he discarded a diamond, then led the king of diamonds. Barbara won with the ace and returned a club. Henry trumped and then led a diamond to the queen, and had a trump left for the last trick. Henry had taken nine tricks, receiving credit for tricks taken by either him or dummy. The defenders had taken four tricks. Consequently Henry "made" his contract with a trick to spare. I pointed out that Henry and Jerry would get their bonus for fulfilling the contract, and I wrote down the score but did not stop at this time to explain it.

"Barbara, take the deck of cards Jerry shuffled a while ago. Give them to Henry to cut, and then deal them out. Alice, shuffle the deck you have just played and place them on your right, ready for Jerry to deal next time."

Barbara dealt the following hand:

```
                         NORTH
                         ♠ K Q 8 4
                         ♡ J 7 6
        WEST             ◇ 5 3              EAST
        ♠ 9 7 5          ♣ J 9 8 4          ♠ J 6 3
        ♡ A K Q 8 4 2                       ♡ 9 5
        ◇ A 6                               ◇ K 10 7 4
        ♣ A 7            SOUTH              ♣ Q 6 5 2
                         ♠ A 10 2
                         ♡ 10 3
                         ◇ Q J 9 8 2
                         ♣ K 10 3
```

"Your correct opening bid is one heart, Barbara."

"You told us that the more we bid, the better score we get if we make it," said Barbara. "It looks to me as though I ought to make eight tricks at hearts all by myself unless one of my opponents has four hearts or more. And if I get any help from partner I ought to make nine or ten tricks. Why don't I bid two or three hearts?"

"I don't want to explain the bidding to you yet, but you are right in a way. This is a good hand. However, when you open the bidding, your partner will bid with very little strength, and you can take strong action next time."

Jerry passed without being told, and Alice bid one no trump.

"What does 'no trump' mean?" asked Jerry.

"It means there will be no trump suit if the final bid is no trump. Consequently, whoever plays the highest card of the suit led will always win the trick."

"How does no trump rank with the suits?" asked Barbara. "Mom bid one no trump, which apparently means that no trump outranks hearts."

"That is right. No trump ranks higher than any suit. Your mother could have bid one spade as well as one no trump. If she had wanted to bid clubs or diamonds, she would have had to bid two clubs or two diamonds."

Henry passed and it was Barbara's turn to bid.

"You can hardly be expected to know what to bid because

you don't know what your partner's no trump response means, and you don't know how to score. You receive approximately the same score for bidding and making three no trump as for bidding and making four hearts. Your correct bid is three no trump."

Everyone else passed, and Henry started to lead.*

"It is my lead, isn't it?" asked Jerry. "Barbara bid three no trump, and I am on her left."

"Alice bid no trump first, so she is the declarer. Consequently it is Henry's lead."

Henry led the queen of diamonds. Barbara spread her hand as dummy. Since there was no trump suit, it did not matter which suit was on the left. Alice won the first trick with dummy's ace. She led the three top hearts in succession. After three rounds of hearts, no one but dummy had any hearts, and the remaining three hearts all took tricks. Alice cashed six heart tricks, the ace of clubs, and king of diamonds—then lost the last four tricks. (To "cash" is to play a winner.)

"It would never have occurred to me to play this hand in no trump with all those beautiful hearts," said Barbara. "Yet, now that I see how the play went, it looks easier to take nine tricks at no trump than ten tricks at hearts. The only way the opponents could have defeated us was to take the first five spade tricks. Or for one opponent to hold four or five hearts."

"If one of us had held four or five hearts, you couldn't have made either three no trump or four hearts," Henry commented. "So you would still be no worse off in no trump."

"As Barbara pointed out," I said, "assuming that the heart suit will 'run,' the only thing that can defeat three no trump is for the opponents to take the first five spade tricks. And even if

_____
* The complete bidding is shown in the following diagram. "P" stands for "pass."

WEST	NORTH	EAST	SOUTH
1 ♡	P	1 NT	P
3 NT	P	P	P

Jerry held five spades, Henry might have led a diamond just as he did. Remember, Henry must make his opening lead before seeing the dummy, and he may often fail to make the best lead. With these two hands, there is no chance to make four hearts unless someone misdefends. I haven't tried to explain when you should play no trump and when you should play in a suit, but you can see the advantage in playing no trump with certain types of hands."

Jerry dealt the next hand, which was as follows:

		NORTH		
		♠ 7 5		
		♡ J 10 4		
		◇ A K Q 8 3 2		
WEST		♣ K 4		EAST
♠ K 2				♠ A J 10 3
♡ K 6 5 3 2				♡ A 9 8 7
◇ 9 5 4		SOUTH		◇ 6
♣ A 8 6		♠ Q 9 8 6 4		♣ Q J 7 2
		♡ Q		
		◇ J 10 7		
		♣ 10 9 5 3		

I told the players to bid as indicated:

NORTH	EAST	SOUTH	WEST
1 ◇	DBL	P	2 ♡
P	4 ♡	P	P
P			

"We had a new type of bid introduced on this hand," I explained. "When Alice doubled, that was supposed to mean, 'I don't think you can make one diamond. Let's double the stakes.' Actually, many bids have a meaning other than their natural meaning. We call these bids 'conventional bids.' Alice did not really want to defend against one diamond, doubled. What she wanted was for Barbara to bid her longest suit. Many years ago someone decided that it would be more useful to use a double for this purpose than to attempt to penalize the opponents at the one-level. But if Henry, Barbara and Jerry had passed the double, the final contract would be one diamond, doubled."

"Where does the double rank compared to a suit or no trump?" asked Barbara.

"The double does not have any rank. Over the double, South could have bid anything he would have bid without the double plus one additional bid, a redouble. A redouble is supposed to mean, 'I think you are crazy. Let's double the double or quadruple the stakes.' Oh, I see what was bothering you, Barbara. You could have bid just one heart. The reason for bidding two hearts was to show a pretty good hand. Remember, the more you bid the greater the reward for making your bid, as a general rule."

"My hand doesn't look as good to me as Mom's or Jerry's hand. Why is it worth a jump bid?"

"Because it is stronger than your partner has a right to expect under the circumstances, since both she and Jerry have shown pretty good hands; also, because you know that *combined* strength of the partnership is fairly high. Whether a hand is considered good or bad depends upon the bidding of the other players. However, it will be several lessons before you will fully understand why that is true."

"How do we know when a double has its natural meaning?" asked Jerry.

"That is a very complicated problem which you could not understand now even if I were to explain it. All that I want you to learn now is that there is such a bid. Let's continue with the play."

Jerry led the king of diamonds and Barbara trumped with the seven.

"How many trumps do your opponents have, Barbara?"

"Five."

"How did you arrive at that figure?"

"The dummy has three and I have five, so I subtracted eight from thirteen since there are thirteen cards in each suit."

"Your method is correct, but you forgot one detail. The dummy had four hearts. You just trumped with one of them."

"What a stupid mistake I made!" said Barbara, blushing.

"No, that is a very easy mistake to make. You learn by making mistakes. Remember the hand that Henry played? We said that he should draw the opponents' trumps as fast as he could. Does that seem like a good idea here?"

"It does if I can draw them in two leads, but I still have a little diamond to trump. Besides," she continued, her face lighting up, "if two leads do not draw the opponents' trumps, the remaining trump or trumps will be good, and they will take tricks anyway. The purpose in drawing trumps is to prevent the opponents from trumping my high cards with their small trumps, isn't it?"

"Yes, that is right."

Barbara played the ace and king of trumps, then trumped her remaining diamond. She led the queen of clubs, losing to Jerry's king.

"All you can take now is your high trump," she said.

"That concludes the rubber," I announced. "You don't know what a rubber is yet, but it is time for you to draw again for partners. Even if the gentlemen draw the two high cards or the two low cards, they will split up. On second thought, I think we have covered enough ground for one lesson. Do you have any questions?"

"What is a 'ruff'?" asked Jerry.

"'Ruff' is both a verb and a noun. It means to play a trump on a trick when you cannot follow suit or it may refer to the trump thus played. I said that Barbara trumped two small diamonds in the last hand, but it would have been equally correct to say that she 'ruffed' them.

"Now," I went on, "if you have no more questions, let me ask you a few. How many tricks must declarer take to make six spades?"

"Twelve" was their immediate answer.

"How many tricks to make three diamonds?"

"Nine."

"How many tricks to make three diamonds, doubled?"

"Nine."

"How many tricks do the defenders have to take to defeat a three diamond contract?"

"Five."

"Do you know what 'set' means?"

"It means to defeat the contract," answered Alice and Henry.

"The contract is four hearts, and the opening lead is the queen of diamonds. How many cards can possibly win this trick?"

"Fifteen," replied Barbara. "The ace or king of diamonds and all thirteen trumps."

"Very good. Till our next lesson, practice dealing out hands. Decide what the final contract should be after looking at all four hands, and try playing out the hands to best advantage for both sides. You will discover several principles of play and defense that way which will stick with you better than if I were to explain them to you. Good night."

CHAPTER 2

Play of the Hand

THE next lesson was on the following Wednesday. I was greeted like a son returning home from the war. Such enthusiasm! So many questions! They had been very badly bitten by the bridge bug.

"Wait, don't be so impatient," I said, laughing. "You can't learn the game in two easy lessons. However, I'll answer your questions about 'finesses,' since that is part of the lesson for this evening.

"Suppose that the heart suit is distributed as follows:

	NORTH	
WEST	A Q	EAST
K 10 x x		J 9 x x
	SOUTH	
	x x x	

"If North leads hearts, how many heart tricks can North-South take, Jerry?"

"One. If North leads the ace, West will play small and save the king to capture the queen. If North leads the queen, West will win right away."

"Suppose that South leads to the first heart trick. How many tricks will North-South take?"

"Two. Because if West plays small, the queen will win, while if he plays the king, North will play the ace—I mean South will play the ace from dummy."

"It is all right to say 'North will play the ace.' In bridge terminology we often say that dummy plays a card, even though we know that declarer actually plays dummy's cards for him. Also, you must have been reading the bridge column in the newspaper or you wouldn't know that South is the declarer and North is dummy in most bridge diagrams. Returning to the problem of finessing, suppose that the East and West heart holdings were exchanged. How many tricks could North and South take?"

"Do you mean, if South leads to the first heart trick?"

"Yes."

"Just one. But if East were to lead, North would take two tricks."

"Right. That illustrates the tremendous advantage in playing last. What advantage, if any, is there in playing first?"

"You can choose which suit to lead."

"When playing bridge, if you were South you would see only your own cards and dummy's cards. Either East or West might have the king of hearts. Some of the time you could take two tricks by leading from the South hand toward the ace-queen; other times you could only take one trick. At least by leading from the South hand you have a chance to take two tricks; usually you will still win a trick with the ace later, when the queen loses to the king. Leading toward the ace-queen, and playing the queen when West plays low, is called 'finessing.' The finesse will win or lose depending upon who has the king.

"Suppose that the contract is three no trump. West leads the king of clubs, and the North-South hands are as follows:

NORTH
♠ A x x x
♡ A Q
♢ K J 10 x x
♣ A x

SOUTH
♠ J x x
♡ x x x
♢ A Q x x
♣ x x x

"How many tricks can you count for sure, Alice?"

"Eight—five diamond tricks and three more aces."

"How many do you need for your contract?"

"Nine."

"What is your best chance for the ninth trick?"

"The heart finesse."

"How often would you expect the heart finesses to work?"

"About half the time. Each opponent is equally likely to have the king of hearts."

"Suppose that the opening lead is a club. How would you play the hand?"

"Upon winning with the ace of clubs, I would take my five diamond tricks and then—no, I would take just four diamond tricks, ending up in my own hand so as to be able to take the heart finesse. If I were to take all five diamond tricks I would be stuck in the dummy and would eventually have to lead away from the ace-queen of hearts."

"Do all of you see how declarer must plan ahead so as to be able to lead hearts from the South hand?"

"Yes."

"Henry, can you give us other examples of finesses? If so, explain how the finesse should be taken."

Henry laid out the following combinations:

NORTH	NORTH	NORTH	NORTH	NORTH
A x x x	A 10 9 x	K x	x x	x x x

SOUTH	SOUTH	SOUTH	SOUTH	SOUTH
K J x	Q J x x	x x x	K J	K J 10

"I could construct more examples, but they would just be variations of those already given. In the first example, the lead should come from the North hand, and if East plays small, the jack is finessed. The ace could be played first, and that might be how North obtains the lead. Low to the ace, and low back to the king-jack.

"In the second example South leads the queen, intending to

play small from the North hand unless West covers with the king. If the queen wins the trick, the jack will be led next time. That way declarer can take four tricks provided West has the king."

"Why not lead low to the nine the first time instead of leading the queen?" I asked.

"That would be all right; that would still be a finesse. But if the finesse should work, the lead would be in the North hand, and I would have to discontinue playing the suit till the South hand had regained the lead."

"Your third combination is not usually called a finesse," I said, "but according to my definition it is a finesse. The fact that you used it indicates an understanding of the problem involved. Naturally, you are going to lead toward the king."

"What is your definition of a finesse?" asked Alice.

"It is not a very technical one. A finesse is the act of leading toward one or more high cards with the intention of varying third hand's play depending upon what second hand does. For example, when you lead toward the king, you intend to play the king if West plays small, but to play small if West plays the ace. An element in any finesse is the expectation, or at least hope, that second hand, rather than fourth hand, will hold a certain key card. Let's let Henry continue to explain his examples."

"In the next example, the lead should be from the North hand. If East plays small, South must guess whether to play the king or the jack. If he thinks East has the ace, South should play the king. If he thinks East has the queen, South should play the jack. When East has both honors or neither honor, South's play is immaterial—but in the former case it is still important for the lead to come from the North hand."

Barbara now spoke up. "Dad, you said, 'If South thinks East has the ace . . .' or 'If South thinks East has the queen . . .' Did you mean to imply that South may have reason to know or believe something about an opponent's hand, or is it just a matter of guesswork?"

"I'd better pass your question on to our teacher," Henry replied.

"Your father stated the matter very accurately," I said. "Declarer may have good reason to believe that certain honors lie with one opponent rather than with the other. I doubt that I will explain in detail in this course of lessons how declarer can tell, because it is too difficult a subject for beginners. A general answer is that the bidding and discarding will give declarer important clues. A player who has bid is more likely than his passing partner to have a particular high card. Or if two high cards are missing, the player who has bid probably has the higher card, if not both. In the hand just given, you are missing the ace and queen. If West has bid you would usually play him for the ace and East for the queen. Now let's let Henry explain his last example."

"With the last combination I am sure to win one trick eventually, however I play. To get two tricks, I should lead toward the king-jack-ten and finesse the jack or ten. I hope the ten will win the trick or drive out the ace. In either case I'll return to the dummy by playing another suit, and I'll lead toward the king-jack, intending to finesse the jack. This would be a repeated finesse against the queen. There wouldn't be any guesswork whether to play the king or the jack the second time. If the ten did not lose to the queen the first time, I would know that East had the queen."

"That was a very good explanation, Henry. Now, Barbara, I am going to give you several combinations to consider, and I'll ask you some questions about them.

NORTH	NORTH	NORTH	NORTH
♠ A Q 10	♡ A J 10	◇ K Q 10	♣ Q x x
SOUTH	SOUTH	SOUTH	SOUTH
♠ x x x	♡ x x x	◇ x x x	♣ A x x

"In the first example, how would you play to take three tricks?"

"I would lead low and finesse the ten, hoping that West had both the king and the jack. If the ten wins the trick, I would return to my hand to finesse the queen."

"How do you play to take three tricks in the second example?"

Barbara answered after a few moments of thought, "You are pulling my leg. You can't take three tricks with this combination. Even if West has both missing honors, all he has to do is to play an honor, and he is bound to win one trick."

"How many tricks can you take with this combination?"

"It depends upon who has the king and queen. If West has them, I can take two tricks. If East has them, unless he leads the suit I can only take one trick."

"Suppose that East has one missing honor and West has the other?"

"Aha! I play this combination like the last one in order to win two tricks. I finesse the ten, and even if it loses to an honor I return to my hand and finesse again."

"How often would you expect to take two tricks with this combination?"

"Hmm—about seventy-five per cent of the time. I would win two tricks when West had the king-queen, when West had the king, and when West had the queen. I would lose two tricks only in one case out of four—when East had both missing honors. Is that right?"

"Yes, that is right. Furthermore, the method you used to determine your chances has many other applications. How would you play the third combination?"

"I would lead toward the North hand. If West plays small I would play the queen. If the queen loses to the ace, I would finesse the ten next time."

"Suppose that your queen wins. What would you do then?"

"I would return to my hand and lead toward the king-ten. If West played low I would—I started to say I would play the king, but it is really a guess, isn't it? Just like Dad's king-jack combination. If East were smart, he wouldn't take his ace the first time. In fact, he wouldn't have to be too smart if the king-queen-ten were in the dummy. If they were in my hand, West would not know whether to take his ace or not. For all he could tell, I might have just queen-small or king-small."

"You are going to be an excellent bridge player, Barbara! Some people play for years without being able to figure out that sort of thing. Suppose that the lead were in your hand and you had no possible way of leading from your hand again. How would you play to take two tricks in the suit?"

"I would finesse the ten, since that might be the play I would make eventually, anyway. If I were to play the queen, whether it won or lost, I would have to lead away from the king-ten later."

"All right, how would you play the last combination?"

"I would lead up to the queen, either before or after cashing the ace."

"Why not lead the queen for a finesse?"

"Because the queen would never take a trick that way. If East had the king he would capture my queen. If West had the king he could play it, and still the only trick I could win would be the ace."

"Can you give me a rule on when to lead a high card for a finesse?"

"You have to have the card below it, or at least some high cards that will be good if the high card is covered."

"Barbara, I think you've been holding out on me. Either you have played bridge before, or else you have been studying very industriously during the week."

"You said to deal hands, play them out, and try to discover some principles of play. That's what I did. Besides," she admitted, "I got a bridge book on play from the library. I didn't think a book on play would interfere with your lessons."

"You don't need to apologize. I am pleased that you are enthusiastic enough to put forth the effort. You didn't have the time to do all of this studying, did you, Jerry?"

"No, but I might have picked up something from Barbara. She has talked about nothing but bridge during dinner every night."

"The next subject for discussion is how to establish tricks. Anyone can take tricks with aces and kings, but it requires skill and planning to take tricks with spot cards. Consider the following example, which shows how many tricks' difference it can make whether you establish winners or just cash high cards.

```
                    NORTH
                    ♠ A x x
                    ♡ K Q J
                    ◇ x x x
    WEST            ♣ A x x x           EAST
♠ Q J 10 x x                          ♠ x x
♡ A x x                               ♡ 10 x x x
◇ J x x                               ◇ Q 10 x x
♣ Q x               SOUTH             ♣ J x x
                    ♠ K x x
                    ♡ x x x
                    ◇ A K x
                    ♣ K 10 x x
```

"The contract is three no trump, and West leads the queen of spades. Suppose that declarer wins this trick and takes the next five tricks by cashing his high cards. The remaining cards will then be as follows:

```
                    NORTH
                    ♠ x
                    ♡ K Q J
    WEST            ◇ x                 EAST
♠ J 10 x            ♣ x x              ♠ —
♡ A x x                               ♡ 10 x x x
◇ J                 SOUTH             ◇ Q 10
♣ —                 ♠ x               ♣ J
                    ♡ x x x
                    ◇ x
                    ♣ 10 x
```

"Now, whatever is led, East and West can take the remaining tricks—three good spade tricks, the ace of hearts, the queen and ten of diamonds, and the jack of clubs. If declarer had won the opening lead in either his own hand or dummy, and had played the king of hearts—followed by the queen if West had refused to take his ace right away—declarer could be sure of at least eight tricks instead of six. As it happens, he can take nine tricks.

West wins the ace of hearts and returns another spade. Declarer plays the ace of clubs, king of clubs, and a third round of clubs. East wins and cannot return a spade. Now the fourth round of clubs will take a trick.

"There are two ways to establish tricks," I went on to explain. "One is by brute force. With king-queen-jack, as in the last example, lead one of these cards to force out the ace, and the other two will be good. With queen-jack-ten, lead the suit twice to force out the ace and king.

"The other way is to establish 'long cards' of a suit. Suppose I have A K Q x x opposite two small hearts in the dummy. How many hearts do the opponents have, Jerry?"

"Six."

"How can these six hearts be divided?"

"Several ways. Each opponent could have three of the suit. Or one opponent might have all six. Or—"

"Let me interrupt for a moment. Suppose that each opponent has three hearts. How many tricks can you take in the suit?"

"Five. They will all fall under the ace-king-queen, and my two spot cards will be good."

"Suppose that one opponent has four hearts and the other two. How many tricks can you take?"

"Just three. The opponents would win the fourth round."

"But if you regained the lead later, wouldn't your remaining spot card be good? By 'good' I mean the highest remaining card of the suit—therefore good for taking a trick."

"Yes, it would be good, so this holding would produce four tricks if the suit were to split 4-2."

"Suppose that the hearts were A K Q x x opposite three small. How many tricks could you take?"

"Three, four, or five, depending upon how the suit splits."

"Would you expect your chances of taking five tricks to be better or worse with A K Q x x opposite x x x, as opposed to A K Q x x opposite x x?"

"So far as I can see, the chances would be the same. I would still need to find no more than three cards of the suit in an opponent's hand."

"That doesn't sound right to me," said Barbara.

"Why not?" I asked.

"The more hearts we have, the less the opponents have. Consequently, neither opponent is quite so likely to have length in the suit. I don't know how to explain it, but I'm pretty sure I am right."

"You *are* right, Barbara. Perhaps I can explain it so that it will be obvious to all of you. Suppose that I have A K Q x x of hearts and dummy has x x x. Fortunately the suit splits nicely for us, with one opponent holding three hearts and the other opponent holding two hearts. Now I take one of dummy's hearts and offer to give it to one of the defenders chosen at random. You can see that this increases their chances to take a heart trick, can't you?"

"Yes," said Jerry. "That convinces me."

"Suppose that your heart holding was A K x x x opposite x x x. How many tricks would you expect to take?"

"Two, three, or four. Exactly one trick less than with A K Q x x opposite x x x. Of course, this time I would have to give up the lead for sure."

"And with A x x x x of hearts opposite x x x you would keep leading the suit in an effort to take two or three tricks instead of just one. Correct?"

"Yes, that is correct. But it looks to me as though you might have more trouble when you have to give up the lead a time or two."

"There are many more difficulties. For one thing, the opponents might establish their suit before we can establish ours. We are disregarding other problems for the moment and are only considering potential tricks—tricks that can be won if we have the time and opportunity to establish them. Now consider the following two holdings:

             x x x   K x x x x
             A Q x x x   x x x

"Alice, how would you play these combinations in order to take a maximum number of tricks?"

"I would start by leading toward the ace-queen or toward the king—then continue to lead the suit in an effort to establish the spot cards."

"In other words, you would combine the two types of plays I have taught you today—leading toward strength to finesse, and establishing length by repeated plays. How many tricks could you expect to make with these combinations?"

"With the first combination I could take no more than four tricks and possibly as few as one, if all five missing hearts were behind me. In the second combination I could take anywhere from no tricks to three tricks."

"Fine. Now, Henry, I'd like for you to play a hand. I am going to give you the first hand you played last week, but don't try to remember your opponent's hands.

NORTH
♠ Q 9
♡ A Q 10 5
♢ K Q 8 4
♣ 8 4 3

SOUTH
♠ K J 10 7 4 2
♡ K 2
♢ 7 5 3
♣ J 2

"Your contract is two spades. How many tricks can you afford to lose?"

"Five."

"How many tricks do you expect to lose?"

"Four. Two club tricks, the ace of diamonds and the ace of spades."

"How many tricks do you expect to win?"

"Nine. Five spade tricks, three heart tricks, and a diamond trick after the opponents take their ace. In fact, I might be able to take two diamond tricks if West has the ace."

"Can anything happen to prevent you from taking nine tricks?"

"Yes, the opponents might ruff one of my winners. That is why I want to pull their trumps as fast as I can. Or if they lead diamonds right away and East has the ace, they might establish five defensive tricks. It won't do me any good to have nine winners if the opponents have already taken five tricks. I would merely have to discard one of dummy's winners on one of my own or vice versa."

"So you pull the opponent's trumps. How do you know how many trumps to play?"

"I count them. The opponents have five spades. If they are split 3-2 it will take three leads to pull them. If they are split 4-1 it will take four leads. Naturally, I watch to see whether both opponents follow suit each time so that I'll know whether to play three or four rounds of trumps. If the trumps split 5-0 I am in trouble and probably can't make the hand."

"Play the hand and 'think aloud.' In other words, state your thoughts so that the other players can benefit. The opponents have taken the first two club tricks and West has led a high club to the third trick."

"I wait until my right hand opponent has played. It is very embarrassing to play too fast—and perhaps ruff small when an opponent has ruffed with a higher trump."

"East discards a heart on the third round of clubs."

"I win the trick by trumping small and I lead a low spade to the queen."

"West follows suit. East takes the ace and returns a trump. Which hand do you win in?"

"I win in my own hand with the ten in order to continue to draw trumps. If I were to win in dummy and attempt to return to my own hand by leading another suit, there is a remote chance that an opponent would ruff. I can afford to waste the nine of trumps by overtaking because West followed to the previous round, and there are only three trumps out, including the one that was led. The king, jack and ten will pick up those outstanding trumps."

"West follows suit. How many trumps have been played, and how many are outstanding?"

"Nine trumps have been played—one at the third trick when I trumped in, and four on each of the next two tricks. There are always four cards of a suit played each time the suit is led, provided everyone follows. Since nine trumps have been played, and I still have three left, there must be one trump outstanding, so I pick it up. Then I play three rounds of hearts, discarding a diamond from my hand, and I give up a trick to the ace of diamonds."

"You just told us how to count. Wouldn't this same method work for the other suits?"

"Yes, it would. I count long suits at no trump the same way. I guess I could count any suit, using this method. But trumps are always important, and sometimes the other suits are not. Maybe I'm just lazy."

"Well, after all, you are learning bridge to have fun. Don't do anything you don't want to. However, if you play bridge seriously, you will notice what everyone plays and keep a count of all suits. Once you get in the habit you do it almost subconsciously, and it does not require as much effort as you might imagine."

"We have covered a lot of material. Shall we quit for the evening?"

"Please give me one hand to play," said Barbara.

"All right. I'll just deal one out."

NORTH
♠ A Q 4
♡ J 10 6
♢ Q 7 6 5
♣ K 4 2

SOUTH
♠ 8 5 2
♡ Q 3
♢ A K 8 4 2
♣ A 7 5

"Suppose that your contract is three no trump, Barbara, and you get a club lead. How many tricks do you expect to win?"

"At least eight, and perhaps as many as ten. In spades I have one or two tricks, depending upon whether the spade finesse works. In hearts, one sure trick—eventually. In diamonds I probably have five tricks, but four tricks for sure, even if all four outstanding diamonds are in one hand. In clubs, I have two tricks, neither more nor less."

"The opening lead is the six of clubs, which you can win in either hand. Let's just say that you play small from dummy and win East's queen with your ace. You lead the ace of diamonds, and both opponents follow suit. How many tricks can you count now for sure?"

"Nine. The spade finesse may or may not work."

"Actually, I threw you a curve when I asked how many tricks you could count for sure. Suppose that West holds Q J x x x of clubs and A K of hearts. By playing clubs at every opportunity, the opponents can take three club tricks and two heart tricks before you can establish your 'sure' heart trick. Anyway, you are now sure of nine tricks provided the opponents do not take five tricks first. Getting back to the play, you won the opening lead with the ace of clubs, you played a high diamond to which everyone followed suit, and you now lead the queen of hearts. East wins with the king and returns a small club. I won't try to explain why, but suppose that you let the opponents win that trick, and you win the next club trick with the king. *Everyone has followed suit to all three rounds of clubs.* You lead the jack of hearts, losing to West's ace. West leads a low spade. What do you play?"

"How many tricks have I lost?"

"Three—two hearts and a club."

"Then I would play the ace. If I were to finesse, East might win and cash the remaining club. At this stage I have nine tricks for sure without taking the finesse—so why should I risk it?"

"You are absolutely right. The extra trick is of almost no importance. It does not pay to jeopardize your contract to try for an overtrick."

"Then what is the rule?" asked Alice. "When should we finesse and when shouldn't we?"

"There is no easy answer. Your objective is to make your contract. Count your winners and losers, and form a general plan as to how you will accomplish your objective. If a finesse is necessary, or it can't hurt you to take it, go ahead and take it. But don't lose sight of your objective, which is to make your contract. I have written out some problems for you to work on between now and your next lesson. We shall discuss them as the first order of business next time."

QUIZ

1. How should you play the following combinations to take two tricks?

(a)	*(b)*	*(c)*	*(d)*
A Q	A J	A 2	J 10 9
3 2	Q 2	Q J	K 5 3

(e)	*(f)*	*(g)*
J 10 9	K J 3	K J 3
A 6 4	7 6 5	7 6 5 4

2. How should you play the following combinations to take three tricks?

(a)	*(b)*	*(c)*	*(d)*
Q 10 6	A Q 10	K J	K 7
A J 4	8 7 6	Q 10 5 4	8 6 5 4 2

(e)	*(f)*	*(g)*
Q J 4 3	A J	A J
A 6 5	K 7 6 5	K 7 6 5 4

3. How will the cards have to be distributed in the opponents' hands in order for you to make the following contracts? How should you plan the play?

(a)

♠ 7 6
♡ 8 5
◊ A Q J 7 6 5
♣ 8 4 3

♠ A Q 3
♡ A 7 4
◊ 4 3
♣ Q 9 6 5 2

Contract is 3 NT with the queen of hearts lead.

(b)

♠ 7 6
♡ 8 5
◊ A Q J 7 6 5
♣ 8 4 3

♠ A Q 3
♡ A 7 4
◊ 4 3 2
♣ Q 9 6 5

Contract is 3 NT with the 4 of spades lead.

(c)

♠ A 10 9 5 4
♡ A 6 4
◊ A 6 4
♣ 5 3

♠ K 7
♡ K 8 2
◊ K 7 3
♣ A 8 7 4 2

Contract is 3 NT with queen of hearts lead.

(d)

♠ A x
♡ K Q 6 5
◊ 7 6 4
♣ Q J 10 3

♠ 7 4
♡ A 7 4 2
◊ A 8 3
♣ A 7 5 4

Contract is 4 ♡ with spade lead.

(e)

♠ Q 7 6
♡ K J 8 4 3
◊ 7 6 5
♣ A 4

♠ A K J 4 3 2
♡ Q 10 5
◊ 4 3
♣ 7 6

Contract is 4 ♠. West leads king, ace and queen of diamonds.

CHAPTER 3

Trumps

"Everything you said last week made sense to me when you said it," said Jerry. "But when the lesson was over, I forgot a lot of it."

"I am sorry," I replied. "We have been moving along very rapidly, and the last lesson covered quite a bit of material. There just didn't seem to be any logical way to break it up. However, for tonight's lesson anyway, we won't cover quite so much."

"Could you give us more rules to follow?" asked Alice.

"Alice has a good memory and is very good at remembering rules," Henry explained.

"Unfortunately, most rules in the play have so many exceptions, they are of little value. I'll try to give you rules whenever I can, but the important thing is to understand the reason for whatever is done. Let's consider the problems I gave you last week. Alice, how did you play the combinations to take two tricks?"

"The first three examples were very easy. I led from the South hand, intending to play small from the North hand provided West should play small."

"Remember, I told you that in taking any finesse it is necessary to hope that second hand, rather than fourth hand, holds a certain card or cards. There is a rule for you. What card or cards did you hope that second hand would hold?"

"I hoped that West would hold the king."

"Can you think of an exception to the rule I just stated?"

"No, I can't. The card or cards I would want him to hold might differ, but I would always want the player playing second to hold one or more key cards."

"Suppose that North holds A Q of diamonds opposite South's small diamonds, and West leads a diamond. Would it be possible to finesse the queen?"

"Yes."

"Who would you want to hold the king?"

"West."

"Would West be the person to play second to the trick?"

"No, I see what you mean. If he were to lead, he would be the first person to play to the trick."

"Then perhaps I should state that when you take a finesse, you want the person playing first or second, rather than the person playing third or fourth, to hold a certain card or cards. Or I could state the rule in alternatives, depending upon who leads to the trick. The important thing is for you to understand the reason why a finesse works, and if you do you will automatically figure out exceptions, even though the rule is stated to you in general terms. How would you play the next combination, jack-ten-nine opposite king and two small?"

"I would lead a card from dummy, intending to play small if East played small. I would hope that East has the queen."

"Do you care who has the ace?"

"No, only the location of the queen is important. If the jack loses to the ace, I would finesse against the queen next time."

"How would you play the next combination, jack-ten-nine opposite ace and two small?"

"I would lead from dummy, playing small if East played small. If West were to win I would later lead from dummy again, hoping that East had the remaining honor."

"With which of the last two combinations would you expect to have the best chance for two tricks?" I then asked.

"With the latter. I could take two tricks if East had either the king or the queen—or both. With the former he would have had to have specifically the queen. Two chances are better than one."

"Which combination is more likely to produce two tricks for you, king-jack-small opposite three small, or king-jack-small opposite four small?"

"The latter. In each case I would lead twice toward the king-jack, intending to play the jack the first time and the king the next time. But even if the ace and queen were not both on one side, I would still have a chance to take two tricks with the latter holding. If the suit were divided evenly, the last spot card would be good."

"Jerry, how would you play the next combinations to take three tricks?"

"The first combination is just a finesse against the king. The second is a repeated finesse against the king and jack. The third combination I just have to keep leading the suit. After the ace is driven out I have three good tricks."

"I know you would play the next combination correctly—king-small opposite five-small. My question is, how many times South will have to be on lead to take your three tricks, assuming that the suit lies favorably for you."

"First, I must be in the South hand to lead toward the king. It is necessary that West have the ace for me to take three tricks. If he plays small, the king will win and I can lead next time from dummy. If West plays his ace immediately, the next time the suit is led I can play the king from dummy. Then I must return to the South hand a second time to lead the third round of this suit, and I must return to the South hand a third time in order to play my two good spot cards."

"That is right. You must lead three times from the South hand.

"If the two hands were

♠ A x x
♡ K x
◇ x x x
♣ x x x x x

♠ K Q J
♡ x x x x x
◇ A K x
♣ A K

you might be able to take three heart tricks with a lot of luck.

"If the hands were

♠ A K Q J
♡ K x
◇ A K x
♣ A x x x

♠ x x x
♡ x x x x x
◇ x x
♣ K x x

you would have no chance to take three heart tricks because you could not lead from the South hand often enough. How would you play the next combination, Q J 4 3 opposite A 6 5?"

"I would lead the queen, intending to play small, of course, if East played small. And I would continue leading the suit in an effort to establish the three or four spot."

"Since you are leading the queen, I assume that you want East to have the king."

"That is right."

"Suppose that the suit splits 3-3. Would it make any difference who had the king?"

"Let's see . . . No, it wouldn't make any difference who has the king if the suit splits 3-3."

"Suppose that the suit splits 4-2, and East has the king. How many tricks can you take?"

"Who has the doubleton, East or West?"

"Try it both ways and see if it makes any difference."

"I guess it doesn't make any difference. If East covers the queen with king I can only take two tricks."

"Suppose that the suit splits 4-2 and West has the king. How many tricks can you take?"

"The same two tricks. He will win the queen with the king, and I can win just the ace and jack."

"Is there any way to play the suit so as to take three tricks when West has K x or K x x x?"

"Oh, yes. I can play the ace and lead twice toward the queen-jack."

"Would this latter line of play work if the distribution were 5-1 or 6-0?"

"Yes. The latter play would work whenever West had the king, regardless of distribution—also when East held the singleton king."

"Since leading the queen or jack can never gain, and since leading the ace, then toward the queen-jack, can never lose, the latter play is preferable, right?"

"Yes, it must be."

"Can you think of any time when it would be correct to lead the queen from dummy with this combination?"

"No, you've convinced me."

"But it could be right. Barbara, when would leading the queen be the right play?"

"When I only needed two tricks, and could not afford to lose the lead."

"Henry, let's hear your answers to the next group of problems."

"I would need a lot of luck to make the first hand. The diamonds would have to split 3-2 with the king on-side, and the spade finesse would have to work. I would win the opening lead, take a diamond finesse, finesse the queen of spades, and repeat the diamond finesse.

"The next hand would be played the same way, but my chances would be better. Assuming that both finesses work, diamonds could split either 3-1 or 2-2.

"In the next example," he continued, "I have seven top tricks and can attack either spades or clubs for my two extra tricks."

"Which would give you a better chance?" I asked.

"Spades, for two reasons. If I were to establish club tricks I would have to give up the lead at least twice, and the opponents might take enough heart tricks to defeat me. Besides, in spades I do not necessarily need a 3-3 break. If someone has Q x or J x, I can make four tricks by playing the king and ace, then forcing out the remaining honor with the ten-nine.

"To make four hearts with the next hands," Henry continued, "I need a 3-2 break in both hearts and clubs, plus the club finesse. I draw the opponents' trumps, ending in dummy, then lead a club honor for a finesse."

"How would your prospects be at three no trump compared with your prospects at four hearts?" I asked him.

"Actually, I would have a better chance to make three no trump. I would still need the club finesse and a 3-2 break in *either* clubs or hearts, but not both.

"In the last example I have a cinch for my contract since the opponents did not lead a club. I'll pull trumps and drive out the ace of hearts. My club loser will be discarded on a good heart."

"Now we shall take up a new topic—how to handle the trump suit. Remember the first hand that Henry played.

	NORTH	
	♠ Q 9	
	♡ A Q 10 5	
WEST	◇ K Q 8 4	EAST
♠ 6 5	♣ 8 4 3	♠ A 8 3
♡ 9 3		♡ J 8 7 6 4
◇ A J 6	SOUTH	◇ 10 9 2
♣ K Q 10 9 7 6	♠ K J 10 7 4 2	♣ A 5
	♡ K 2	
	◇ 7 5 3	
	♣ J 2	

"In this case trumps were used to prevent the opponents from running a suit. At no trump East and West could take eight tricks, including all six of their club tricks. At a spade contract they can take only two club tricks because declarer will trump the third round of clubs. Henry also pointed out to you that he should lead the trumps out as quickly as possible to prevent the opponents from trumping his good tricks. At least he should play trumps till the opponents have no more— then save his remaining trumps to prevent them from cashing more club tricks upon regaining the lead.

NORTH
♠ Q 9
♡ A Q 10 5
◇ K Q 8 4
♣ 8 4 3

WEST
♠ 6 5 3
♡ 9
◇ A J 6
♣ K Q 10 9 7 6

EAST
♠ A 8
♡ J 8 7 6 4 3
◇ 10 9 2
♣ A 5

SOUTH
♠ K J 10 7 4 2
♡ K 2
◇ 7 5 3
♣ J 2

"Now the defenders can take five tricks with a heart lead. When East wins the ace of spades, he can lead a heart for West to trump. After the king and ace of clubs, East will lead another heart, but South can trump high and still make his contract. Change the hand again.

NORTH
♠ Q 9
♡ A Q 10 5
◇ K Q 8 4
♣ 8 4 3

WEST
♠ 6 5 3
♡ 9
◇ A J 6
♣ K Q 10 9 7 6

EAST
♠ A 8
♡ J 8 7 6 4
◇ 10 9 3 2
♣ A 5

SOUTH
♠ K J 10 7 4 2
♡ K 3 2
◇ 7 5
♣ J 2

"The defenders can actually defeat two spades with a heart lead. The defenders' objective with hands of this kind is *not* to lead trumps. And declarer should try to lead out trumps as quickly as possible to prevent his good tricks from being trumped."

"The general rule seems to be that declarer should draw trumps as fast as he can," said Alice.

"Before you form any conclusions," I said, "or attempt to generalize, consider the following hand.

NORTH
♠ 5
♡ A K 7
◇ A 7 6 5
♣ 8 7 6 4 2

WEST
♠ A Q 10 6
♡ 8 4 3
◇ Q J 10 8
♣ Q 5

EAST
♠ K J 9 3 2
♡ 9 6
◇ 9 3
♣ K J 10 3

SOUTH
♠ 8 7 4
♡ Q J 10 5 2
◇ K 4 2
♣ A 9

"West leads the queen of diamonds against a four-heart contract. If declarer draws trumps, how many tricks can he take, Alice?"

"Eight—five heart tricks, two diamonds and a club."

"Consequently, declarer has no chance to make his contract if he draws trumps. How many tricks can declarer take if he trumps two of his spade losers?"

"Ten. That way declarer would take seven trump tricks altogether. But how would declarer know that the defenders would not trump one of his winners if trumps were not drawn immediately?"

"Declarer wouldn't know. However, he can see a maximum of eight tricks and a sure set if he pulls trumps. Consequently, his only chance is to ruff his spade losers first. He may still be set, but leaving the trumps out is a risk he must take.

"Now consider this hand," I then said.

```
                   NORTH
                 ♠ K 7 5 4
                 ♡ A Q 8
                 ◇ 6 5 3 2
   WEST          ♣ 9 2            EAST
 ♠ J 9 8 3                      ♠ Q 10 6
 ♡ 3 2                          ♡ 6 5 4
 ◇ J 10 9 7      SOUTH          ◇ Q 8
 ♣ K J 4         ♠ A 2          ♣ A Q 10 7 5
                 ♡ K J 10 9 7
                 ◇ A K 4
                 ♣ 8 6 3
```

"Again the contract is four hearts. Declarer can count only nine winners if he draws trumps. He must lead clubs at every opportunity so as to ruff a club loser while dummy still has a trump."

"It looks to me," said Barbara, "as though both this contract and the other one could be set if the defenders should lead trumps at every opportunity."

"That is right. With these two hands the declarer's objective is to delay the drawing of trumps until he can trump one or more of his losers, while the defenders' objective is to play the trumps. In both of these examples, once the opening leader failed to lead a trump, declarer could make his contract with proper play. Barbara, can you give me two more examples similar in principle to the latter hand?"

"I'll try."

NORTH	NORTH
♠ K 7 5 4	♠ 8 7 5 4
♡ A Q 8	♡ A Q 8
◇ 6 5 3 2	◇ 6 5 3 2
♣ 9 2	♣ A 2

SOUTH	SOUTH
♠ 8 2	♠ A 2
♡ K J 10 9 7	♡ K J 10 9 7
◇ A K 4	◇ A K 4
♣ A 6 3	♣ 8 6 3

"Now that I have looked them over closely," I said, "these hands are different in one respect. The defenders cannot prevent a ruff even if they lead a trump on opening lead. But they are similar from declarer's point of view. He ought to ruff a club before drawing trumps, and in both examples he should lead clubs immediately.

"Jerry, how would you play the following four-heart contract? The opening lead is the ten of diamonds."

♠ 7 4
♡ A J 8 4 3
◇ K Q 8 4
♣ K 5

♠ 8 5 3
♡ K Q 7 5 2
◇ A 6 2
♣ Q 8

"I can only count nine winners unless I ruff a spade. So I lead a spade immediately."

"I'll show you all four hands so that you can see what would happen.

```
                         NORTH
                         ♠ 7 4
                         ♡ A J 8 4 3
        WEST             ◇ K Q 8 4            EAST
     ♠ K J 9 6 2         ♣ K 5             ♠ A Q 10
     ♡ 10 9 6                              ♡ —
     ◇ 10                 SOUTH            ◇ J 9 7 5 3
     ♣ A 9 7 2           ♠ 8 5 3           ♣ J 10 6 4 3
                         ♡ K Q 7 5 2
                         ◇ A 6 2
                         ♣ Q 8
```

"East would win the spade trick and give his partner a diamond ruff. West would lead another spade. East would win and lead another diamond. The defenders would take two spade tricks, two trump tricks, and the ace of clubs. Now that you see all four hands, can you determine how the hand should be played?"

"Yes. Declarer should play three rounds of trumps immediately so as to exhaust West's trumps. Declarer could still give up two spade tricks and obtain a ruff."

"That is right. Because declarer has so many trumps in the combined hands, he can draw the opponent's trumps without losing the ruff he needs for the tenth trick."

"Can you give us a rule on when to draw trumps?" asked Alice.

"I believe I can state a rule that works pretty well.

(a) When you have no losers to ruff in the dummy, play trumps immediately;

(b) When you have one or more losers to ruff, try to ruff the loser(s) before drawing trumps—unless dummy has four or more trumps;

(c) When dummy has four or more trumps, play trumps immediately.

"A more accurate rule, though more difficult to apply, is to draw the opponents' trumps immediately whenever you will still have enough trumps left to ruff all your losers. Let me ask you some questions.

NORTH
♠ J x x
♡ x
◊ A x x x x
♣ x x x x

SOUTH
♠ A K Q x x x
♡ A x x
◊ K x
♣ x x

"Alice, your contract is five spades, and the opponents take the first two club tricks and continue a third round, which you trump. Will it help you to trump hearts in the dummy?"

"Yes."

"Why?"

"Because if I draw trumps I will take only six trump tricks. If I trump a heart or two, I'll take seven or eight trump tricks."

"In other words, you are sure to take six trump tricks in your hand, and whatever trump tricks dummy can take will increase the total?"

"Right."

"Will it help you to trump the fourth round of clubs or the third round of diamonds in your hand?"

"No. I am going to take six trump tricks with A K Q x x x whether I trump with them or lead them. It never does any good to trump with the longer trump holding. Why are you looking at me like that?"

"I didn't mean to upset you. I just naturally cringe when you say 'never' or 'always.' But what you said is probably true eighty per cent of the time. Henry, can you think of any reasons to trump with the greater trump length?"

"The main one is to gain the lead. That is why you would trump the third round of clubs. This time you wanted to gain the lead from the opponents, but you might also ruff so as to transfer the lead from the declarer to dummy or vice versa."

"Can you think of any other reason?"

"Yes, to establish a suit."

"This time," I said, "I shall provide the example.

NORTH
♠ x x
♡ K x x x x
◊ A J x x
♣ x x

SOUTH
♠ x x
♡ A x
◊ K Q x x x x
♣ A Q x

"West cashes the ace and king of spades then shifts to his singleton trump against your five-diamond contract. The correct play, after drawing another round of trumps, is to play the ace of hearts and a low heart to the king, and to trump the third round of hearts. If hearts split 3-3 you can discard the queen and small club on dummy's two good hearts. If the hearts do not split 3-3 you will lead a trump to dummy for a club finesse, planning to trump the third round of clubs with dummy's last trump. If the contract were no trump you could not establish the heart suit without giving up the lead, but at a suit contract it is often possible to establish a suit by ruffing, even when you need all the tricks.

"Barbara, can you guess what a ruffing finesse is?"

"No, I can't."

"Suppose that your contract is four spades with the following hands.

NORTH
♠ A Q x
♡ A Q J 10
◊ x x x
♣ x x x

SOUTH
♠ K 10 x x x x
♡ x
◊ A x x
♣ Q x x

"West leads the king of diamonds, which you win with the ace. Remember, you need ten tricks. Where will those tricks come from?"

"I have six spade tricks, probably, and a diamond. The queen of clubs might take a trick if East has both the ace and king, but my best chance is to take three heart tricks."

"How can you take three heart tricks?"

"I could lead toward dummy and finesse the ten, then hope the king will drop the next round or two. But that doesn't look very likely. . . . Oh, I see what I could do! Play a heart to the ace and lead another heart. If East has the king he will cover it, and I'll trump it. Then the dummy will have two good hearts."

"Why is this better than finessing West for the king of hearts?" I asked.

"Because I could only take one finesse against West, but I can keep finessing against East regardless of his length in the suit."

"That is right. If East has the king of hearts and doesn't play it, you can continue leading hearts through him and discarding until he covers. However, you must leave a high spade in the dummy so that you can get back to use the good hearts after ruffing out East's king.

"That is enough material to cover for this evening. For homework look at the following hands and try to decide whether declarer should pull the opponent's trumps as fast as possible or whether he should try to ruff his losers first. In each case the contract is four spades and the opening lead is the king of hearts."

	(a)		(b)		(c)
♠	Q J	♠	K Q 4	♠	K Q 4
♡	8 6 4	♡	6	♡	6 5
◇	7 6 4	◇	8 7 6 4	◇	A Q 6 4 2
♣	K J 6 5 3	♣	A 8 6 5 3	♣	7 6 4
♠	K 10 9 8 4 2	♠	A J 8 6 3	♠	A J 8 6 3
♡	A 5	♡	8 5 2	♡	A 8 4
◇	A 5	◇	A K 5 2	◇	9 8
♣	A 8 7	♣	7	♣	A 8 2

	(d)		(e)		(f)
♠	K Q 4	♠	K Q 6 5	♠	K Q 4
♡	6 5	♡	6	♡	A 8 5
◇	A Q 6 4 2	◇	8 7 6 4	◇	7 6 4
♣	7 6 4	♣	8 6 4 3	♣	8 6 4 2
♠	A J 8 6 3	♠	A J 8 7 4 3	♠	A J 10 7 3
♡	A 8 4	♡	A 9 7	♡	7 4
◇	K J 5	◇	Q J 10	◇	A K 3 2
♣	9 8	♣	9	♣	A 5

CHAPTER 4

Entries

"Did you have any trouble with your homework problems?" I asked.

"No," Alice replied. "You gave us some good rules to follow. With problems (a), (d), (e) and (f) we should pull trumps immediately. With (b) and (c) we should not."

"Does everyone agree?" I asked.

Jerry readily agreed but Henry remained silent and Barbara said no.

"What is bothering you, Henry?" I asked.

"Problem (f). It doesn't seem to fit clearly into either category. I am not much worried about getting my ace of clubs trumped, and if someone has a singleton diamond, I can't make the hand anyway. But I suppose I should pull the trumps."

"What do you think, Barbara?"

"Dad explained why there is little or no necessity for drawing trumps. If trumps are drawn, declarer can't make the hand unless diamonds split 3-3. But if declarer plays the ace, king and another diamond he can make his contract even if diamonds split 4-2. He can trump his last diamond high in the dummy."

"All right, let's move on to the subject to be discussed this evening: entries. An entry is a means by which a hand may gain the lead. It does no good for a player to hold established high cards if he is not on lead and if he cannot gain the lead. For example:

NORTH
♠ 8 5
♡ 9 7 4
◇ A 8 5 4 3
♣ 7 6 5

WEST
♠ J 10 9 7 4
♡ Q 10 5 2
◇ Q 9
♣ J 4

EAST
♠ 6 3 2
♡ 8 6 3
◇ K 10 6
♣ K Q 8 2

SOUTH
♠ A K Q
♡ A K J
◇ J 7 2
♣ A 10 9 3

"The contract is three no trump, and the opening lead is the jack of spades. Declarer wins and leads a diamond to the ace and plays another diamond. Both defenders follow suit, West, winning with the queen. West plays another spade, won by declarer, who then plays a third diamond. East wins this trick, and dummy's remaining two diamonds are both good. However, dummy will never gain the lead, and these two good diamonds will never take tricks.

"Declarer has played incorrectly. How should he play, Alice?"

"He has to lose at least two diamond tricks anyway, so he should concede them right away, saving the ace until the suit is established. Proper play is to lead a diamond at trick two, and to play *small* from dummy. Declarer will win the spade return and play another diamond. Again he will play small from dummy. When he regains the lead he can play a third diamond, this time winning with the ace. Dummy is now on lead and can cash the two remaining diamonds."

"That was a very clear explanation, Alice. If dummy's diamonds had been A K 5 4 3 opposite three small, declarer should duck* the first round of diamonds. It might even be correct to duck two rounds if only three diamond tricks are needed. This would be the only way to take three diamond tricks—assuming no outside entries to dummy—if the suit were split as follows.

---

* To "duck" means to fail to play a high card; usually the term implies that one deliberately concedes a trick that could be won.

NORTH
A K 5 4 3

WEST
Q 10 8 6

SOUTH
9 7 2

EAST
J

The general principle is that, when there are no entries on the side, the high cards of a suit should be saved until the suit is ready to run.

"Now, Jerry, I have a hand for you. The opening lead against three no trump is a small club. How many tricks can you count for sure?"

NORTH
♠ 9 8 3
♡ A K Q 7 4
♢ 7 6 4
♣ 8 2

SOUTH
♠ A 7 4 2
♡ 6 5
♢ A K 3
♣ A Q 7 4

"Eight. Two clubs, two diamonds, three hearts and a spade."
"So that means you only have to establish one additional trick. You need four heart tricks, not five. How would you plan to take four heart tricks?"

"I would win the opening lead and duck a heart completely. Upon regaining the lead, I would lead another heart and hope that all of the opponents' hearts would fall under the ace, king and queen. The only thing that bothers me is that I might be giving away a heart trick unnecessarily. If hearts split 3-3 I could take five heart tricks just by playing off the ace, king and queen immediately."

"That is true," I said. "However, the extra trick is not important compared to making your contract. Besides, a 4-2 split is more common than a 3-3 split.

"Henry, how would you play the next hand at three no trump with a club lead?"

> **NORTH**
> ♠ K 8 5
> ♡ A K 7 6 5
> ◇ 8 4 3
> ♣ 7 2
>
> **SOUTH**
> ♠ A 7 6 2
> ♡ 4 2
> ◇ A K 7
> ♣ A Q 6 4

"If I were to play ace, king and a small heart, all would be well, provided the suit should split 3-3. The king of spades would be an entry. However, if the hearts should split 4-2 I would need to use my last entry, the king of spades, to establish the long heart, and there would be no entry to use it. Since I only need three heart tricks, I would duck the first heart trick. Upon regaining the lead, I would play the ace-king and another heart. Unless the suit were to split very badly, this would establish one long heart with the king of spades entry to use it."

"You said, 'since I only need three heart tricks,' you would duck the first heart trick. Could it cost you anything to duck a heart even if the suit were to split 3-3?"

"No, I guess that is the right play regardless of the number of heart tricks I need."

"Suppose dummy's hearts were A Q 7 6 5 instead of A K 7 6 5. How would that affect your play?"

"I would plan to finesse the queen eventually, but I would play the five of hearts on the first heart trick so as to concede my sure loser while retaining all possible entries to dummy.

This would be the only way to make the hand if West had K x
of hearts or four hearts headed by the king."

"I don't believe I see why that is true," said Jerry.

"Let's lay out a typical hand and play it through," I suggested.

```
                      NORTH
                    ♠ K 8 5
                    ♡ A Q 7 6 5
    WEST            ◇ 8 4 3                    EAST
  ♠ Q 4             ♣ 7 2                    ♠ J 10 9 3
  ♡ K 10 8 3                                 ♡ J 9
  ◇ J 6 2           SOUTH                    ◇ Q 10 9 5
  ♣ K 10 8 5        ♠ A 7 6 2                ♣ J 9 3
                    ♡ 4 2
                    ◇ A K 7
                    ♣ A Q 6 4
```

"Suppose that upon winning the club lead with the queen,
South finesses the queen of hearts. He then plays the ace and
another, but his suit is not established. He has one more entry
with which to establish the long heart, but no entry left to use
it. But suppose that South ducks the first heart completely. He
wins the club return and finesses the queen of hearts. The ace
of hearts is followed by a small heart, and there is now a good
heart in dummy with the king of spades as entry. It is odd that
everyone can see that it is right to duck the first trick with ace-
king in dummy, but it is harder to see with ace-queen. Yet the
situation is substantially the same."

"I see it now."

"Here is a hand for you, Barbara," I then said.

NORTH
♠ Q 8 4
♡ 8 5 3
♢ K Q 7 6 4 2
♣ 9

SOUTH
♠ A K 5
♡ A K J
♢ 8 3
♣ A 10 8 5 4

"How would you play three no trump with a spade lead?"

"Obviously, I would win in my hand, saving the queen until I need it. Then I would lead a diamond. What does West play?"

"Small."

"I play the queen. Does it hold?"

"Yes."

"Then I return to my hand with a heart to the ace and lead another diamond. Wait! No, I take everything back. I would have played the seven of diamonds, not the queen the first time."

"Why?"

"Because East wouldn't, or at least shouldn't, take the queen even if he has the ace. If East had A J x or A 10 x, for example, he would let me win the first trick. He would take the second trick, and the suit still would not be established. However, if I play small the first time and an honor the second time, he cannot prevent me from establishing and using the suit if it splits 3-2."

"Suppose the suit splits 4-1?" I asked.

"Then I couldn't make the hand. Consequently, it must be right to duck the first diamond trick. Playing an honor the first time loses whenever East has the ace."

"If East had only the doubleton ace, he would have to win the first trick, wouldn't he? And you would still be all right."

"No, he would *not* have to win the first trick. It is true that he would lose a trick by ducking if I were to play small next time, but I would never guess to play small. Unless he is a terrible coward, East should always refuse the first trick. After all, I can't tell what he has."

"Very, very good reasoning, Barbara! Now it is Jerry's turn again.

NORTH
♠ 5 4 2
♡ 9 8
◇ A K Q 4 3
♣ 8 6 4

SOUTH
♠ A 8 7
♡ A K 4
◇ 8 7 6 2
♣ K Q 5

"Jerry, suppose you only need four diamond tricks. Would you duck the first round?"

"No, because that would probably give away a trick unnecessarily. I would win the first round, and if someone were to show out I would duck the second or third round of the suit."

"Your contract is three no trump, and West leads a low club upon which East plays the jack. The diamonds do not split 4-0. Can you possibly be set?"

"No, I can count nine sure tricks."

"Play it out," I said. "I'll play the opponents' cards for them."

Jerry won with the queen of clubs and played out the ace, king and queen of diamonds. West discarded a spade on the second trick, but that only left East with three diamonds. To Jerry's dismay, he won the fourth diamond trick with his own eight-spot and could not get back to dummy for the last diamond trick.

"Horrors! What did I do wrong?" asked Jerry.

"You blocked the diamond suit. Correct play is to drop the six, seven, and eight under the ace, king, and queen. Then the four will beat your deuce and the lead will remain in dummy.

A suit is blocked when the hand with the shorter length in the suit must win the trick. Suppose you are in a three no trump-contract with three small spades opposite three small. It looks as though the opponents can take at least four spade tricks however the suit may be split. But if one player has the ace-king alone, and his partner has no entry, the opponents can only take two spade tricks. On rare occasions a suit is blocked and nothing can be done about it. More frequently the problem is to avoid blocking the suit. Alice, can you give me a typical example of how to handle a suit so as not to block it? Come to the blackboard."

Alice wrote the following diagram.

NORTH

A Q x x x x

SOUTH

K x

"If I were to lead low from my hand and win in dummy," she explained, "I would have to win the next round of this suit in my hand. Then I would need to use another entry to get to dummy and continue the suit. The proper way to play this suit is to lead the king from my hand first, then a small one. It is always proper to play your high cards from the shorter holding first."

Barbara was smiling at me. She must have noticed me wince when Alice said "always," but I made no comment except that her example was a good one.

"Henry, can you give me some examples where you play a suit in such a way as to conserve or create entries?"

Henry had a blank look on his face, so I provided the example for him.

NORTH

A 6 5 3

SOUTH

K Q J 4

"Suppose you need two entries to the North hand," I said. "How would you play this suit?"

"I would lead the king, then the queen. If the opponents followed suit to both tricks, there would be only one card of the suit outstanding. I could then lead the jack to the ace and later lead the four to the six."

"Correct! How would you play the following hand at three no trump with a spade lead?"

> **NORTH**
> ♠ 8 7 4 2
> ♡ J 7 6
> ◇ Q 9 5 4
> ♣ A 5
>
> **SOUTH**
> ♠ A 10
> ♡ A 4 3
> ◇ A J 10 3
> ♣ K Q 4 2

"I would lead a club to the ace and take the diamond finesse."

"Which diamond would you lead from dummy?"

"The queen or the nine so that the lead would stay in dummy."

"Would it ever matter whether you were to lead the queen or the nine?"

"I don't think so. Oh, yes—it would if East had four or five diamonds. If I should lead the queen I would have to win the next round in my hand. Consequently, I should lead the nine the first time and the queen the second time."

"That is right. Suppose that East holds the K 8 7 2 of diamonds. Only by leading the nine first can you take all four diamond tricks."

"What about leading the queen the first time and dropping the ten or jack under it?" asked Barbara. "Then you could lead the nine from dummy. Oh, I see why that wouldn't work.

After you had wasted an honor, East could cover the nine with the king and eventually establish his eight-spot."

"Barbara, how would you play the next hand at three no trump after a heart lead, East playing the jack? Explain your problem and think aloud for the benefit of the others."

NORTH
♠ K J 9 4 3
♡ 9
◇ 9 7 4
♣ Q 8 4 3

SOUTH
♠ A Q 6
♡ K 7 4
◇ A Q J 5
♣ K 9 2

"I would win the first trick; otherwise, East would continue hearts through my king and I might never take a heart trick. If I give up the lead, the opponents can take at least four more heart tricks, so my problem is to take nine tricks without losing the lead. The heart trick I've won plus five spade tricks bring my total in those two suits to six. So I shall need three diamond tricks. I can get three diamond tricks if East has the king *and if I can lead diamonds twice from dummy*. The problem is how to get to dummy twice."

"Does everyone see the problem? Barbara has explained it quite well."

Everyone nodded, and Barbara continued.

"If spades split 3-2 I can play the ace and then low to the jack for a diamond finesse. Then the queen of spades can be overtaken by the king to run the suit, after which I will repeat the diamond finesse."

"You have the right general idea, Barbara. However, your play will not work when the spades split 4-1. Can you see any way of improving your chances?"

After long thought Barbara replied, "Yes. I should lead the

ace, followed by the queen of spades. If both players follow to
the first spade trick and if West follows to this trick, I can safely
overtake with the king. Then if East shows out I can finesse
next round against West's ten-spot."

"Suppose West fails to play a spade on the second round?"

"In that case I could not afford to overtake the queen. I
would just run my five spade tricks and hope that East has
the singleton or doubleton king of diamonds."

The hand I gave them actually came up in a tournament
recently, and only two players out of thirteen made the right
play. The full hand was as follows.

```
                      NORTH
                      ♠ K J 9 4 3
                      ♡ 9
                      ◇ 9 7 4
                      ♣ Q 8 4 3
   WEST                                    EAST
   ♠ 10 8 5 2                              ♠ 7
   ♡ A 10 8 6 3                            ♡ Q J 5 2
   ◇ 8 2                                   ◇ K 10 6 3
   ♣ J 7                                   ♣ A 10 6 5
                      SOUTH
                      ♠ A Q 6
                      ♡ K 7 4
                      ◇ A Q J 5
                      ♣ K 9 2
```

"Here is another hand for you to play, Barbara. A small
spade is led against your three-no trump-contract. Again, express
your thoughts aloud."

```
                      NORTH
                      ♠ J 6
                      ♡ 8 7 4
                      ◇ A 6 5
                      ♣ Q J 10 9 3

                      SOUTH
                      ♠ A K Q
                      ♡ A K 5 2
                      ◇ J 10 9 4 3
                      ♣ K
```

"I'd lead a club at the second trick. If the opponents should take my king my problems would be over, but I suppose they let my king hold, don't they?"

"Right."

"I can get to dummy with the ace of diamonds to establish the club suit, but there would be no way to get back to use the good clubs. My best chance is to establish the diamond suit. I would lead the jack, planning to take two finesses. However, I only need three diamond tricks, and unless the suit splits 5-0 I am sure to take three tricks."

"The important point is that you don't have enough entries to use the club suit. After the king holds, you must abandon the suit. Once you see this, you can hardly go wrong.

"Thus far," I continued, "our concern has been in saving or creating entries for declarer. It is equally important to destroy the defender's entries. While we have not studied the defender's problems yet, it is important to know that one usually leads from a long suit at no trump. In the following examples we shall assume that the opening leader has the greater length in the suit led."

I wrote the following hand on the board.

NORTH
♠ 8 5
♡ A K 4
♢ A Q J 10 6
♣ 7 5 4

SOUTH
♠ A 9 4
♡ 8 7 6
♢ 9 8 4
♣ A K 8 2

"West leads a spade against your three-no-trump contract. He will establish several spade tricks, the exact number depending upon how long a suit he has. After he establishes his suit, what possible entry will he have, Jerry?"

"The only entry will be in the spade suit itself."

"Suppose he has a five- or six-card spade suit? What can you do to prevent him from taking enough spade tricks to set you?"

"I should refuse to win the ace till the third round. Then, even if the diamond finesse loses, East will have no spades to return. Or if he does, it will mean that the suit has split 4-4 and I can afford to lose three spade tricks."

"Assuming that West has the greater length, your contract is one hundred per cent safe by holding up the ace of spades till the third round. Is your contract safe in the following example—same contract, same lead?"

NORTH
♠ 8 5
♡ A K 4
♢ K Q J 10 6
♣ 7 5 4

SOUTH
♠ A 9 4
♡ 8 7 6
♢ 9 8 4
♣ A K 8 2

"No," replied Jerry. "West might have the ace of diamonds as entry to his long spades."

"So how should you play this hand?"

"The same way as the other hand. Hold up the ace of spades as long as possible and lead a diamond. If *East* has the ace of diamonds my contract is safe; if not, the hold-up will neither gain nor lose."

"It is occasionally correct to hold off with a double stopper," I said. "The conditions have to be just right."

I then drew the following hand on the board.

NORTH
♠ 8 6 4
♡ A 6 5
◇ Q J 10 9 4
♣ A 7

SOUTH
♠ A K 3
♡ K J 7 4
◇ 8 3
♣ K 10 9 3

"West leads the queen of spades. It is necessary to give up the lead twice in order to establish the diamond suit. Suppose that the diamond honors are split. If you can win the first spade trick, East should win the first diamond trick and return a spade, forcing out your remaining spade honor. Then, if West started with five spades, he will obtain the lead with his diamond honor and set you. Alice, how can you guard against a five-card spade suit in the West hand?"

"I don't know."

"I'll put a hand on the blackboard meeting the conditions just mentioned—West with five spades and the diamond honors split.

NORTH
♠ 8 6 4
♡ A 6 5
◇ Q J 10 9 4
♣ A 7

WEST
♠ Q J 10 7 5
♡ Q 3 2
◇ K 7 5
♣ 8 2

EAST
♠ 9 2
♡ 10 9 8
◇ A 6 2
♣ Q J 6 5 4

SOUTH
♠ A K 3
♡ K J 7 4
◇ 8 3
♣ K 10 9 3

"When you allow West to win the first spade trick," I explained, "he plays another one, which you are forced to win. However, if East wins the first diamond trick he no longer has a spade to return. That was the purpose of your hold-up play. Of course, West could win the first diamond trick with the king, but it would do him no good. Although he could establish his spade suit he would have no entry left to cash his good spades."

"Why did you say the conditions have to be just right for us to hold up with a double stopper?" Henry asked.

"Because in the example given, West could not hurt you by shifting to another suit. The following hand represents a much more typical case.

```
                        NORTH
                      ♠ x x x
                      ♡ x x x
                      ◊ x x x
        WEST                              EAST
      ♠ Q J 10 x      ♣ A K Q x         ♠ x x x
      ♡ J 10 x                          ♡ Q x x x
      ◊ K x x                           ◊ A x
      ♣ x x x           SOUTH           ♣ J 10 x x
                      ♠ A K x
                      ♡ A K x
                      ◊ Q J 10 9 x
                      ♣ x x
```

"Suppose that declarer allows the queen of spades to win the first trick. If West shifts to hearts he can establish five tricks for the defenders. On the other hand, no lead can defeat the contract provided declarer wins immediately."

"How would West know to lead a heart at the second trick?" asked Barbara.

"He might not know. As a practical matter, it is not as dangerous to hold up with a double stopper as it appears. Perhaps my example was not too clear-cut. The principle is that in deciding whether to hold up with a double stopper, you have to weigh the risk that a defender, having already been given one trick, will successfully turn his attack elsewhere.

NORTH
♠ 9 4
♡ K Q 6
♢ A Q J 10 4
♣ 7 6 3

SOUTH
♠ A K 6
♡ J 7 3
♢ 9 8 6
♣ A K 9 5

"The opening lead against three no trump is the queen of spades. Would you duck it, Jerry?"

"I guess so. It doesn't look as though the opponents can hurt me by shifting suits."

"In this case it makes very little difference whether you duck now or later. Let's say you duck now and win the second spade trick. What entry can West have outside of the spade suit?"

"The ace of hearts."

"How should you play the hand?"

After long thought, Jerry replied, "I should lead a heart right away to make West take his ace. Then if he continues spades he cannot run a long spade suit, even if the diamond finesse loses."

"Here is a possible hand," I said.

NORTH
♠ 9 4
♡ K Q 6
◊ A Q J 10 4
♣ 7 6 3

WEST   **EAST**
♠ Q J 10 8 3   ♠ 7 5 2
♡ A 7 2   ♡ 10 8 5 4
◊ 7 3   ◊ K 5 2
♣ J 4 2   ♣ Q 10 8

SOUTH
♠ A K 6
♡ J 9 3
◊ 9 8 6
♣ A K 9 5

"If you had taken the diamond finesse before playing a heart, East would win and return a spade. You could only take eight tricks before letting West in with the ace of hearts to cash his good spades. Barbara, suppose when you played a heart at the third trick you were allowed to hold the trick. What would you do next?"

"I would play another heart to force out West's only possible entry."

"Aren't you being a bit greedy? After you win one heart trick you have a cinch for your contract by going back to diamonds."

"Yes, that is true. But if a play may gain and cannot lose, it is worth trying, even if just for overtricks. Can it hurt anything to play another heart?"

"Try to answer your own question. Can playing another heart place your contract in jeopardy?"

"Yes, I see now that it could. East might have five or six hearts headed by the ace. When I continue hearts, he simply wins and plays another heart. Then he would take the setting tricks in hearts when the diamond finesse loses. I suppose the moral of this hand is not to be greedy. Really, the moral is to count your tricks. If I had realized that I had nine sure tricks once I had stolen a heart trick, I think I would have shifted back to diamonds."

"In all of the example hands I've shown you tonight the contract was no trump. The same principles apply to suit contracts, but there are other factors as well."

I then drew the following illustration on the board.

NORTH
♠ A 8 4
♡ K 6
◇ A K 8 4 2
♣ 8 6 5

SOUTH
♠ K 7
♡ A Q J 10 9 4
◇ 6 3
♣ A 10 3

"The contract is six hearts and the opening lead is the king of clubs. Not only must declarer be careful not to waste his entries; he must use them in the proper order. It would be a very serious mistake to play trumps right away, since the king of hearts is needed as an entry to establish the diamonds. The diamond entries must be used first. Actually, one of the diamond entries will be wasted since both top diamonds have to be cashed before you can start ruffing diamonds. In other words, the hand would play just as well with A x in declarer's hand and K x x x x in dummy. The proper play is to play the ace and king of diamonds, ruff the third round high, enter dummy with the king of hearts, and—if the diamonds are not good— ruff another diamond high, pull trumps, and use the spade entry last. This is the normal order of using entries to establish a suit. First use the entries to the suit being established, then use the entries in the trump suit, and last, use the entries in the side suit or suits. Alice, apply these principles to the next hand.

NORTH
♠ 8
♡ A 7 5
◇ 8 6
♣ A 10 9 7 5 4 2

SOUTH
♠ A 7 3
♡ Q 9 4
◇ A K Q J 4 3
♣ J

"West leads a trump against your six-diamond contract. You will probably make seven or be set at six. It is necessary to establish the club suit. With these clues, how would you plan the play?"

"I would play the ace and ruff a club. Next, the ace of spades and a spade-ruff, followed by a club-ruff. Then pull the trumps, after which the ace of hearts will be an entry to the good clubs—assuming that they split 3-2."

"Very good. You applied what I told you quite well. There is one detail. When you led a club to the ace and ruffed a club, which diamond did you ruff with?"

"Heavens, I don't know! A high one, I suppose, to avoid the risk of an over-ruff. Is that right?"

"What would you say, Jerry?"

"Wouldn't that depend upon what clubs and diamonds had already been played?"

"Perhaps. Let's say that West led a small diamond and East played the nine at the first trick. On the club lead to the ace, both opponents played small clubs."

"I guess I agree with Alice. I would ruff high."

"What do you think, Henry?"

"I would ruff with a low trump. I can't make the hand unless clubs split 3-2, so I won't worry about West's having a singleton club. The reason for not ruffing high this time is that

I may have to ruff high next time, and if I ruff high twice, I'll surely lose a trump trick."

"Henry mentioned two very important principles," I said. "First, if you need a certain break to make your contract, assume that it exists and save your worrying for factors over which you have some control. Henry didn't worry about, or attempt to guard against, a singleton club in West's hand, because if clubs split that badly, the contract was hopeless. Second, if you are going to have to ruff a suit twice, and if you can only afford to ruff high once, you should ruff high the second time rather than the first time. Obviously, if there is a danger of being over-ruffed the first time, the danger must be much greater the second time. The whole hand is as follows:

```
                    NORTH
                    ♠ 8
                    ♡ A 7 5
                    ◇ 8 6
   WEST             ♣ A 10 9 7 5 4 2        EAST
♠ K J 9 6 2                                ♠ Q 10 5 4
♡ K 10 2                                   ♡ J 8 6 3
◇ 10 7 2            SOUTH                   ◇ 9 5
♣ Q 3              ♠ A 7 3                 ♣ K 8 6
                   ♡ Q 9 4
                   ◇ A K Q J 4 3
                   ♣ J
```

"Note that if you ruff a spade before playing a club to the ace and ruffing a club, you cannot make the hand. Ruffing the spade is a form of trump entry which should not be wasted by using it too early. Also note that the first club-ruff must be with a low trump, and the second club-ruff with a high trump.

"Barbara, the last hand of the evening is a difficult one because you have to remember and apply several different principles."

I drew the following on the board.

NORTH

♠ K 5
♡ A 8 7 5 3
♢ J 9
♣ Q 7 4 2

SOUTH

♠ A Q J 10 9 4
♡ 6 2
♢ A 10
♣ A K 8

"Your contract is six spades, and the opening lead is the queen of hearts. How would you plan the play?"

Barbara studied the hand almost five minutes before saying a word. The other players were growing restless.

"Don't become impatient," I cautioned. "Declarer should plan the play of the entire hand before playing to the first trick. Normally, one or two minutes will be sufficient, but this is a difficult hand. It is wise to do your thinking before you make a misplay, since then it is too late. Besides, you won't really waste any time, since you won't have to think after each trick."

"I duck the first trick," said Barbara almost defiantly.

"Then what?" I asked.

"West might as well continue hearts. I win with the ace and ruff a heart high. Suppose the hearts split 4-2. Then I must play the ace of spades, the four of spades to the king, and ruff another heart. Next the opponents' trumps are drawn. The queen of clubs will be my entry to the good heart, upon which I can discard the ten of diamonds."

"Weren't you afraid of a heart ruff?" I asked her.

"No, not particularly. The way I played I could make the hand if hearts split 3-3 or 4-2. It would not be right to win the first trick, because for this play to be right hearts must split 5-1 and clubs must split 3-3. There is no reason to assume that hearts will split very badly and clubs will split perfectly."

"The hand was nicely played, and your analysis was clear

and logical. This has been a long and difficult lesson. When we get to bidding, it will seem very easy by comparison."

"Wait," Barbara said. "You're not going to leave without giving us a homework assignment, are you?"

"You ornery little dickens," said Henry. "I had to threaten and cajole you to do your homework when you were in school. Now you beg for it. Well, better late than never."

"First," I asked, "how should the following holdings be played to give North the maximum number of entries?"

(a) NORTH	(b) NORTH	(c) NORTH	(d) NORTH
A Q J 4	A J	A 10 5	A Q 9

SOUTH	SOUTH	SOUTH	SOUTH
9 8 7 3	K 2	K Q 3	K 3 2

West's opening lead in example (d) is the jack of diamonds. (Hint: lead of the jack normally guarantees possession of the ten also.)

"Next, how should declarer plan the play of the following four hands?"

(a)	(b)
♠ A 8 5 3 2	♠ A 9 8 5 3
♡ 6 4 3	♡ A 7
◇ A 7 5	◇ 5 4 3
♣ Q 4	♣ 6 5 4
♠ 7 6	♠ K Q
♡ 9	♡ K 8 3
◇ K 8 3	◇ A 7 6 2
♣ A K J 10 6 5 2	♣ A K 8 3
CONTRACT: 5 ♣	3 NT
LEAD: ♡ K and ♡ A	♡ Q

	(c)		(d)
	♠ 7 6 2		♠ 7 4
	♡ A		♡ 8 5
	◇ 9 8 5		◇ A K Q 4 3
	♣ 9 8 7 5 4 3		♣ A 9 7 6
	♠ K Q 10		♠ A 8 6 5 2
	♡ K 5 3 2		♡ A K 6
	◇ A K Q J		◇ 9 8 7 5
	♣ A 6		♣ 4

CONTRACT: 3 NT   3 NT
LEAD: ♡ Q   ♣ K

CHAPTER 5

Defense

"ALICE, did you have any trouble with the first group of problems?" I asked.

"Not except for the last one," she replied. "In problem (a) I can get four entries if the suit breaks favorably. The nine is led to the jack, the eight to the queen, the seven to the ace, and the three to the four. In problem (b) I lead the deuce and finesse the jack. However, if I were really playing the hand, I don't think I would do that, because I might lose a trick that would not otherwise be lost."

"That would not bother me," said Henry. "If I should need the finesse and an extra entry to make my contract, I would gladly risk being set an extra trick. But West could foil my attempt by playing the queen when I lead low. Consequently my only chance is to lead the king to the ace and hope that the queen is a singleton."

"What do you think, Barbara?"

"Obviously, Dad is correct in saying that West *could* play the queen so as to prevent North from gaining an extra entry. But how would West know when to make the play? With Q x x x x , for example, wouldn't he normally play small? I don't know what the chances are of finding eight diamonds in one hand and the singleton queen in the other, but I think I'd rather lead low toward the ace-jack and hope that West wouldn't play the queen."

"You are right, Barbara," I said. "When I show the distribution of a suit on the blackboard, you can see all four hands, and it is obvious what each player should do. When you are playing or defending a hand, you only see your own cards and dummy's. Suppose you hold Q x x x and see A J in the dummy. For every time declarer has K x and needs an extra entry to the dummy, there will be ten times that he holds K 10 x x and needs to take three diamond tricks without losing the lead. Hopping up with the queen would not only avoid a guess, it would give him *four* tricks. Even when West ought to see what the right play is, it is better to hope that he will make a mistake than to play for a remote legitimate chance—like dropping a singleton queen with nine diamonds outstanding. Jerry, could you get three entries from A Q 9 opposite K 3 2?"

"Yes—with the clue you gave us that West should have the ten, win with the ace or queen. Later I would lead low and finesse the nine."

"West could stymie you by playing the ten when you lead low, couldn't he?"

"Yes. But as you just pointed out, West probably would not do this."

"What I said was to play for an error, *if necessary,* or at least not expect the defenders to play as though they could see your hand. When there is a safe way to play, by all means take it. Also, in this case West would not have too much difficulty in figuring out what you have. Henry, do you see a better play?"

"The jack should be won with the ace, South dropping the king. Later the nine may be finessed."

"Very good, Henry. How did you play the next group of hands?"

"The five-club contract is easy. I ruff the second trick and duck a spade. If a diamond is returned, I win in my hand to save the ace of diamonds for later. A spade to the ace and a spade ruff, followed by a club to the queen and another spade—"

"I hate to interrupt you," I broke in, "but what club would you use to ruff the third spade?"

"It depends upon what East does. If he discards on the

third spade, I can ruff low, since I know West still has spades. If East follows suit I would ruff high. A 4-2 spade split is more likely than a 4-1 trump split."

"How did you know that?"

"I once saw a table of probabilities. Someone figured out what the percentages were for all sorts of suit breaks. I don't remember the figures, but I do remember that doubletons occur more frequently than singletons, and singletons more frequently than voids. Somehow it makes sense to me, but I can't explain why."

"What about the other hands?"

"Hand (c) is also easy. At trick one I am in the dummy for the last time. My best chance for two spade tricks is to finesse the ten.

"Hand (d) is sort of cute," he continued. "The diamonds are apparently blocked, no matter how I play them. If they split 2-2 I can win the third round in my hand and the fourth round with an honor in dummy. But if they split 3-1 I must win the fourth round in my hand, unless I can somehow get rid of a diamond. The key to the hand is to duck the opening club lead. Whether clubs are continued or not, I plan to discard a diamond on the ace of clubs. That will unblock the suit."

"Hand (b) bothers me because I don't see the problems," said Henry. "I simply cash the queen and king of spades, enter dummy with the ace of hearts, and cash the ace of spades. In order to make the hand, the spades must split 3-3, or else the jack-ten must drop doubleton."

"Barbara, how would you play the hand?"

"I wouldn't put all my eggs in one basket. Upon winning with the king of hearts, I would cash the king and queen of spades, then play the ace, king, and another club. This might establish a small club for my ninth trick. If the spades break for me, fine—but there is no hurry to play them. Once the ace of hearts is played, the opponents can probably take the setting tricks in hearts before I can establish a club trick."

"You continue to amaze me, Barbara That is not what I had

in mind with this example, but your play is just about as good
as the play I intended to recommend. However, let's assume
that someone has bid clubs, so you are pretty sure they won't
split 3-3. Is there any way you can increase your chances of
taking at least four spade tricks?"

"Aha, I see it now! Play the king of spades, then overtake
the queen with the ace to lead the nine. If the suit splits 3-3,
this will lose a trick, but I'll still get four tricks, which is all
that I need. However, this play will also work if the suit splits
4-2, provided the doubleton is headed by the jack or ten. If the
jack or ten drops on the second round, the nine will force out
the remaining honor, after which the eight and the five will
be good."

"Excellent! Now we shall consider the new subject for this
evening: defense. In most of the examples given to you so far,
the defenders have played quite well. When declarer had a
weakness, they plugged away at it; when the correct play was
to lead trumps, they usually led trumps. However, good defense
is very difficult. The play of the cards is the same whether by
declarer or defenders. In other words, the defenders have the
same problems as declarer regarding suit establishment—leading
up to strength rather than away from it, preserving their own
entries and destroying their opponent's, and so on. What makes
the defenders' problems unique is that they do not know the
extent of their combined assets, while declarer does. In order
to defend well, the defenders must give each other all the
information they can.

"Before going further, let me explain that the only proper
way to give information to partner is by bidding or by playing
a certain card. The *manner* in which you bid or play is not
supposed to give partner any information. If you acquire any
such information from partner, even though it was unintentional
on his part, you are honor bound to disregard it."

"When I first started to play bridge in the Army," said
Henry, "some of the fellows suggested playing 'two no trump'
to mean one thing and 'two no' to mean something else. They

weren't sneaky or crooked about it. In fact, we all thought this was a brilliant idea until some kill-joy came along and showed us the rules."

"It is obvious that there are many ways other than those mentioned which you could use to describe your hand," I said. "But it would ruin the game to allow them. For example, you are not supposed to play a card with particular emphasis or uncertainty, nor with excessive speed or deliberation, to indicate your holding. It would be easy to work out signals along these lines, but to do so would constitute cheating. Furthermore, you are not supposed to do anything to deliberately mislead the opponents—except, of course, by bids made or cards played. In other words, you are not supposed to appear confident when you are afraid of being doubled, or pretend to have a choice of plays when you do not—for instance, when you hold a singleton. I think the rules should be changed to allow you to mislead the opponents so long as you do not give information to your partner—for example, when you are declarer. However, most people do not agree with me. You have to play bridge according to the way it is usually played or you risk being ostracized.

"Getting back to signals which *are* allowed, the two basic ways of describing your hand on defense are by the card you lead and by the card you play when partner leads. Let's start with leads. Any time you have three or more cards in sequence headed by an honor, lead the top card of the sequence, other than the ace. With the following holdings, lead the card italicized. K Q J, Q J 10 7 5, J 10 9 4, 10 9 8 7 5 3 2, K J 10 9 6, A K Q 6. With a broken sequence—two touching cards followed by a skip—it is usually correct to lead the top of the sequence. Q J 9 4, J 10 8 5 3, K Q 10, A K J 7. As you can see, the lead of an honor denies possession of the honor immediately above it, with one exception. The lead of the king does not deny possession of the ace; in fact, it is the other way around—leading the ace denies possession of the king! Against suit contracts, the top card should be led from two card sequences if the suit is led at all. Q J 4, K Q 8 5, J 10 7, A K 7 3.

The latter holding is a desirable lead. Partner may have the queen or a doubleton. Even when he has neither, the lead seldom costs anything.

"Alice, against a heart contract, would you prefer to lead a club or a spade with the following holding

♠ Q J 10 7   ♡ Q 7   ◇ x x x   ♣ K J x x?"

"A spade."

"Why?"

"Culbertson said that top of a sequence is a desirable lead. A lead from a ten-ace is not."

"Yes, but why? Can you think of anything I told you in an earlier lesson that would be relevant to this problem?"

"No, you haven't discussed leads."

"Can you help her, Jerry?"

"You pointed out that it's desirable to lead up to strength rather than away from it, particularly when it's broken strength. If your right hand opponent has the ace-queen of clubs, you would lose a trick by leading away from the king-jack. However, it ought to be pretty safe to lead the queen from Q J 10 x."

"Culbertson had a list of leads in order of preference," I said. "A lead from K J x x against a suit contract was near the bottom of the list and as I recall, A x x and A J x were holdings that should never be led from. The table of leads was intended only as a general guide. When you don't have a sequence to lead from, lead fourth best from a four-card or longer suit. The proper lead is italicized: K J 7 *5* 3, Q 10 8 *7*, A J 8 *5* 4 2, K Q 8 *6* 4. In the last two examples, the indicated lead was against a no-trump contract. It would be highly undesirable to lead from A J 8 5 4 2 against a suit contract, since it is seldom correct to try to establish a long suit on defense except against no trump. The opponents can probably trump the second or third round of the suit. If you do lead the suit, the ace is the correct lead. By leading small, you might lose your ace. In the last example the king would be the proper lead against a suit contract. After leading fourth best, the next time you play to the suit play the fifth best, provided you do not need to play a high card for any reason. Thus, if you lead the four of spades and play the deuce next time, there are only two possibilities. You started with five spades or two.

"With a doubleton or three small cards, lead your top card. After leading your eight from 8 6 4, play the six next time; in other words, play from top to bottom. With three cards to an honor—J 8 3, Q 10 7, and so on—lead your smallest card.

"All of these rules have a purpose," I continued. "Not only do they give the defenders direct or positive information, they also provide inferential or negative information. Jerry, suppose that you are East, and partner has led the jack of diamonds; dummy has K 5 4 of diamonds and you hold A 8 3. Who has the queen?"

"It must be declarer. Partner's lead of the jack denied possession of the queen, since you always lead the higher or highest of touching honors."

"Jerry, you are still East. This time partner leads the seven of diamonds and dummy plays small. Yours and dummy's diamonds are as follows:

NORTH
K J 8 5

EAST
Q 9 4 2

"Can you figure out how the diamonds are distributed? First, can partner's seven be his fourth-best diamond?"

"No. Because there are only two missing diamonds which are higher than the seven."

"Could partner have led the seven from A 10 7?"

"It seems unlikely. You told us you seldom underlead an ace, at least against suit contracts."

"There is an even more convincing reason. Suppose West had A 10 7, leaving declarer with 6 3. As declarer, what would you play from dummy when the seven is led?"

"Probably the jack. At least I wouldn't play the five."

"In the very unlikely event that partner *has* led the seven from A 10 7, his seven will win the trick. If his lead is from the singleton 7, the 7 6, 7 3, or 7 6 3, playing the queen will give declarer all four diamond tricks. The principle is that you should decide whether partner's lead of a spot-card can be fourth best. If not, it must be third best from three to an honor or top of a short holding. Usually, the bidding and de-clarer's play from the dummy will provide additional clues.

"Now let's consider third-hand play. As a general rule, third hand should play high provided he can beat the card played from dummy and partner's card, although there are many ex-ceptions such as the one just mentioned. The following diagram illustrates why it is usually correct for third hand to play high. West leads the deuce of hearts. If East plays small, South will make two heart tricks. If East plays the queen, declarer can be held to one heart trick—provided West does not lead the second round of hearts.

NORTH
♡ 9 8 5

WEST
♡ K 10 7 2

SOUTH
♡ A J 6

EAST
♡ Q 4 3

"There are four main exceptions to the third-hand-high rule. Henry, can you state one of them?"

"You play the lower or lowest of equals. If partner leads a low spade and I have Q J x, I should play the jack rather than the queen. With Q J 10, the correct play is the ten. Con-sequently, the play of a card in third position denies pos-session of the card immediately below it."

"Can you state a second exception?"

"Sometimes you finesse against partner."

"I know what you mean, but more accurate terminology is that you finesse against dummy. Suppose that you are de-clarer, and your and dummy's club holdings are as follows.

NORTH
♣ K 10 7

SOUTH
♣ J 9 6 4 2

You would lead low from the South hand and finesse the ten, hoping that West has the queen. Perhaps the whole suit will be distributed as follows.

NORTH
♣ K 10 7

WEST   **EAST**
♣ Q 5 3   **SOUTH**   **♣ A 8**
            ♣ J 9 6 4 2

Next time you will lead the jack or nine to repeat the finesse against West's queen. *Whether you are declarer or defender, the suit should be played the same way.*

NORTH
♣ Q 5 3

EAST
♣ K 10 7

Partner leads the four of clubs and dummy plays small. You should still play the ten in order to hold declarer to one trick in the suit if he has A x or A x x. Despite this exception to the third-hand-high rule, your play of the ten denies possession of the nine. With K 10 9, you would play the nine.

"A third exception to the third-hand-high rule is when dummy will play last to the trick. In that case, you play your smallest card that will force an honor or win the trick. This exception is difficult to state, but an example should clarify it. Suppose that you are West. Partner wins the fourth trick and returns a small heart. At that time, your and dummy's hearts are as follows.

NORTH

♡ A 7 3

WEST

♡ K 10 8

"If South plays the jack or queen you will play the king. If he plays the nine you will play the ten, since the ten will force out the ace just as well as the king would. If declarer plays small and the eight will drive out the ace—or win the trick if declarer refuses to play the ace—then you would play the eight."

"What is the last main exception to the rule of third-hand-high?"

"It is when you recognize partner's lead as top of nothing, and you can tell that playing a high card will not establish a trick for either you or partner. The hand where East had Q 9 x x of diamonds and dummy had K J x x was an example.

"Another example is as follows.

NORTH

♡ J 10 9 8 6

EAST

♡ Q 4 3

"Partner leads the seven of hearts, which you know is his highest heart. He would not lead the seven from A K 7. Dummy plays the eight. You should play small for several reasons. First, declarer may have ace-king alone, in which case playing the queen would lose a trick in the suit. Second, if declarer has A K x, playing the queen gives him an entry to the long suit, while if the eight is allowed to win, the suit is, at least temporarily, blocked. Third, since there is no purpose in covering with Q x x, partner will assume that you also have the king if you play the queen—provided declarer is shrewd enough to win with the ace. You certainly do not want to give partner any encouragement or excuse to play hearts again.

"It is not always clear-cut which card you should play."

I then drew the following diagram on the board.

NORTH
♠ K J 5

EAST
♠ Q 9 8

"Partner leads the three of spades and dummy plays small. If partner is leading low from the ace, your winning play is the queen. If declarer has the ace you should play the eight, hoping that partner has the ten. But the nine can never be the right play. Notice that the only time these problems arise is when dummy has a high card, or high cards, to finesse against. When dummy has two or three small cards the queen would always be the right play from Q 9 8.

"Barbara, let's see what inferences you can draw from partner's play.

NORTH
◇ 8 7

WEST
◇ Q 10 6 3 2

You lead the three of diamonds, partner plays the jack, and declarer wins with the ace. Who has the king?"

"Declarer."

"How can you tell?"

"Because partner would play the king, if he had it, with K J x."

NORTH
◇ 8 7

WEST
◇ J 10 6 3 2

"Again you lead the three of diamonds, partner plays the king, and declarer wins with the ace. Who has the queen?"

"Declarer. Partner would play the queen from K Q."

NORTH
◊ 5 7

WEST
◊ J 10 6 3 2

"You lead the three of diamonds, partner plays the queen, and declarer wins with the ace. Who has the king?"

"I can't tell."

"It is true that you cannot tell from partner's play. Suppose that the contract is no trump. Who would you suspect has the king?"

"Declarer. Because with A x x, for example, he would probably duck the first couple of tricks."

NORTH
◊ Q 7 4

WEST
◊ J 10 6 3 2

"You lead the three of diamonds, dummy plays low, partner plays the nine, and declarer wins the ace. Who has the king?"

"I can't tell. The nine might be partner's highest card, or he may have played the nine from K 9 x. The only card I can be sure of is the eight-spot. It must be in declarer's hand."

"All the examples of third-hand play thus far have had one thing in common. Third-hand at least had a chance to play a higher card than the one led or played by second hand. Suppose that partner leads from a sequence or dummy plays a card that you cannot beat. What should you play then? For example:

NORTH
♠ 8 4 2
♡ Q J 7 5
◇ K Q J 4
♣ 7 5

EAST
♠ Q 9 3
♡ 8 4
◇ 9 8 6
♣ J 8 6 4 2

"Partner leads the king of spades against a four-heart contract. You cannot beat the king, so what should you do? You should decide whether to encourage partner to play more spades, or discourage him so that he will shift to another suit. Partner's lead could be from the ace-king or the king-queen, but since you have the queen you know it is from the former holding. Maybe you can take the first three spade tricks if partner continues spades, and you surely do not want him to shift to another suit. So you should play the nine of spades. When it is not necessary to play a high card to win a trick or to force out a high card from an opponent's hand, the play of an unnecessarily high card asks partner to continue the suit. The play of your lowest card suggests a switch, or at least tells partner to continue at his own risk.

"The contract, the opening lead, and dummy are the same, but this time your hand is ♠ 9 3 ♡ 8 4 ◇ 9 8 6 2 ♣ J 8 6 4 2. What spade would you play, Barbara?"

"The nine. Partner may be leading from ace-king. When he continues the suit, I'll ruff the third round."

"True. But suppose partner is leading the king from K Q 10 x x. When he continues the suit, declarer will take a trick with his jack."

"I didn't think of that. Besides, the hand looks rather hopeless for the defense unless partner has the ace-king. So far as I am concerned, a spade continuation looks like our best chance. Surely I have no reason to encourage partner to lead something else."

I then drew the following on the board.

NORTH
♣ K 7 4

EAST
♣ Q 8 5

"Partner leads the three of clubs against a no-trump contract, and dummy plays the king. You have a reasonable amount of strength in partner's suit and should encourage him to continue, the next time he is on lead, by playing the eight. Suppose that your club holdings were Q J 5. In that case, you should play the *queen!* Whenever you are playing high to win a trick or force out a high card, you should play the lower or lowest of equal honors. When you are discarding or signaling, you should play your highest! Playing the jack under these circumstances would deny possession of the queen. Why the different rules? The reason why you play lowest of equals to force out a high card from fourth hand is that partner can figure out what you had to a certain extent by what the fourth hand played.

"For example, if he were to lead low from the king and your jack were to force declarer's ace, he could be pretty sure that you had the queen—otherwise declarer would have won the trick with the queen. When third hand's play does not affect fourth hand's play, this clue no longer exists. Consider an extreme example. Suppose declarer leads a heart. I have no hearts, but I do have K Q J 10 in clubs. If I discard the ten partner cannot tell what I have, since my ten won't force out one of declarer's honors. Similarly, if partner leads a club and dummy's ace is played, the ten could be played from J 10, Q J 10, or K Q J 10, if the bottom card of the sequence were played. Discarding or signaling with the king gives more information. It is more important for partner to know the top card of your sequence than for him to know the bottom card.

"Alice," I then said, "the contract is four spades. Which club would you lead from the following holdings?"

(a) K Q J   (b) Q J 9 8   (c) 7 6 4 2   (d) J 9 7 5 3   (e) A K 9
(f) 8 5   (g) 9 7 5   (h) K J 10 8   (i) Q 10 9 7 3   (j) Q 10 8 6 4 2
(k) A J 9 5 2

"My top card in (a) and (b). My fourth-best in (c) and (d). My king in (e). My top card in (f) and (g). My fourth-best in the next three examples, and the ace in the last example."

"All of those leads could be right. However, with K J 10 8 most players would lead the jack, and with Q 10 9 7 3 most players would lead the ten. This is the top card from an interior sequence. If you did not have the king or queen, that is the card you would lead. So it is still the correct lead. Suppose the whole suit were distributed as follows.

```
                   NORTH
                   ♣ Q x x

   WEST                              EAST
   ♣ K J 10 8      SOUTH            ♣ A x x
                   ♣ 9 x x
```

```
                   NORTH
                   ♣ J x x

   WEST                              EAST
   ♣ Q 10 9 7 3    SOUTH            ♣ K x x
                   ♣ A 8
```

"In both cases, the fourth-best lead could cost you a trick. Now suppose the contract is three no trump. Would this cause you to make a different lead?"

"Only in the last example. I would lead my fourth-best instead of the ace."

"Jerry, the contract is three no trump. Partner leads the two of spades, and dummy plays small from Q 7 3. What do you play with each of the following holdings?"

(a)	(b)	(c)	(d)
J 9 4	J 10 4	K J 8	K J 10

(e)	(f)	(g)	(h)
K 10 8	K 10 9	A 10 6	A 9 6

"The first six are easy. The jack, the ten, the jack, the ten, the ten and the nine. The last two I don't know about. How deep do you finesse?"

"Let me ask you a question in return. How many spades does declarer have?"

"Three. I assume that partner has led from a four-card suit."

"Could partner have had more than four spades?"

"No. If he had more than four spades, the deuce would not be his fourth-best."

"Let's assume first that partner has the king of spades. What would your correct play be?"

"The nine or ten. I wouldn't expect the nine to win the trick, but the ten might, if partner led from king-jack. In any event, if I play the ace declarer must win a trick later with the queen."

"In other words, playing the nine or ten gives you a chance, however remote, of running the suit, while going up with the ace gives declarer a trick for sure. Now suppose that declarer has the king."

"In that case, it is surely correct to play the ten or nine. Playing the ace gives declarer two tricks, while the finesse may hold him to one trick if partner has the jack-nine or jack-ten."

"If the contract were four hearts instead of three no trump, would your play be different in any case?"

"I don't think so."

"What do you think, Henry?"

"In the last two examples I might play the ace. The assumption at no trump is that whatever tricks you have coming you will get eventually. Even that is not always true. The right play might be to win with the ace and shift to another suit. However, usually the finesse is right at no trump. Usually at a suit contract

I would not be willing to let the declarer win the first trick cheaply for fear he would get rid of his remaining losers on a long suit."

I next drew the following diagram.

NORTH
♠ Q 7 5

WEST
♠ 10 8 6 4 2

"Henry, you lead the four of spades, dummy plays the five, partner the king, and declarer the ace. Who has the jack?"

"Declarer. If partner had the king-jack, he would have played the jack."

"Suppose that dummy plays the five, partner the king, and declarer the three. Who has the ace?"

"I couldn't tell. Declarer might be holding off."

"Who has the jack?"

"Declarer."

"Would declarer let the king win if he had the ace-jack?"

"No, I guess he wouldn't. Partner is pretty well marked with the ace. Declarer surely would not duck with A J 3, since it would cost him a trick. With A J 9 3, a duck would be rather pointless, to say the least."

"You lead the four, dummy plays the queen, partner the king, and declarer the ace. Who has the jack?"

"Probably partner. With A J, A J 9, A J 3, or A J 9 3, declarer would almost surely play low from dummy."

NORTH
♡ K 8

WEST
♡ 9 7 5 4 3

"You lead a heart, dummy's king wins, partner plays the jack. Who has the ace?"

"Declarer. Because partner would have won the king with the ace if he had it."

"Who has the queen?"

"Declarer."

"How do you know?"

"Because you said that East should play the higher or highest of touching honors when he cannot beat one of the cards already played. He must have started with J 10 or J 10 x. With Q J x, if he were to signal at all, he would play the queen."

NORTH

◊ J 8 3

EAST

◊ 9 4

"Partner leads the king of diamonds. Which diamond do you play, Barbara?"

"It depends upon what the contract is, doesn't it? If it were a suit contract I would probably play the nine to encourage partner to continue diamonds so that I could ruff. If the contract were no trump, there would be no reason to encourage partner with this diamond holding."

CHAPTER 6

Introduction to Bidding Theory

"TONIGHT we shall discuss bidding. After the last few lessons, this lesson is going to seem very easy indeed."

"Are you trying to use psychology on us?" asked Jerry. "If bidding is so much easier than play, why didn't you teach us how to bid first?"

"The reason I didn't take up bidding first is that you need to know something about the play in order to be able to tell when you are in a good contract. Also, you ought to know something about scoring so as to understand the objective of bidding. Otherwise my comments on bidding would not be very meaningful to you.

"Alice, why are clubs and diamonds called 'minor suits' while hearts and spades are called 'major suits'?"

"Because clubs and diamonds are only worth 20 points a trick while the majors are worth 30 points a trick."

"How would you expect that to affect the bidding?"

"We have to bid higher in a minor suit and take more tricks to get the same score as we would for bidding less in a major."

I then drew a typical score sheet.

"Do you remember what the purpose of the horizontal line is?" I asked.

"Yes," said Henry. "The score for the tricks we bid goes below the line. Everything else goes above the line."

"What difference does it make whether the score goes above or below the line?"

"Only the score below the line counts toward *game*."

"What is a *game*?"

"It is what you receive when you score 100 points or more below the line. I started to say it is a bonus, but you don't get a bonus for game, only for rubber."

"Okay, I'd better take over with the explanation now. As you remember from your first lesson, declarer must take six tricks before he can start counting his 'trick score.' Let's suppose the contract is two diamonds and declarer takes nine tricks. We say he has made three diamonds—we don't count the first six tricks unless he fails to take them. If he should only take five tricks altogether at this two-diamond contract, he would be down three because he failed to take the eight tricks he was supposed to.

"Suppose you bid two hearts and make five—eleven tricks in all. You receive points for each trick taken, but the score for the contract goes below the line. Thus, the score would look like this.

```
        WE  |  THEY
            |
            |
        90  |
        60  |
            |
```

"When 100 points are scored below the line, it entitles the side that scores these points to a *game*, which is worth roughly 300 additional points. As it happens, these additional points are not scored immediately. Instead, the side which first scores two games wins the *rubber* and receives a 500- or 700-point bonus. There is also a slam bonus for bidding and making six or seven, but don't worry about that for a while. Incidentally, the first trick at no trump counts 40 points and subsequent tricks count 30 points. Consequently, in order to make game in one hand you must bid three no trump, four of a major, or five of a minor.

"The important thing is that you have to bid approximately what you think you can make in order to be successful. In the example just given, you bid *two* hearts and made *five*. As a result of bidding just two hearts you scored 60 points below the line—not enough for game. If you had bid four hearts, you would have scored 120 points below the line, which would have been enough. For that matter, you could have bid five hearts, but it would not have done any good to bid more than four. The objective is to get *100 points or more* below the line. Since five is harder to make than four, and it carries no additional rewards, five hearts and five spades are undesirable contracts. Jerry, can you think of any reason for bidding five hearts or five spades?"

"Yes, the opponents might have bid up to five clubs, and if I wanted to play the hand I would have to outbid them."

"Alice, what is the disadvantage in not bidding enough?"

"You only get credit *toward game* for what you bid."

"Right! In our example where you bid two hearts and made five, you scored 60 points below the line. On the next hand, if you were to bid and make two diamonds, you would score an additional 40 points below the line, and it would complete the game. The trouble is that the opponents may score a game before you do, in which case your 'leg' or 'part-score' is cut off or canceled, and you have to start all over. If you had bid four hearts you would already have scored game. Besides, if you bid two hearts and make four, then again bid two hearts and make four, you will have scored *one* game. If you had bid four hearts each time, you would have scored two games. What is the disadvantage in bidding too much?"

"There is a penalty for being set. If the opponents realize you have bid too much, they can increase this penalty by doubling you."

"Yes. Not only do you lose points as a penalty, you fail to

receive the points below the line you would otherwise have received. Suppose you bid four spades and only take nine tricks. The next hand all you can make is three diamonds. These points, added to the points from the previous hand which you threw away by bidding too much, would be enough for game.

"Consequently, your objective is to bid game when you can make it or to stop at a safe, comfortable part-score as soon as you discover that you do not have enough strength for game. How can you tell? When you look at your partner's hand and yours, you can tell pretty well—although even then it may depend somewhat upon the opponents' hands."

"Suppose a game contract depends upon a finesse," Jerry said. "Should you bid game or stop in a part-score?"

"You should bid game whenever you have an even chance, or slightly less than an even chance. The system of scoring rewards aggressiveness. The problem is that you can't see partner's hand till the bidding is over, so you have to talk to partner in bridge-bidding language to find out what the two of you have. It is seldom that you can tell for a fact that your game contract will depend upon a finesse. However, by evaluating your hands, finding the proper spot, such as diamonds, hearts or no trump, and adding the worth of your two hands, you can usually determine whether the total value is sufficient to justify a game bid.

"How is this evaluation done? First, count 4 points for each ace, 3 points for each king, 2 points for each queen, and 1 point for each jack. Also, count points for distribution, which will be explained later. Experience has shown that when the two partnership hands add up to 26 points they usually belong in game—either three no trump or four of a major. Five of a minor requires about 29 points, but you usually try to bid game in no trump or a major rather than five of a minor. Let us see how this works.

"Would you like to be in game with the following pairs of hands, Jerry?"

(1)	(2)	(3)	(4)
♠ A Q x	♠ A Q x	♠ x x	♠ x
♡ K Q x x	♡ K Q x x x	♡ Q x x x	♡ K Q x x x
◊ Q x x	◊ Q x x	◊ K x x x	◊ K x x x
♣ x x x	♣ x x	♣ x x x	♣ x x x
♠ K x x	♠ K x x	♠ x x x	♠ A J x
♡ A J x	♡ A x x	♡ A K J x x	♡ A J x x x
◊ K J x	◊ J x x	◊ A x	◊ A x
♣ J x x x	♣ A x x x	♣ A K x	♣ x x x

"Yes, I would. The first hand will provide nine sure tricks by knocking out the opponents' ace of diamonds—unless they can take four club tricks in the meantime, and that possibility does not frighten me. In the second hand, three no trump is cold if the hearts break. The last two hands are excellent four-heart contracts."

"The first hand contains 26 points, 13 in each hand. The second hand contains 26 points counting 1 point for North's five-card suit. You don't know how to count points for distribution yet, so you will just have to take my word for it. In the third hand South has 20 points as a heart bidder and North has 6 points in support of hearts—his ruffing value is worth a point. The combined total in the last pair of hands is 26 points for hearts—North is worth 11 points in support of hearts! —but only 23 at no trump. So you can see that a combined total of 26 points usually provides a good play for game."

"Wouldn't the last group of hands contain the same number of points if South had K Q x of spades instead of A J x?" asked Barbara.

"Yes."

"In that case, the opponents could take the first four tricks."

"Twenty-six points do not guarantee game. Nor do you need 26 points to have a good play for game. In the last example, take away South's jacks, leaving a combined total of 24 points, and the two hands would still belong in game. When the hands are unbalanced, that is, when one or both hands have long suits or singletons, our bidding accuracy suffers. Much depends upon how well the hands fit. In the long run it still pays to bid game in a major with a combined total of 26 points, and to stop in a part-score with less. After you have become more experienced you may occasionally predict how well the hands fit, and may deliberately bid game with less than 26 points or refuse to bid game with more."

CHAPTER 7

Making the Responses Mesh

"BARBARA, how many points would you expect a person to need in order to open the bidding?"

"Probably 13."

"Why?"

"Someone has to open with 13 points, because if both partners pass with 13 points a game would be missed. On the other hand, both partners could afford to pass with less than 13 points since their combined total then necessarily would be less than 26."

"The opening bid of one of a suit should show approximately 13 to 21 points inclusive. Obviously the partner of the opening bidder, whom we shall call the responder, must assume the responsibility for reaching game when he has 13 points or more."

"How do the players show their points?" asked Jerry.

"Every bid shows some sort of range. It would be possible to play a system like this: An opening bid of one club shows 12-13 high card points; one diamond shows 14-15 points; one heart shows 16-17; one spade shows 18-19; one no trump shows 20-21. Then responder could make the cheapest bid—such as one heart over one diamond—to show 6 points or less, the next cheapest bid to show 7-8 points, and so on. In fact, a long time ago a system called the 'Anchor System' was developed that worked essentially just as described. After each player had shown his point count, each player showed his best suit.

"There are several bad features about this system. For one thing, by using the first round of bidding to show high card strength, there was less time—fewer rounds of bidding—to find out about distribution. Another serious disadvantage was that when the opponents entered the bidding, especially with a jump bid, before the partnership had completed its message, it was very difficult to guess what to do. Playing standard bridge, if my partner should bid one heart and my right-hand opponent should bid two spades, I could bid three hearts with ♠ x x ♡ K J x x ◇ A x x x x ♣ x x. With a minimum opening bid partner would pass. With extra values he would bid game. But I could bid hearts because I know my partner has hearts. Similarly, I could raise if he had bid diamonds. But if I knew neither what his best suit was nor his approximate distribution—merely that he held 12 to 13 points in high cards, I would have to pass.

"Another reason why we do not use the Anchor System is that often it is not necessary to know exactly how many points partner has. Why wouldn't I need to know, Henry?"

"Perhaps because your hand was so horrible you couldn't bid whether partner's hand was weak or strong."

"That is one reason, but not the only reason. Suppose I open the bidding with 14 points and partner makes a bid which shows 6 to 10 points. Whether he has 6 or 10 points, we are still short of the 26 needed for game. So I am merely concerned with finding a reasonable part-score contract. On the other hand, if I have 17 points and partner makes a bid showing 6 to 10, I am interested in knowing whether he has the top or the bottom of his range. In this case I shall make a bid which will seek this information. Sometimes I will want to know exactly how many points partner has; other times I won't care. Consequently, the first bid usually shows a rather wide range. Subsequent bids narrow the range. It is preferable to have fairly wide high-card ranges, but to start giving information about distribution right away, than to use narrow high-card ranges and keep your distribution a secret. Jerry, I told you that an opening bid of one of a suit shows a range of 13 to 21 points. What would you expect responder's range to be for a bid at the one-level?"

"I am afraid I don't get the point. I don't know."

"Barbara?"

"Five to 27."

"How did you arrive at that answer?"

"Responder has to bid with 5 points. Otherwise game might be missed when opener has 21 points. And 27 would be his maximum because opener has at least 13, and there are only 40 points in the deck."

"How did you arrive at the 40-point total?"

"There are 10 points in each suit—4 for the ace, 3 for the king, 2 for the queen, and 1 for the jack."

"Your reasoning is logical and I am pleased with your answer because it shows you have a grasp of the basic principles. However, your answer is not correct. Some players do respond with as few as 5 points to avoid the possibility of missing game when opener is very strong. Most of us are convinced that it is better to pass without 6 points or more. Partner doesn't have 21 points very often, and when he has less strength we usually get too high by responding with 5 points. We are willing to risk missing game on rare occasions in order to narrow the range, increase our accuracy, and avoid getting too high on the rest of the hands. Regarding the upper range, you have no way of knowing, but responder almost always jumps the bidding so as to suggest a slam with 17 points or more. Also, you were overlooking something when you assumed that 27 points was the most responder could have."

"Well, the most he could have is 27 points in high cards. We haven't learned yet how to count distribution."

"No, you haven't. But you were assuming that opener has 13 *high-card* points. He may have only 10 or 11 provided his distribution is good. Now is a good time to tell you how the opener evaluates his hand. After counting up his high card points, opener should add points for distribution as follows: 1 point for each card in excess of 4 in his long suit, and 1 point for each card in excess of 3 in the other suits. For example: ♠ K Q x x x ♡ K x x ◊ A x x ♣ x x. There are 12 high-card points, and 1 point is added for the fifth spade, making 13 'basic' points. ♠ K Q x ♡ K x x x x x ◊ A x ♣ x x has 14 basic points. Two distributional points are added for the fifth and sixth hearts. ♠ K Q x x x ♡ K x x ◊ A x x x ♣ x also has 14 basic points. One point is added for the fifth spade, another for the fourth diamond.

$$\spadesuit \text{ K Q x x} \quad \heartsuit \text{ K x x x x x} \quad \Diamond \text{ A x x} \quad \clubsuit -$$

has 15 basic points, the same as

$$\spadesuit \text{ K Q x x} \quad \heartsuit \text{ K x x x x x} \quad \Diamond \text{ A} \quad \clubsuit \text{ x x.''}$$

"What about ♠ K Q x x x ♡ K x ◊ A x x x x ♣ x?" asked Henry. "Which is considered the long suit?"

"It doesn't matter. Call either your 'long' suit and the other suit the 'other' suit. In either case, you get the same answer —15 basic points. Similarly, with

$$\spadesuit \text{ K Q x x} \quad \heartsuit \text{ K x x x} \quad \Diamond \text{ A x} \quad \clubsuit \text{ x x x,}$$

you get no points for length on your 'long' suit and 1 point for length in your 'other' suit. With

$$\spadesuit \text{ K Q x x} \quad \heartsuit \text{ K x x x} \quad \Diamond \text{ A x x x} \quad \clubsuit \text{ x}$$

you get no points for length in your 'long' suit but one point for length in each of your 'other' suits. Alice, can you give me the basic points for each of the following hands?"

(a)
♠ K Q J x x   ♡ A Q J x   ◊ x x   ♣ x x

(b)
♠ A Q 10 x x   ♡ A K x x   ◊ —   ♣ x x x x

(c)
♠ K Q J x x x x   ♡ A J x x x   ◊ x   ♣ —

(d)
♠ Q J x   ♡ K Q x x   ◊ A J x   ♣ J 10 x

(e)

♠ x x   ♡ A x x x   ◊ A x x x   ♣ x x x

(f)

♠ x   ♡ x x   ◊ x   ♣ K J 10 9 x x x x x

Without hesitation she replied, "Fifteen, 16, 16, 14, 9, 9. That was easy. You gave us a rule to follow."

"Opening one-bids fall into three main categories. The minimum opening, or 'minny,' contains 13 to 15 basic points, at least 10 of which must be high-card points. The intermediate openings contain 16 to 18 basic points, and the strong openings contain 19 to 21 basic points. Powerhouse openings —22 basic points or more—are usually opened by two no trump or two of a suit.

"The minimum response contains 6 to 10 points—not necessarily basic points as will be explained later. But for the present let us overlook that distinction. The intermediate response contains 11 or 12 points, and the strong response shows 13 to 16 points."

"This is going to be very hard to remember," said Jerry. "Why are there two groups of categories?"

"There is a good reason for these ranges. A minimum opening bid opposite a minimum response will not make game. At most, you would find 15 points opposite 10. A minimum opener opposite a strong response is enough for game, just as a strong opener opposite a minimum response is enough for game—25 points at least, and more likely 26. It is possible for the opener, if at the top of the minimum range, to make game opposite an intermediate responder, while a minimum response, if at the top of the range, can make game opposite an intermediate opener.

OPENER	RESPONDER	or	OPENER	RESPONDER
1 ♡	1 NT		1 ♡	2 ♡

(NOTE: When no bidding is shown for the opponents, it is assumed that they pass.)

"Both the one-no-trump and two-heart responses *guarantee* a minimum response. If opener has 13 to 15 points and a balanced hand, he will pass one no trump. If he has 13 to 15 points and an unbalanced hand—♠ x x ♡ K Q 10 x x x ◇ A Q x ♣ x x or ♠ x x ♡ K Q 10 x x ◇ A Q x x x ♣ x—he will bid two hearts or two diamonds, looking for a safer contract than one no trump. Whichever type of hand he has, he will pass a raise to two hearts. This is an example of minimum opposite minimum. If——"

"Before you continue, please define a 'balanced hand,'" Alice said.

"A balanced hand is one not containing a void, a singleton, or two doubletons. In other words, 4-3-3-3, 4-4-3-2 or 5-3-3-2 distribution.

"Jerry, suppose responder had bid one spade. What would his range be?"

"From what you told Barbara, I imagine 6-16 points."

"Would one spade be forcing?"

"It would have to be. Otherwise a game would be missed whenever responder had 13-16 points, even when opener had a bare minimum."

"How can opener rebid intelligently when the response covers such a wide range? Should opener assume a minimum or maximum response?"

"I suppose he should assume an average—about 11 points."

"What do you think, Barbara?"

"Opener should assume a minimum."

"Why?"

"Because if responder has extra strength he can show it on the next round over opener's rebid. With 13 points or more he can jump to game. With 11 or 12 points responder can try for game. So opener should assume a minimum until responder says he has more than a minimum."

"Barbara is right. Opener assumes a minimum response, and if opener is minimum he should rebid in such a way as to allow the bidding to drop at a low level. After a one-heart opening and a one-spade response he may rebid one no trump, two clubs, two diamonds, two hearts, or two spades. All of these rebids will allow the bidding to die at the two-level. The rebids—one no trump, two hearts, and two spades—all *guarantee* a minimum opening bid, and if responder has a minimum response he should pass. Two clubs and two diamonds are ambiguous; they would show a minimum *or* intermediate opening bid. As Barbara said, when responder has an intermediate or strong hand, he bids again even over opener's minimum rebid because he knows that game is still possible. I won't go into further detail now.

"Alice, what is opener's range for a bid of one of a suit?"

"Thirteen-21 points."

"What are the three categories for opener and his ranges?"

"Thirteen-15, minny; 16-18 intermediate; 19-21 strong."

"What is the range for a minimum response?"

"Six-10."

"Suppose you were to forget the range. Could you figure out what it had to be?"

"Yes. Six is the lower range because if you pass with 6 you are likely to miss game when opener has 20 or 21. Ten is the upper limit because 15 is the upper limit of a minimum opener, and a minimum opener opposite a minimum response should not produce game."

"Very good, Alice. When either player can tell there is no game, what does he do?"

"He looks for the safest part-score contract. If he is in a good part-score contract already, he passes."

"Henry, when the response is ambiguous what does the opener do?"

"He assumes that responder has a minimum until responder tells him otherwise. However, opener must bid again over any ambiguous response such as:

OPENER	RESPONDER
1 ◇	1 ♠

"Opener can only pass when the response is weak and

unambiguous such as a no trump-response or a raise of opener's suit."

"When opener has enough strength to make game opposite any response, including a bare minimum, what does he do?"

"He either bids game or makes a bid that is forcing to game."

"What does opener do with an intermediate hand over a minimum or ambiguous response?"

"He makes a bid which invites responder to clarify his response and to show whether he is near the top or the bottom of his range."

"You have played more than anyone else in your group. Can you give me some examples of bids by an intermediate opener which request a clarification?"

"Yes. This may be done by rebidding two no trump

(1 ♡   P   1 NT   P   or   1 ♡   P   1 ♠   P);
2 NT   2 NT

by jumping in opener's suit

(1 ♡   P   1 NT   P   or   1 ♡   P   1 ♠   P);
3 ♡   3 ♡

by jumping in partner's suit

(1 ♡   P   1 ♠   P)
3 ♠

or by rebidding opener's suit after a raise

(1 ♡   P   2 ♡   P)."
3 ♡

"If responder has a minimum, what does he do?"

"He makes only one bid unless opener later shows a strong or intermediate hand."

"What you said is substantially, but not literally, true. Responder may have to make another bid with a bare minimum, but he makes no encouraging bid with a minimum. For example:

OPENER	RESPONDER
1 ◇	1 ♠
2 ♣	?

"Responder, with ♠ A J x x x ♡ x x x x ◇ J x x ♣ x, has a minimum, but he would return his partner to two diamonds rather than leave him in clubs with a singleton. What does responder do with a strong hand?"

"He makes certain that the partnership reaches game."

"Barbara, when the combined hands add up to 26 points, should game always be bid?"

"No," she said, laughing. "You gave away the answer when you said 'always.' Apparently there is no such thing as 'always' or 'never' at bridge. You are careful to avoid both words."

"Can you think of any reason why you shouldn't bid game with a combined partnership total of 26 points?"

"I suppose because the hands fit badly or the only playable spot is a minor. You told us last week that we needed 29 points for game in a minor."

"Several times it was stated: When a player can tell that the combined partnership assets are enough for game, he should bid game or make a forcing bid. Your father said, 'He makes certain that the partnership reaches game.' Why not just bid game?"

"I suppose there are times when you know the hands should play in game but you are not sure where—in your suit, partner's suit, or no trump. There must be certain bids that show your strength and do not allow partner to pass. By using them you could obtain additional information before making a final decision."

CHAPTER 8

Opening the Bidding

"WHEN can we start to play?" asked Barbara. "I can hardly wait to apply what you have been teaching us."

"Don't rush him," said Henry, coming to my defense. "Our teacher knows best. If we were to start playing now, we would form bad habits which might be difficult to break. The rules will be easy to remember when we can understand the reasons for them."

"Thank you for your support, Henry. I really do not believe that unsupervised play would be good for you since you, as a group, know very little about bidding. However, if you want to play a few hands, I'll watch and tell you what to bid. The practice in playing and defending should be helpful."

An hour and a half—and ten hands later—the regular lesson commenced.

"In the last two lessons, we discussed the theory of bidding in general terms. It was necessary for you to have a general idea of bidding objectives and how they are accomplished. Now it is time to become specific and to learn what to bid with various hands.

"As Barbara said last week, to open the bidding you need a basic count of 13. At least 10, preferably 11 of these points should be in high cards. There are 40 high-card points—10 in each suit—and you need at least your share of these to open the bidding. If you were always to play the hand in the longest suit, you could forget about a minimum high-card requirement. For playing in hearts, ♠ x ♡ K Q J x x x ◊ Q J x x x ♣ x is at least as good as ♠ x x ♡ A K x x x ◇ K Q x ♣ x x x, but the difficulty is that partner may wish to play the hand in spades or no trump, or the opponents may insist upon playing the hand. Unless you play the hand in hearts or diamonds, the first hand is not worth very much. Later you will be taught when and how to bid hands with a long suit and little defensive strength so that you won't mislead your partner. Just remember, for now, that such hands do not qualify as an opening one-bid.

"All right, suppose you have 13 basic points, at least 10 of which are in high cards. Which suit do you open? With one long suit, bid your suit. With two long suits, bid your longer one. Thus, with ♠ Q J x x x x ♡ A x ◇ K Q x ♣ x x, bid one spade. With ♠ x x x x x x ♡ A K Q J x ◇ K x ♣ —, bid one spade. Does this look right to you, Alice?"

"Yes. You said the rule is to bid your longest suit. I have no reason to question the rule."

"It looks odd to me," said Jerry. "In this case, the hearts are so *good*. Doesn't that make any difference?"

"Instead of answering you directly," I said, "let me ask you a question. Suppose that partner has an equal holding in both majors. Let's give him the following hand:

♠ 10 x   ♡ 10 x   ◇ A 10 x x x   ♣ Q x x x.

Would you rather play four hearts or four spades?"

Jerry thought for quite a while. "Four spades, I guess. At first it looked as though hearts would be better, but if the opponents keep leading clubs and forcing me to trump, I'll run out of hearts and won't be able to use my spades, even if the hearts split 3-3. Besides, there is more chance of four hearts in one hand than there is of four spades in one hand because the opponents have more hearts between them."

"In other words, your high cards will take tricks at either a heart or spade contract, but you prefer the longer trump suit to withstand forces from the opponent's suit. If partner knows that you tend to open your longest suit, when he has the same number of cards in both your suits, he will choose the suit you open for the final contract. If you bid spades first and later bid hearts, he will return you to spades, which is where you can best play the hand."

"What do I bid when I have two suits of equal length?"

"With two five-card suits—or two six-card suits—bid the higher ranking. With two four-card suits—and I'll arbitrarily define a 'suit' as being Q x x x or better—bid the higher ranking if they are touching, the lower ranking if they are not touching. Suits are touching when they are next to each other in order of rank, such as spades and hearts, hearts and diamonds, or diamonds and clubs. With three four-card suits, bid the one below the singleton."

"Is there any reason for these rules?" asked Jerry. "Or are they arbitrary, like deciding whether to drive on the left or right side of the street?"

"There are sound reasons for all of these rules. Suppose you were to open one diamond with five hearts and five diamonds. Partner has a weak hand and responds one spade. Naturally, you want to show your heart suit, so you bid two hearts. Let's say partner likes diamonds better than hearts. He must bid three diamonds to show his preference. If you had bid one heart, then two diamonds, he could show that he preferred diamonds by passing, and if he preferred hearts, he could bid two hearts. Opening the higher-ranking touching suit with equal length permits you to show both suits and obtain a preference at a low level."

"You keep talking about keeping the bidding low, as though that were a great virtue in itself," said Jerry. "I should think at times you would want to raise the level of the bidding."

"That is true, sometimes you do. In fact, sometimes you jump the bidding. However, any time you have a minimum hand, you want to furnish your information at a low level. Even with a good hand you usually want to make several bids before you reach the game level so as to give partner a choice of contracts. So ordinarily it *is* a virtue to plan the bidding so as to show as much as possible about your distribution at a rather low level."

"What is the reason for the other rules—about non-touching suits, and why bid non-touching four-card suits one way and non-touching five-card suits another way?" asked Barbara.

"Let's start with four-card suits. With

♠ A Q x x   ♡ A K x x   ◇ x x x   ♣ J x,

I can show both suits and get a preference at the two-level by bidding spades first. When the suits are touching and of equal length, it is always correct to open the higher-ranking."

"I heard you say 'always' and I have witnesses," said Barbara, laughing. "This must really be a reliable rule."

"It is," I said.

"Now change my hand to

♠ A Q x x   ♡ J x   ◇ x x x   ♣ A K x x.

Suppose I open one spade and partner bids two hearts. Now if I want to show my club suit I must bid it at the three-level. Had the opening bid been one club, partner would have bid one heart and I could have bid one spade.

"Change my hand to ♠ A Q x x ♡ J x ◇ A K x x ♣ x x x and the rule calls for a one-diamond opening. Does this look right to you, Barbara?"

"I don't know. If partner bids one heart I can bid one spade, and everything is dandy. But suppose he bids one no trump or two clubs?"

"Try to answer your own questions. What would you do if partner should respond one no trump?"

"I would pass because my hand is balanced and we couldn't have game."

"That's right. Besides, partner is unlikely to have four spades. With ♠ K x x x or ♠ J 10 x x, he would have bid one spade rather than one no trump. Anyway you can safely pass, while if you had bid one spade you would not be permitted to pass a two-heart response—yet you have no satisfactory bid. Now suppose partner responds two clubs?"

"I don't know what I would bid. Should I know?"

"Not yet. The fact is that you hope partner will not respond two clubs. However, if he does, you are not in quite as bad shape as if you had opened one spade and received a two-heart response. The rule about opening the lower, non-touching four-card suit always works when the two suits are clubs and spades. It works reasonably well when the suits are spades and diamonds or hearts and clubs. Now why don't we follow this rule when the non-touching suits are five-card suits? Without going into great detail, the reason is that it is very important to show a five-card major. If you open your major and partner makes an inconvenient response, you may not get to show your second suit—a minor. You will have to rebid your major suit instead. But if you were to open the minor, you might not get to show your major suit. It is worse not to show a five-card major than it is not to show a five-card minor. Why do you suppose that is true, Barbara?"

"Because it is easier to make game in a major."

"Alice, what is your opening bid on the following hands? Give us your bid and an explanation in each case."

(a)

♠ Q J x x x x   ♡ —   ◇ x   ♣ K Q x x x x

(b)

♠ A J x x x x   ♡ —   ◇ A   ♣ A Q x x x x

(c)

♠ A K J x x   ♡ A x   ◇ —   ♣ J 10 x x x x

(d)

♠ x x x   ♡ Q J x x   ◇ x   ♣ A K Q x x

(e)

♠ —   ♡ J x x x x   ◇ A K x x   ♣ A Q x x

(f)

♠ K J x x   ♡ Q J x x   ◇ A Q x   ♣ x x

(g)

♠ K J x x   ♡ A J x   ◇ x x   ♣ A Q x x

(h)

♠ K J x x   ♡ J x x   ◇ A Q x x   ♣ x x

(*i*)

♠ K J x x   ♡ x x   ◇ A Q 10 x   ♣ Q 10 x

(*j*)

♠ K J x x   ♡ x   ◇ A Q 10 x   ♣ Q 10 x x

(*k*)

♠ x   ♡ K J x x   ◇ A Q 10 x   ♣ Q 10 x x

(*l*)

♠ K J x x   ♡ A Q 10 x   ◇ Q 10 x x   ♣ x

(*m*)

♠ x x x x   ♡ A Q 10 x   ◇ A K x x   ♣ x

"Hand (*a*) is not an opening bid."

"Why not? Doesn't it have 13 basic points?"

"Yes, but you said we needed at least 10 high card points, and this hand only has 8. Hand (*b*) should be opened one spade. With two long suits equal in length bid the higher ranking. The next two hands should be opened one club, the longest suit. Hand (*e*) should be opened one heart for the same reason—"

"I thought a suit had to be headed by a queen or better to be biddable," interjected Jerry.

"No, that is just when it is a four-card suit," Alice replied.

"The next hand should be opened one spade, the next one club. Hand (*h*) is not an opening bid because it doesn't have 13 basic points. Hand (*i*) is a diamond opening because the four-card suits are not touching. Hand (*j*) should be opened one diamond; (*k*) should be opened one heart. In both cases the suit under the singleton is the correct bid. But I don't know what to do with (*l*)."

"Can you tell her, Henry?"

"I imagine one spade is right. The bidding goes in cycles —like one club, one diamond, one heart, one spade, two clubs, two diamonds, etcetera. Spades would be below clubs. The purpose in the rule of bidding the suit below the singleton is to make it easy to rebid if partner bids the suit where you have the singleton."

"Very logical reasoning, Henry," I said.

"I read it somewhere," he admitted sheepishly. "And since it made good sense, I remembered it."

"What do you bid with the last hand?"

"One heart. Spades are not a 'suit' because they are not headed by the queen. So I have to go down the line till I hit a suit."

"While we haven't mentioned it yet, it is possible to open the bidding by saying one no trump. When you have the requirements for the bid, it is a very desirable bid. It shows partner immediately that you have a balanced hand and are in the intermediate zone. When one particular bid gives a good description of your hand, that one bid is more accurate and desirable than a combination of bids. The requirements for a no-trump opening are 4-3-3-3, 4-4-3-2 or 5-3-3-2 distribution and 16 to 18 high-card points. There is one additional requirement. If your five-card suit is a major, your doubleton must be no weaker than Q x."

The following are all good examples of opening one-no-trump bids:

♠ Q x x	♡ A J x x	◇ Q x x	♣ A Q J
♠ x x	♡ Q J x	◇ A K x	♣ A Q x x x
♠ A x x	♡ A Q	◇ A Q x x	♣ Q x x x
♠ K J x x	♡ J x	◇ A K J	♣ A 10 x x
♠ K Q 10	♡ A J x	◇ K x	♣ A x x x x
♠ Q x	♡ K Q x x x	◇ A Q x	♣ K J x

The following two hands should be opened with the major suit because of the weak doubleton:

♠ A Q x	♡ Q 10 x x x	◇ A K x	♣ J x
♠ K J x x x	♡ A Q x	◇ A K x	♣ x x

The requirements for a two-no-trump bid are the same as

for an opening one-no-trump bid—except that you need more points. The range is 22 to 24. Examples:

♠ A Q x	♡ K Q x	◇ A Q x x	♣ K Q x
♠ K Q x	♡ A x	◇ A Q x x	♣ A K x x
♠ x x	♡ A K x	◇ A K Q J x	♣ K Q x
♠ A K x	♡ K Q x	◇ A Q x	♣ A Q x x
♠ A Q J x	♡ x x	◇ A K Q x	♣ A Q J
♠ Q x	♡ A K Q x x	◇ A Q x	♣ K Q x

With an unbalanced hand and 22 basic points, including a good major suit, or 23 points otherwise, open with two of a suit. This bid is forcing to game. If partner has nothing, you may not make your bid; on the other hand, he would not keep the bidding open with three or four points, so it is worth the gamble. In fact, with very solid suits you may bid two with less strength. Bid two spades or two hearts with the following hands:

♠ A K J x x x　　♡ A　　　◇ A Q J x　　♣ x x
(22 basic points)

♠ K Q J 10 x x　♡ x　　　◇ A　　　♣ A Q 10 9 x
(20 basic points)

♠ A Q　　　♡ A Q J x x　◇ A Q 10 x x　♣ x
(22 basic points)

With ♠ A Q ♡ A Q J x x ◇ A Q J ♣ Q x x, bid 2NT so that partner can pass if he has nothing. With

♠ x ♡ K x ◇ A K x x x ♣ A K Q x x

bid one diamond. If your suits were majors, you would open with a two-bid.

"Barbara, what would you expect an opening three-no-trump bid to show?"

"Better than a two-no-trump bid. Enough to make game almost by myself, or possibly with the right queen or jack in partner's hand. Since an opening two-no-trump bid shows 22 to 24 points, an opening three-no-trump bid should show something like 25 to 27 points."

"We haven't discussed responses to no-trump bids, but let me test your intuition. Partner bids two no trump and you hold ♠ x x x ♡ J x x x ◊ x x x ♣ x x x. What would you bid?"

"I would pass. We can't have 26 points, and I don't see any reason to bid a suit with this hand."

"Suppose partner opens one no trump and you hold

♠ Q x x   ♡ K x x   ◊ J x x   ♣ x x x x."

"I would pass for the same reason. We can't have a combined total of 26 points."

"Again partner opens one no trump and you hold

♠ J 10 x x x x   ♡ x x   ◊ x x   ♣ x x x."

"I would like to play two spades. It looks safer than one no trump because partner may get no tricks out of my hand at no trump, and it should be worth a few tricks at spades. But I don't know what partner would think if I were to bid two spades. Maybe he would think I was interested in game."

"You don't know what two spades would mean. We shall discuss responses next week. You have the right idea—that it would be desirable to play two spades rather than one no trump. Next question. Partner is the dealer and passes. Would you rather hold ♠ x x ♡ A K x x ◊ K Q x ♣ J x x x or

♠ x   ♡ K Q J x x x   ◊ Q J x x x   ♣ x?"

"I would prefer the first hand. It is doubtful that we can make game once partner has passed, and the first hand has enough high cards to give us a good chance to defeat any game the opponents might bid."

"Suppose partner had opened one no trump. Now which hand would you prefer?"

"The second one. Both hands should give us a cinch for game, but the second one might give us a chance for a slam. Anyway, once partner bids one no trump I am no longer worried that the opponents will outbid us."

"I'll write several hands on the blackboard for your homework. In each case, compute your basic points and decide what the opening bid should be."

(a)

♠ A K 10 x   ♡ x x   ◇ Q J x x   ♣ Q 10 x

(b)

♠ A K x x x   ♡ A Q x x x x   ◇ x   ♣ x

(c)

♠ x x   ♡ Q J x x   ◇ A K Q x   ♣ Q x x

(d)

♠ J x   ♡ A Q x   ◇ K J x   ♣ A J 10 x x

(e)

♠ A x   ♡ Q J x x   ◇ A x   ♣ 10 9 x x x

(f)

♠ K Q x x   ♡ Q J x x   ◇ K x x   ♣ x x

(g)

♠ K Q J x x x   ♡ A J x   ◇ x x   ♣ x x

(h)

♠ Q J x x x   ♡ A Q x   ◇ K x x   ♣ Q x

(i)

♠ Q J x x x   ♡ A Q x   ◇ x x x   ♣ A 10

(j)

♠ Q x x x   ♡ Q 10 x x   ◇ x   ♣ A K x x

(k)

♠ A K x x   ♡ x   ◇ 10 x x x   ♣ A J x x

(l)

♠ Q J x x   ♡ A Q x x   ◇ A Q x x   ♣ Q

(m)

♠ A x x   ♡ K Q x x   ◇ A Q x   ♣ x x x

(n)

♠ J 10 x x x   ♡ A   ◇ Q J 10 x x x   ♣ J

(o)

♠ A Q x   ♡ K Q x   ◇ K x x   ♣ 8 x x x

CHAPTER 9

Responses to No-Trump Opening Bids

"ALICE, what comments do you have regarding your homework problems from last week?"

"The first few were easy. All we had to do was follow the rules you gave us. Hand (f) should not be opened."

"What did you bid with hand (d)?"

"One no trump. If it meets the requirements, that is what you are supposed to bid in preference to a suit."

"What did you bid with hand (k)?"

"One club. The diamonds are not a *suit* because they are not headed by the queen or better. The first *suit* below the singleton is clubs. Hand (l) should be opened one spade. Hand (m) is a heart opening bid. Hand (n) should be passed because it lacks 10 high-card points. Hand (o) stumps me. I guess I have to pass because it is too weak to open one no trump, and there is no suit."

"Does anyone else have any comments?"

"I don't know what I should bid with the last hand, but I think I should bid *something*," said Barbara. "We might easily miss a game if I pass with this hand."

"What do you think should be bid?"

"I can't see much wrong with bidding one club. It is quite likely that we will play this hand in no trump, or partner's suit anyway, and he will be just as happy to find me with the queen of spades as with the queen of clubs."

"Barbara, you have no respect for rules. If a suit is not biddable, it just can't be bid," said Alice.

"Well, Marshall, what should you do with this hand?" asked Henry. (Couldn't the man see that the two women's comments had put me in an embarrassing position?)

"The correct bid is one club," I replied. "There is an exception to the rule about biddable suits which I had not mentioned. You had no way of knowing about the exception, Alice. Rather than pass a hand with enough strength for an opening bid, you are allowed to bid an 'unbiddable' minor suit, even a three-card suit. With ♠ A K x ♡ x x x x ◊ x x x ♣ A K x you could bid one club. There is less danger in bidding a weak or short minor suit than in bidding an unbiddable major suit. Partner is not likely to insist upon your playing game in the minor suit. If you have enough strength for game, you will find out where you belong. The only danger is that you may reach an inferior part-score contract. If partner raises to two clubs, you must pass. Another bid by you would show that you were interested in game, not that you were nervous about playing the hand in two clubs."

"Is this the 'short club' system?" asked Alice.

"There is no system I know of called the 'short club.' In all standard American systems it is permissible to bid one club —or occasionally one diamond—with only three cards in the suit when the alternatives are less desirable. However, partner treats your minor suit openings as though they were normal, since most of the time they are. If partner bids with a hopeless hand just because he has a singleton in opener's suit, the results are chaos."

"It looks to me as though bridge is a logical game," said Henry. "Barbara was able to predict an exception before she knew about it. She realized that there was more danger of missing game or otherwise getting to the wrong contract if she were to pass than if she were to bid an unbiddable suit. Also, she guessed how to respond to one- and two-no-trump openings before you explained it to us. What she said last week was right, wasn't it?"

"Yes," I said. "I would have spoken up if she had said something wrong rather than leave you with a false impression. Let's continue to consider responses to no-trump opening bids. You were told that an opening bid of one of a suit could show as much as 20 or 21 points. Consequently, responder must bid with 6 points or risk missing game. However, an opening one-no-trump bid shows a maximum of 18 points. After a no-trump opening, responder does not need to bid with 6 or 7 points to avoid missing game. With 7 points or less and a balanced hand—4-3-3-3, 4-4-3-2 or 5-3-3-2 distribution—responder should pass. With fewer than 8 points and an unbalanced hand, including a long suit, responder should bid his long suit unless it is clubs. The reason for the 'club' exception will be explained later. Pass partner's one-no-trump bid with

♠ A x x   ♡ K x x   ◇ x x x x   ♣ x x x

or

♠ J x x   ♡ J x x   ◇ x x x x   ♣ x x x.

Bid two hearts with

♠ x   ♡ J 10 x x x x   ◇ Q x x x   ♣ x x

or

♠ x x x   ♡ Q 10 x x x x   ◇ x   ♣ K x x."

"The first hand looks strong enough to give us a good play for two no trump," said Jerry. "Isn't it worth bidding more so as to have more points below the line?"

"No, it is not practical to try for larger part-score than a part-score of 40, because partner would not know whether you were trying for game or just more points below the line. It is more useful to have a raise show an interest in game. Thus a raise to two no trump says, 'Partner, if you have a maximum opening no-trump go on to game.' The only time you stretch is when you already have a part-score. Thus, if you already had a 30 or 40 part-score, you would raise partner's opening no-trump to two with 6 or 7 points. Incidentally, in all future discussions, assume there is no part-score unless I tell you otherwise."

"Even with the fairly narrow ranges of no trump bidding, I don't see how you can always get to game with 26 points without occasionally getting to game with less," said Henry.

"You are right," I said. "But explain why this is true for the benefit of the others."

"The opening no-trump range is 16-18 points. Suppose responder has 8 points. He must raise to two no trump or miss game when opener has 18. Let's go back to opener. Naturally, when responder bids two no trump, opener will bid three when he has 18 points. What should he bid with 17?"

"He should pass with only 17," said Jerry.

"What should responder bid with 9 points?"

"He should bid three no trump," Jerry replied, "since opener would pass a raise to two with 17 points."

"Then, if opener had 16, the partnership would be in game with 16 opposite 9, or a total of 25 points."

"What is the solution to this problem?" asked Jerry.

"The solution is to try to reach game whenever you have, or may have, 26 points, even though this may result in your reaching game sometimes with 25 points. There is nothing sacred about 26 points. In fact, in England they try to reach game with 25 points, and don't mind getting there with 24. I've often wondered whether it was because their declarer play is better than ours or because their defense is worse."

"Was I right about passing a raise to two no trump with 17 points?" asked Jerry.

"The rule to adopt is arbitrary. You could raise to two no trump with 8 points and to three no trump with 9. In that case, opener should pass a single raise with 17 points. My tendency is to raise to two no trump with a bare 9 points; I need an extra ten-spot or some good feature—the equivalent of 9½ points—to raise to game. Consequently, opener is expected to bid three no trump over two with 17 points, since responder might have 9 points."

"How do we count points for raising no trump?" asked Alice.

"The same way we count basic points, except that you count

nothing for four-card suits, and if you have two long suits you only count one of them. Thus

♠ A x x x x   ♡ K x x   ◇ x x   ♣ x x x

worth 8 points, one for the five-card suit. But

♠ A x x x x   ♡ K x x x   ◇ x x x   ♣ x,

♠ A x x x   ♡ K x x x   ◇ J x   ♣ x x x,

and

♠ x   ♡ A x x x x   ◇ K x x x x   ♣ x x

are all worth only 8 points in support of no trump."

"Why don't you count the second long suit?" asked Barbara.

"What I said was that you don't count the second suit *for no trump*. If you play the hand in a suit contract the hand will be worth the full basic count. Hands with 5–5 distribution should normally be played in a suit rather than no trump. As to the reason for not counting both suits, you seldom have time to establish and use two suits before the opponents get their suit established. If you are only going to establish one suit, it does not make sense to count points for length of a suit you do not expect to establish. Besides, when you have two long suits you have a shortage elsewhere, which is a compensating disadvantage.

"Jerry, if partner opens one no trump, what would you bid with the following hands?"

(a)

♠ K Q x   ♡ K 9 8 x   ◇ 10 9 x   ♣ x x x

(b)

♠ K Q x   ♡ K J x x   ◇ x x x   ♣ x x x

(c)

♠ K Q x   ♡ K J 10 9   ◇ x x x   ♣ x x x

(d)

♠ K Q x   ♡ Q 10 9 x x   ◇ x x   ♣ x x x

(e)

♠ x x   ♡ x x x   ◇ A K 8 x x x   ♣ x x

(f)

♠ Q x x   ♡ A x x   ◇ J 10 x x   ♣ x x x

(g)

♠ A K x   ♡ Q x   ◇ A x x x x   ♣ x x x

(h)

♠ Q x x x x x   ♡ J x x x   ◇ x x   ♣ x

(i)

♠ J 10 x   ♡ x   ◇ Q x x   ♣ J 10 x x x x

"With the first two hands I would bid two no trump. I suppose the next hand is strong enough to raise to three no trump."

"Yes, it is. Does it make any difference to you that your ten is in hearts rather than clubs, for example?"

"Not so far as I can see."

"What do you think, Henry?"

"I would much rather have the ten with other honors and in my long suit. Suppose partner has Q x or Q x x opposite my K J 10 x. I am sure to take three tricks instead of two, which is all I would probably take without the ten-spot. But give partner Q x or Q x x—or A x x—opposite my 10 x x, and the ten is quite likely worthless."

"Do you mean to imply that I should raise to three no trump with ♠ K Q x ♡ K J 10 x ◇ x x x ♣ x x x but only to two no trump with ♠ K Q x ♡ K J x x ◇ x x x ♣ 10 x x?"

"It is very close with the latter hand, and neither bid could be criticized. But it would be a mistake not to bid three with the former hand or to bid more than two with

♠ K Q x   ♡ K x x x   ◇ J x x   ♣ 10 x x.

With this hand both the jack and the ten are dubious values. Continue with your comments, Jerry."

"Hand (d) is surely worth a raise to two no trump. Besides

having a five-card suit, your ten is in your long suit. Hand (*e*) is a maximum raise to two no trump. Hand (*f*) should be passed. The next hand is quite good; my guess is that it is worth a raise to four no trump."

"There is no point in bidding four no trump unless it is to suggest to partner that he bid six. It doesn't hurt to have a few extra values occasionally. You should just raise to three no trump. Let's go back to hand (*e*). It is worth a raise to three no trump because your honors are together and they are in your long suit. The sixth card of a suit, if you can get the suit established, is worth a *trick*—roughly three points. The one point we give it takes into consideration the uncertainty of being able to establish the suit. With ♠ A K ♡ x x x ◇ x x x x x x ♣ x x, a raise to two no trump would be quite adequate. Give opener a typical 16-point minimum—♠ Q J x ♡ A K x x ◇ Q x x ♣ A x x—and imagine how the play would go opposite each dummy. When partner has ◇ A K x x x x, you have nine top tricks unless diamonds split 4–0. When he has six small of the suit, he needs a 2–2 break to have any chance for game against good defense, and even then the opponents might be able to establish enough club tricks for themselves in the meantime to set you. Continue, Jerry."

"With hand (*h*) I bid two spades. The hand might take no tricks at no trump, but should take several tricks at spades—not enough for game, however. With the last hand I bid two clubs for the same reason."

"You forgot a rule, Jerry," Alice said. "With hands like this, you are supposed to bid your long suit *unless it is clubs*."

"What difference does it make when the suit is clubs?" Jerry asked.

"I don't know. Marshall didn't tell us why, but I remember the rule, or the exception to the rule."

"Alice is right, and I'll explain why in just a moment. Last week Barbara mentioned that with six spades to the jack-ten and nothing else, she would like to play two spades, rather than one no trump, when her partner had opened one no trump. But she was not sure whether partner would pass. One heart by opener, one spade by responder, is forcing. Why shouldn't one no trump by opener, two spades by responder, be forcing?"

Alice and Jerry shook their heads. Even Henry appeared to be stumped.

"Responder has a pretty good idea of opener's hand when he bids a no trump," Barbara said tentatively. "If he wants to bid more, he can just bid more himself."

"How is the situation different from when opener bids a suit?"

"When opener bids a suit, he may have all sorts of hand patterns from 8-4-1-0 to 4-3-3-3, and his strength may range from 13 to 21 points. Responder usually can't tell what to do until he hears at least one rebid from opener. However, an opening no-trump bid shows opener's distribution and strength quite accurately. Consequently, responder can tell immediately where the hands belong—or at least he has a very good idea."

"You are right, Barbara. Almost all no-trump bids are called 'limit' bids. When one player has described his hand within narrow limits, his partner is usually expected to make the final decision and 'place' the contract. Now we shall discuss the two-club response. Henry, what contract would you prefer with the following hands?"

(a)	(b)	(c)
♠ Q J x x	♠ A x x x	♠ Q J x x x
♡ K x	♡ x x x x	♡ K x x x
◇ K x x x x	◇ A x x x	◇ x
♣ x x	♣ x	♣ A x x
♠ A K x x	♠ K x	♠ K x
♡ A x x	♡ A K x x	♡ A Q x x
◇ A J x	◇ K x	◇ Q x x
♣ J x x	♣ A x x x x	♣ K Q x x

"With the first set of hands, four spades is the best contract by far. At three no trump the opponents might take the first five club tricks. Even if the clubs split 4-4 or the opponents do not lead a club originally, I would need to be lucky in diamonds. At four spades I could stand any opening lead and could make the contract even with a diamond loser. With the second and third sets of hands it is obvious that the best contract is four hearts."

"In all three cases the opening bid would be one no trump," I said. "How can responder find the suit fit? We said that if he bids two diamonds, for example, he is asking opener to pass.

"The solution is to make an artificial bid of two clubs, known as the Stayman Convention. *The Stayman Convention is used only when responder is interested in game.* Over the two-club response opener must rebid a major suit if he has one—Q x x x or better. With no major suit, opener rebids two diamonds. In the first example the bidding would be

SOUTH	NORTH
1 NT	2 ♣
2 ♠	4 ♠

"In the second and third group, opener would rebid two hearts and responder would raise to four. The primary purpose of the Stayman Convention is to find a 4-4 major fit. Responder never bids a four-card suit himself, but he may raise if opener shows a four-card suit. A secondary purpose is to find out whether or not the hands belong in game when responder has eight or nine points with an unbalanced hand. For example, the first responding hand could be weakened by changing one of the kings for a queen. Then if opener should bid two spades, responder would bid just three spades, giving opener a chance to pass with only 16 points. Or if opener rebids two hearts or two diamonds, responder should bid two no trump—again giving opener a chance to stop short of game with a minimum. Henry, what would you respond with

♠ Q J x x x   ♡ K x x x   ◇ A x x   ♣ x?"

"I would bid two clubs."

"Why don't you just jump in spades with a five-card suit?"

"Because the hand should play better in hearts if opener has four hearts, especially when he only holds two spades. If partner rebids hearts or spades, I will raise him to game."

"Suppose partner bids two diamonds?"

"I would still want to play this hand in game. Would two spades be forcing?"

"No."

"Then I would bid three spades to make partner choose between game in spades and no trump."

"Suppose you hold ♠ Q J x x x ♡ K x x x ◊ Q x x ♣ x. Do you want to be in game?"

"I don't know. If partner can bid either major, I'd take a chance and put him in game. But if he rebids two diamonds over my two clubs, I am not sure we would belong in game. Should I bid two no trump?"

"No, two spades would be better. You probably belong in spades, even though partner does not have four. For that matter, he could still have four small spades. He can't bid the suit unless he has Q x x x or better. The fact that you bid Stayman shows that you have at least an *interest* in game. With 16 points, or even 17 points including a doubleton spade, partner will pass. More often than not he will bid again. Suppose that your hand is ♠ Q J x x x x ♡ K x x ◊ x x ♣ x x. If you bid two spades immediately over partner's no-trump opening, partner will pass for sure. If you jump to three spades, partner is forced to bid whether he has a minimum or maximum. The way to *invite* game without committing yourself to game is to bid two clubs. If partner bids two spades—which is not likely when you have six of them yourself—you will raise to three. If he bids anything else, you will bid two spades.

"With

♠ x x   ♡ A 10 x x   ◊ A K x   ♣ A J x x,

opener would pass. With

♠ K x x   ♡ A Q x x   ◊ A J x x   ♣ Q J x,

opener would raise to three spades and you would pass since you have a bare minimum for your bidding. Opener may have a very nice hand in support of spades—something like

♠ K x x   ♡ A x   ◇ A K x x x   ♣ A x x

or

♠ 10 x x x   ♡ A Q x x   ◇ A x x   ♣ A K,

in which case he would jump to four spades himself.

"Barbara, how many points should responder have to bid over two no trump?"

"Three would be my guess. Game might be missed if responder passes with two and opener has 24. On the other hand, if responder should raise with two, he might find opener with 22, and that would be terrible."

"Responder is supposed to have four points to bid," I said. "One reason is that opener has 22 points much more frequently than he has 24. The most common hand contains 10 points, just one-fourth of the total. Twelve-point hands are slightly more frequent than 14-point hands; 6-point hands are more frequent than 4-point hands, and so on. A good system tells you what to do with the hands you are dealt most often. My regular partner and I have no way of accurately describing 27- and 28-point hands. They occur so seldom we haven't bothered to worry about them. Anyway, one reason for not raising a two-no-trump bid with 3 points is that partner seldom has 24 points. Barbara, I think you can give me another reason. Would you rather have 13 points in dummy and 13 points in your own hand, or 3 points in dummy and 23 in your own hand?"

"I'd prefer 13 points in each hand."

"Why?"

"Because when most of the strength is in one hand and very little in the other, it is hard to get back and forth. I might want to take three finesses, but I could only get to dummy once. Or I might want to establish one of dummy's suits and there wouldn't be enough entries to establish and use it."

"That is another reason why you don't mind not getting to game with 23 points opposite 3. With 4-9 points and a balanced hand, raise partner's two-no-trump bid to three. Any suit-response is forcing, since with less than 4 points you just pass. Thus you could respond three hearts with

$$♠ x x \quad ♡ Q J x x x \quad ◇ K x x x \quad ♣ x x$$

to give partner a choice between three no trump and four hearts. A three-club response is still Stayman. Everything is the same except that responder needs much less strength—because opener has much more—and the bidding cannot stop short of game.

"I have several problems for you to look at before next week. The answers are on another piece of paper which you can look at after you have decided what you would do. Next week we can discuss those which you are still uncertain about."

QUIZ

I drew the following problems for them to study.

1. Partner bids one no trump. What would you respond with the following hands?

(a)

♠ J x x x x   ♡ K J x   ◇ x x x   ♣ J x

(b)

♠ Q J 10 x x   ♡ J x x x   ◇ x x   ♣ x x

(c)

♠ x   ♡ K J 10 x x x   ◇ Q J x x   ♣ x x

(d)

♠ A K 10 x x x ♡ x x   ◇ x x x   ♣ x x

(e)

♠ Q J x x   ♡ x   ◇ x x   ♣ Q 10 9 x x x

(f)

♠ K x x   ♡ Q x x   ◇ J x   ♣ K x x x x

(g)

♠ A Q x   ♡ K Q x   ◇ J x x x   ♣ J x x

(h)

♠ A Q x   ♡ K Q x   ◊ A Q 10 x   ♣ x x x

(i)

♠ x x   ♡ x x   ◊ J x x x   ♣ K J x x x

(j)

♠ x x   ♡ x   ◊ J 10 9 x   ♣ Q J 10 x x x

(k)

♠ J 10 x x x   ♡ A x   ◊ x x   ♣ K x x x

(l)

♠ Q x x x   ♡ Q x x x   ◊ Q x   ♣ x x x

(m)

♠ Q x x x   ♡ K x x   ◊ J x x   ♣ Q 10 x

2. Partner bids two no trump. What would you respond with the following hands?

(a)

♠ Q x x   ♡ J x x   ◊ x x x   ♣ x x x x

(b)

♠ K x x x   ♡ x x   ◊ Q x x x   ♣ x x x

(c)

♠ K Q x x   ♡ Q x x   ◊ J x x   ♣ x x x

(d)

♠ x x   ♡ Q J x x x x   ◊ J x x   ♣ x x

(e)

♠ x x   ♡ K Q x x x   ◊ J x x x   ♣ x x

(f)

♠ Q x x x   ♡ K J x x x   ◊ J   ♣ x x x

(g)

♠ K J x x x   ♡ Q x x x   ◊ J   ♣ x x x

(h)

♠ x x   ♡ x x   ◊ A J x x x x   ♣ x x x

ANSWERS

1. (*a*) Pass.
   (*b*) Two spades. You cannot bid Stayman because you are not interested in game.
   (*c*) Four hearts. The hand is unbalanced and worth 10 points (basic points) at hearts. A three-heart bid usually means you are not certain whether the hand should play in hearts or no trump. It can also mean that you are interested in a slam.
   (*d*) Three spades or three no trump.
   (*e*) Pass.
   (*f*) Three no trump.
   (*g*) Three no trump.
   (*h*) Six no trump.
   (*i*) Pass.
   (*j*) Pass.
   (*k*) Three spades or two clubs.
   (*l*) Pass.
   (*m*) Two no trump.
2. (*a*) Pass.
   (*b*) Three clubs.
   (*c*) Three no trump.
   (*d*) Three hearts.
   (*e*) Three hearts.
   (*f*) Three clubs.
   (*g*) Three clubs.
   (*h*) Three no trump.

CHAPTER 10

Responding to Suit Opening Bids

"I HAVE a couple of questions about last week's problems," said Jerry. "In problems 1(m) and 2(c), why didn't we use Stayman?"

"It doesn't pay to play in the 4-4 major fit, provided that you have such a fit, when responder has 4-3-3-3 distribution. Opener may have the same distribution, and when that is the case there is no extra trick to be gained by ruffing. Even when opener has 4-4-3-2 distribution and can gain an extra trick by ruffing in his own hand, you are no better off in the major. You take one more trick, but you had to bid one more trick for game."

"My second question was how we were supposed to know what to bid with the 17-point hand."

"Barbara, did you make the right bid before looking at the answer?"

"Yes. I made up typical hands for partner's opening no trump and put them with mine, and it always seemed as though he would have a good play for six no trump. So that is what I bid!"

"Horrors! Do you mean to say that you tried to visualize possible hands that partner might have instead of just adding up points? That sounds almost un-American!"

"You hadn't told us how many points we would need for a slam, so what else could I do? Besides, I think you are teasing me. How can it matter what method is used if it gives the right answer? It seems quite logical to me that I should try to visualize what partner has—even on game and part-score hands."

"Yes, I was kidding you. Visualizing partner's hand is the

best method of all. The point count is a short cut which saves time and trouble. However, as you become more experienced you will become less dependent upon it."

"I have a question," said Henry. "With hand 1(*k*) your answer was two clubs or three spades. What are the pros and cons of each bid?"

"Three spades is the more direct bid. It gives you the choice between four spades and three no trump. However, I usually save immediate jump responses to show a six-card suit and Stayman, followed by a jump in a suit to show a five-card suit. Every three months—if you play a lot—a hand will come along where this more scientific treatment will pay off. For all practical purposes, you may bid whichever way you prefer.

"Last lesson we discussed the difference between limited bids and unlimited bids. An opening-suit bid shows 13-21 basic points and about 10-21 high-card points. Also, it can show all types of distribution from 4-3-3-3 to 7-5-1-0. Because of the wide range in high-card strength and distribution, the first bid does not describe the hand very well, and it takes at least two bids to give even an approximate description of the opener's hand. On the other hand, an opening no-trump bid showed one of three distributions—4-3-3-3, 4-4-3-2 or 5-3-3-2—and the point count within two points. Responder could tell right away whether there would be a good play for game or no play for game, and if there were no play for game he could pass or sign off in the safest part-score contract.

"Responder also has various limit bids and unlimited bids at his disposal. Suppose the opening bid is one diamond. Both one no trump and two diamonds are limit bids. Both show 6 to 10 points. The no-trump response usually shows no-trump distribution—4-3-3-3, 4-4-3-2 or 5-3-3-2—although not always. Sometimes one no trump must be bid simply because the hand contains 6-10 points and no more appropriate bid is available. The raise to two diamonds shows good support for diamonds, and it is seldom made with a biddable major suit. When opener hears a single raise, if he has a minimum opening bid he should pass; he should pass a one-no-trump response if he has no-trump distribution and a minimum hand. He should try to find a safer spot only when his hand is unbalanced.

"A two-no-trump response is also a limit bid. It shows no-trump distribution and 13 to 15 points. However, since the two hands already add up to at least 26 points, the two-no-trump response is forcing.*

"A new-suit response is an unlimited bid. When partner opens the bidding with one diamond it is correct to bid one spade with

♠ K Q x x x   ♡ x x   ◊ x x x   ♣ x x x

or

♠ A Q x x   ♡ x x   ◊ K Q x x   ♣ A x x.

The range is 6 points to approximately 16. If responder has 6 to 10 points he passes opener's rebid—unless the rebid shows that the combined total may be 26 points despite responder's minimum hand. With 11 or 12 points responder must show an intermediate hand, either by making a bid which immediately shows a hand in this range or by making two bids. How can responder immediately show an intermediate hand? One way is to give partner a double raise: 1 ♡—3 ♡. Another way to show an intermediate *or better* hand is by bidding a new lower-ranking suit at the two-level. When opener bids one diamond, responder can bid one heart or one spade with as few as 6 points, but a two-club bid shows at least 11 points. Alice, what does responder do with 8 or 9 points if his suit is clubs?"

"He must bid one no trump."

"Assume that partner has bid one heart and you hold the following hand: ♠ Q x ♡ x x ◊ K Q x x ♣ x x x x x. What would you bid?"

"One no trump. I must give partner a chance in case he has a strong hand. I am not strong enough to bid two clubs or two diamonds, since that would require 11 basic points."

"What would you respond to partner's heart-bid with

---

* This means that partner must bid again. There are two types of forcing bids, those forcing for one round and those forcing to game.

♠ K Q x x   ♡ Q x   ◇ x x   ♣ x x x x x?"

"One spade. A one-no-trump response denies a biddable suit which can be shown at the one-level."

"If partner shows a minimum hand by rebidding one no trump, two hearts or two spades, what will you bid?"

" I will pass. However, if partner bids two diamonds, I would return him to two hearts, since I like hearts as well as diamonds. A preference does not show extra strength."

"What would you respond to partner's opening heart-bid with

♠ K Q x x   ♡ Q x   ◇ x x   ♣ A 10 9 x x?"

"This hand is strong enough to bid two clubs, and that is what I would bid."

"What would you respond with

♠ K Q x x   ♡ Q x   ◇ x x x   ♣ A 10 9 x?"

"Again I would respond two clubs, because that would show partner right away that I had at least 11 points. You told us that, if possible, we should describe our hand with one bid."

"The trouble is that no one bid will describe the hand. You might have bid two clubs with

♠ x x   ♡ x   ◇ A x x   ♣ K Q x x x x x

or

♠ x   ♡ Q x x   ◇ A x x x   ♣ A K x x x.

The fact that you show at least 11 basic points is not sufficient reason in itself to bid two clubs. On the previous hand it was correct to bid two clubs, because that was your longest suit and the most natural bid. You planned to bid spades later, which would give partner a fairly good description of your hand—more clubs than spades and at least 11 points. However, this time you cannot bid two suits since that implies nine cards or more in those two suits—normally the first-bid suit has five cards, the second, four. The natural way to bid this hand is to bid one of your suits, followed by two no trump next round. Since you are only going to bid one suit, which suit should you bid?"

"Spades. It is more important to show the major."

"How many points does responder show by bidding two no trump on the second round?" asked Jerry.

"Eleven or 12. That is another way to show an intermediate hand. It is just the first-round two-no-trump response which is forcing to game, and which guarantees a minimum of 13 points."

"How do I know I'll get a chance to show an intermediate hand? Partner might pass my one-spade response."

"No, Jerry. Partner is not allowed to pass your one-spade response. You may have 6, 12, or 16 points, so he must bid again to let you clarify your holding."

"What do you mean by 'not allowed' to pass? Is it cheating or against the rules?" Alice asked.

"No," I replied. "What I meant was that it violates the agreement with your partner. It is unwise to pass a forcing bid, and even when it pays off on a particular hand, it destroys partnership confidence. However, the opponents have no redress if you pass a forcing bid any more than if you make some other type of foolish bid. Usually, deviations from good bridge work to the opponents' advantage. I recommend a pass with

♠ Q J x x x x   ♡ —   ◇ A J x x x x   ♣ x

because you don't have 10 high-card points, but it could work out to your advantage to open. If you open and get a good result, the opponents have no basis for complaints.

"Henry, what would you respond to partner's heart-bid with ♠ Q x x ♡ K x x x ◇ J x x x ♣ x x?"

"Two hearts. I have good heart support and a minimum response."

"What would you bid with

♠ K x x   ♡ K x x x   ◇ Q 10 x x   ♣ x x?"

"Two hearts again. I still have a minimum response. However, if partner bids three hearts I'll bid four with this hand, while I would pass with the first hand."

"What would you respond with

♠ K J x x   ♡ K x x x   ◇ x x   ♣ x x x?"

"Two hearts."

"Why?"

"I don't know. It just looks like a two-heart bid."

"Does everyone agree?"

"No," said Alice. "You should not fail to bid a biddable suit which can be shown at the one-level."

"What do you think, Barbara?"

"I don't know what the rule is about showing biddable suits. However, it looks to me as though the hand should play in hearts. The only problem is how many hearts. Why bother with spades when we have already found a nice heart fit?"

"Before I answer you, what should you respond if partner should bid one diamond and you hold

♠ K J x x   ♡ x x   ◇ K x x x   ♣ x x x?"

"One spade. But that's different. I hope to find a spade fit because it should be easier to make four spades than five diamonds."

"Barbara is right. Once you have found a good major suit fit, you need look no further. You don't always show your support right away, but if you are only strong enough for one bid, as is the case here, you show your support. The most important message you can give to partner is that you fit his major.

"In the following examples, partner has opened one heart. What would you respond, Henry? The first hand:

♠ K J x   ♡ Q x x   ◇ K J x   ♣ A x x x."

"Two no trump. I have a balanced hand, all suits stopped, and the right amount of strength."

"What is the high-card range?"

"Thirteen to 15 points."

"Notice how most no-trump bids have a narrow range. The next hand is ♠ K Q x   ♡ x x   ◇ K 10 x x   ♣ A J x x."

"I would bid two no trump again. I don't need a stopper in partner's suit."

"Suppose you hold ♠ K Q x x   ♡ x   ◇ K 10 x x   ♣ A J x x. Would you respond two no trump?"

"No, I would bid a suit, probably one spade. It isn't right to respond two no trump because the hand is unbalanced. There is a good chance that it will play better in a suit."

"What would you respond with

♠ K J x ♡ Q x ◇ K 10 x x ♣ Q 10 x x?"

"I guess two clubs or two diamonds. It is too strong to bid one no trump and too weak for two no trump. If partner rebids his suit, I'll bid two no trump next round."

"How many points would that show?"

"Eleven or 12—an intermediate hand."

"The next responding hand is

♠ K x x ♡ Q x x ◇ A Q x x x ♣ x x."

"I would bid two diamonds, and if partner rebids his suit, I would raise him to three. This sequence would also show an intermediate hand."

"The next hand is ♠ K Q x ♡ Q x x ◇ A Q x x x ♣ x x."

"I would still respond two diamonds."

"If partner should rebid two hearts, what would you bid?"

"This time I would raise him to four hearts. No matter how weak his opening bid is, I would want to be in game."

"The next responding hand is

♠ K x x ♡ Q x x x ◇ A J x x ♣ x x."

"I don't know how to count points for supporting partner, but this hand looks a little bit too strong for a raise to two hearts. I could either bid diamonds and raise hearts next time, or else bid three hearts right away."

"Which do you think better describes your holding?"

"Three hearts. My good four-card support is the outstanding characteristic of this hand. The diamond holding is of less importance."

"You are right in all respects. In support of hearts, this hand is worth 11 points. It is too strong to bid two hearts and too weak to bid four. The correct bid is three hearts, asking partner to go to game if he has 15 points, or 14 if he likes his hand. This is an example of showing an intermediate hand with one bid. How about ♠ Q x x ♡ K x x ◇ J x x ♣ J x x x?"

"It looks as though I could either raise partner's hearts or bid no trump. I don't know which I should do."

"Which would encourage partner more?" I asked.

"The raise would encourage him more because it would indicate that he hands fit."

"Do you want to encourage or discourage partner with this hand?"

"I would rather discourage him. This is not a very good hand, with only 7 points."

"Next lesson I'll show you how to count support points. In support of hearts, this hand is worth only 6 points. It has two bad features—only three-card support, and no shortage on the side to provide ruffing values. You are right; this is a rather poor hand, so you should bid one no trump to discourage partner. With a ruffing value or a stronger hand—

♠ Q x x x ♡ K x x ◇ J x x x ♣ x x

or

♠ A x x ♡ K x x ◇ K x x x ♣ x x x—

you would prefer the raise. As you will discover soon, a raise enables opener to re-evaluate his hand upwards. When you have a very bad hand, you do not want to give partner any excuse for optimism. You have answered this group of problems very well, Henry. Barbara, what would you respond to partner's one-heart opening with

♠ A K Q J x ♡ Q x ◇ A J x x ♣ x x?"

"Two spades. This is stronger than 16 points, so I should jump in order to show a very strong hand."

"One spade would be forcing. Why jump?"

"It tells partner right away that there may be a slam."

"What would you respond to this heart-bid with

♠ A K x x ♡ Q J x x ◇ A Q x ♣ x x?"

"Two spades again. This hand ought to be worth at least 17 points in support of hearts, and I am going to support hearts later."

"Partner bids one diamond. What would you respond with

♠ Q 10 x x   ♡ Q 10 x x   ◇ A x   ♣ K x x?"

"One spade. It is the higher of the touching suits."

"Are you planning to bid both suits?"

"Yes, I am strong enough to bid twice. This is an intermediate hand."

"Take away your king of clubs, leaving

♠ Q 10 x x   ♡ Q 10 x x   ◇ A x   ♣ x x x,

and what would you respond?"

"Hmm . . . One heart? Yes, one heart! I would not be strong enough to *plan* to bid twice. If I should respond one spade, it might prevent partner from bidding hearts because he isn't strong enough, and we might miss our heart fit when he has four hearts. But if I bid one heart and he has hearts, he can raise, and if he has spades, he can bid one spade."

"Suppose he should rebid one spade. Would you pass?"

"No, because his one-spade bid is ambiguous. He might have 17 or 18 points, and my hand looks fairly good in support of spades. I think I could afford to raise to two spades."

"You discovered the general rule in responding, which is to bid the lower of equal suits if you only plan to bid one suit. Now let's go back to the previous hand—

♠ Q 10 x x   ♡ Q 10 x x   ◇ A x   ♣ K x x.

Is this a balanced or an unbalanced hand?"

"Balanced."

"Which gives partner a better picture of a balanced hand, to bid two suits, or to bid one suit followed by no trump?"

"The latter. I should bid one heart and forget the spades unless partner bids them. Though I am strong enough to bid twice, I should bid one suit followed by two no trump, instead of both suits. That seems logical. I should have figured it out without any help, because you told Mom to bid one spade followed by two no trump with

♠ K Q x x   ♡ Q x   ◇ x x x   ♣ A 10 9 x."

"The last topic for tonight is how to respond to an opening two-bid. After an opening two-bid, the bidding must continue until game is reached or an opponent is doubled. When responder has so little strength that he would have passed a one bid, he bids two no trump. This negative response does not promise any values. Any response except two no trump shows at least 6 points and is considered a positive response. After a positive response, opener may become interested in a slam. Henceforth, I shall give you both quizzes and answers, like last time. When we meet for the following lesson, you may ask about anything which is not clear to you."

QUIZ

1. Partner bids two hearts and the next hand passes. What would you bid with the following hands?

(a)

♠ x x x   ♡ x x x   ◇ J x x   ♣ x x x x

(b)

♠ Q J 10 9 8 x   ♡ x x   ◇ x x x   ♣ x x

(c)

♠ K x   ♡ x x x x   ◇ K x x   ♣ x x x x

(d)

♠ K x   ♡ x x x x   ◇ K x x   ♣ A x x x

(e)

♠ K Q x x   ♡ x x   ◇ Q x x   ♣ x x x x

(f)

♠ K x x   ♡ x x x   ◇ Q x x   ♣ K x x x

2. What are the four limit-bids discussed in this lesson which responder can make? What are their ranges?

3. What are the various ways of showing an intermediate responding hand?

4. Partner's opening bid was one heart. What would you respond with the following hands:

(a)

♠ x x   ♡ Q x x x x x   ◇ K x   ♣ x x x

(b)

♠ Q x x   ♡ x x   ◇ K x   ♣ K x x x x x

(c)

♠ K J x   ♡ x   ◇ Q x x x   ♣ J 10 x x x

(d)

♠ K J x   ♡ Q x x   ◇ J 10 x x   ♣ J x x

(e)

♠ A x   ♡ Q x x x x   ◇ K J x   ♣ x x x

(f)

♠ K J x x   ♡ x   ◇ x x   ♣ K x x x x x

(g)

♠ A Q J x   ♡ x x   ◇ Q x x x x   ♣ K x

(h)

♠ Q x x x x   ♡ Q x x x   ◇ Q x   ♣ x x

(i)

♠ Q J x x   ♡ Q x x   ◇ A x x   ♣ Q 10 x

(j)

♠ K x x x   ♡ Q x x   ◇ A J 10   ♣ A Q x

5 Partner has bid one club. What would you respond with the following hands?

(a)

♠ K Q x x   ♡ x x   ◇ x x   ♣ J 10 x x x

(b)

♠ x x   ♡ x x   ◊ J 10 x x x   ♣ K Q x x

(c)

♠ K x x x   ♡ Q J x   ◊ A Q x   ♣ J 10 x

(d)

♠ A x   ♡ x x x   ◊ A x x   ♣ Q 10 x x x

(e)

♠ K Q x x   ♡ Q x x x x   ◊ x x   ♣ x x

(f)

♠ K x x   ♡ K x x   ◊ Q J x x   ♣ J x x

ANSWERS

1. (a) Two no trump.
   (b) Two no trump. Then bid spades next round.
   (c) Three hearts.
   (d) Three hearts. Later you will drive to a slam. A raise is not a limit-bid in this sequence because partner must bid again.
   (e) Two spades.
   (f) Three no trump. Two no trump would promise nothing.
2. One no trump (6-10); two no trump (13-15); single raise of partner's suit (6-10); double raise (11-12).
3. A response at the two-level guarantees *at least* an intermediate hand, but it can also be a strong hand, depending upon what responder bids later. A bid of a new suit (whether at the one- or two-level) followed by two no trump or a raise of partner's suit shows an intermediate hand. The only way to show an intermediate hand in one bid is to give partner a double raise in his suit.
4. (a) Two hearts.
   (b) One no trump.
   (c) One no trump.

- (*d*) One no trump (close between bidding two hearts or one no trump).
- (*e*) Three hearts.
- (*f*) One spade—too weak to bid two clubs.
- (*g*) Two diamonds—you are strong enough to show both suits in normal order, longer suit first.
- (*h*) Two hearts—you are not strong enough to bid spades and support hearts later, so you should support hearts immediately.
- (*i*) One spade, to be followed by two no trump over any minimum rebid.
- (*j*) Three no trump. This bid shows an opening no-trump bid with strength in all unbid suits.

5. (*a*) One spade.
   - (*b*) Two clubs; this hand is only strong enough for one bid. The most important information you can supply is that you have support for partner's suit. If you have a major suit you can show it, but diamonds are no better than clubs.
   - (*c*) Two no trump.
   - (*d*) Three clubs.
   - (*e*) One heart.
   - (*f*) One no trump. This bid describes your hand better than would a one-diamond response. A no-trump response to *one club* shows 9-10 points.

CHAPTER 11

Raising Partner's Suit

"ARE there any questions about last week's problems?"
No one said anything.

"Barbara, I know you have a question."

"You must be able to read my mind," said Barbara, blushing.
"I had decided to be more ladylike, more quiet and retiring, but
since you press me, I am curious about the last problem. Why
should a one-no-trump response to one club show a better hand
than a one-no-trump response to any other opening bid? And
what does responder bid with 6-8 points?"

"Let's consider your last question first. What sort of hand
would present a problem for responder? When would he be
tempted to bid one no trump with 6-8 points?"

"He would have to have no biddable suit. There are two types
of hands I can think of: ♠ Q x x ♡ K x x ◊ Q x x ♣ x x x x and
♠ 10 x x x ♡ Q x x ◊ A x x ♣ x x x. In one case, his four-
card suit is clubs. It seems a distortion to raise clubs with this
sort of hand. In the second case, the four-card suit is not biddable."

"In both cases," I explained, "responder could respond one
diamond. The danger, of course, is that partner will raise. However, that danger is fairly remote, since partner will tend to rebid
a major or no trump in preference to raising a minor suit. The
advantage in responding one diamond is that it permits partner
to show a major suit at the one-level, while he might not be
strong enough to bid two hearts or two spades over one no
trump. Another advantage in responding one diamond is that if
we do play no trump, we prefer to let partner play the hand. It

is easier to defend when the stronger of the two hands is the dummy, and we do want to make things tough for the opponents. Rather than refuse to bid one no trump over a club, we narrow the range so as not to bid it very often. That way, when we do bid one no trump we describe our hand very accurately.

"You have been told that giving partner a single raise shows a minimum response, and a double raise shows an intermediate response. There are other things you ought to know about a raise, and we shall discuss them in this lesson.

"Jerry, what other requirements for a raise can you surmise from the examples shown thus far, plus whatever you may have learned about the play of the hand?"

"The raiser should have fairly good length and strength in the suit he raises."

"Why is that? What do you tell partner when you raise his suit?"

"Aside from showing my strength, I suggest that suit as a trump suit. I wouldn't want us to select a trump suit unless partner and I had more trumps than the opponents."

"Consequently, how many trumps do you need to raise partner?"

"At least three, since he may bid a suit with only four cards in it."

"Suppose partner rebids his suit once or twice or has bid it at a high level?"

"I don't understand your question."

"Would the fact that partner has shown a long suit affect your requirements for a raise?"

"If partner has shown a long suit by his bidding, I should think that I could raise him with fewer than three trumps."

"That is right," I said. "Because it is the *combined* trump length which is important. There are several ways that partner can show a long suit by his bidding, the most common of which is for him to bid the same suit two or three times. The more times he bids his suit, the fewer trumps you need to support it."

"Can you give us some rules instead of talking in generalities?" asked Alice.

"Yes, I believe that I can oblige you. While seven trumps to the opponents' six gives you a majority and may occasionally suffice, you try to find at least an eight-card fit for your trump suit. Seven is too skimpy a majority and can lead to trouble when the opponents' trumps split 4-2 or 5-1. Remember how I told you it was impossible to reach three no trump every time with a combined total of 26 points without occasionally getting there with 25? The same sort of consideration applies to the trump suit. You try for an eight-card fit, but you may sometimes have to play a seven-card fit. When you have only seven trumps, you need most of the high trumps. A Q J x opposite K x x is usually quite satisfactory. Even K Q x x opposite A x x, or A J 10 x opposite K x x, may be all right when there is no better spot, but you surely don't want to play Q x x x opposite x x x. For that reason, you almost never raise partner till he rebids his suit without Q x x or better. If partner refuses to bid a suit without a high honor, and responder won't raise without three to a high honor, the worst possible trump holding will be Q x x x opposite K x x. That still is not very satisfactory, but it seldom is that both partners have the absolute minimum. Throw in a ten and nine, and even the latter combination is fairly playable.

"Consequently, the first 'rule' regarding trump support is not to raise partner with a worse trump holding than Q x x unless his bidding has shown a five-card suit or longer. Even then, you are hoping that he has a five-card suit; if you knew that he only had four, you probably would not raise. Alice, suppose the bidding has gone

OPENER	RESPONDER	*or*	OPENER	RESPONDER
1 ♣	1 ♡		1 ♡	2 ♣
1 ♠	?		2 ◇	?

How many trumps should responder have to raise opener's second suit?"

"As I recall, Culbertson said four."

"Why would Culbertson have required four trumps for the raise?"

"I don't know."

"Jerry, can you tell us?"

"You just said a moment ago that you try to find an eight-card fit, and would not raise what you know, or strongly suspect, to be a four-card suit with three trumps. Opener bids his longest suit first, and his second bid usually shows a four-card suit."

"How many trumps should you need to give partner a double raise?"

"At least four. When I give partner a double raise he ought to be able to assume that we have found an eight-card fit. We would be too high for him to start looking for a better trump suit."

"Very good reasoning, Jerry. To continue with the rules, when partner rebids his suit you may raise with Q x or any three trumps. When he shows a very long suit—for example, by opening the bidding and later jumping in the same suit—you may raise with a singleton honor or two small. When partner opens a minor suit, you should not raise without four trumps. The fact that he may have bid a short suit is not the main reason—it doesn't pay to worry about that possibility. The reason for not raising is that unless you have an exceptionally good fit in a minor suit, there is usually a much better chance to make game in some other denomination."

"Do these rules have exceptions?" asked Barbara.

"Yes. Let's start with the last rule I gave you. What would you respond to partner's opening club-bid with

♠ x x   ♡ Q 10 x x   ◇ A x x x   ♣ K 10 x?"

"One heart or one diamond. I believe the rule you gave us last lesson was to bid one diamond, the lower of equal suits."

"Either bid is all right. The important point is that you would not even consider raising clubs, would you?"

"No."

"Now suppose that partner opens one club and the next hand bids one spade. What would you bid now?"

"Two clubs."

"Why?"

"Because I am not nearly strong enough to bid *two* hearts or *two* diamonds, and partner would never guess that I had nine high-card points if I were to pass."

"Why don't you respond one no trump?"

"It looks dangerous with two little spades after a spade-bid by an opponent. Almost surely the opening lead would be a spade. If we belong in no trump, partner probably should be the declarer. He might have K x or A Q of spades, in which case it would be much better to have the lead come up to his hand."

"Suppose partner bids one club; you respond one diamond; he rebids one heart. Your hand is

♠ x x　♡ A Q x　◇ K x x x x　♣ x x x.

Approximately how many points does partner have?"

"I can't estimate very closely—anywhere from 13 to 18 or 19."

"Consequently, it would be dangerous to pass, wouldn't it?"

"Yes. I wouldn't consider passing."

"Then what would you bid? Or let's hear you tell me what bids you would not make, and why?"

"Naturally, I don't make any jump-bid because my hand is a minimum response—but a maximum-minimum. Of the non-jump bids, I eliminate one no trump for roughly the same reason as for the last hand. The opponents would probably lead the unbid suit, spades, and if we happen to belong in no trump, partner should be the one to bid it. Two clubs is a possibility, since I am only telling partner I like clubs as well as hearts. Actually I don't, but I have equal length in both suits, and partner should have at least as many clubs as hearts, perhaps more. Two diamonds seems rather misleading, since the suit is fairly weak. I don't want to play in diamonds if partner has a singleton or small doubleton. Since partner has bid two suits, I am afraid he won't have very many diamonds. Two hearts looks like the most descriptive bid, provided I am allowed to raise with three trumps."

"You are one hundred per cent correct. Two clubs and two hearts are the only conceivable bids, and some experts would choose two clubs. My preference is for two hearts because I believe there is a greater chance to make game in hearts than anywhere else. The deciding factor is that your hearts are very good. With Q x x of hearts and more strength elsewhere, you would choose some other bid. The two hands might be as follows, in which case four hearts will be the best game contract:

OPENER	RESPONDER
♠ x x	♠ x x
♡ K J x x	♡ A Q x
◇ A x x	◇ K x x x x
♣ A K Q x	♣ x x x

"Another exception is that you may gamble that partner has a five-card suit and raise his opening bid with three small cards, provided you have a singleton, or conceivably a worthless doubleton. You risk a skimpy trump-holding because you figure that a no-trump contract would be even more dangerous.

"Following are typical single raises of partner's opening heart-bid.

1. ♠ K x	♡ x x x x	◇ K x	♣ x x x x x
2. ♠ A x	♡ Q 10 x	◇ Q x x x x	♣ x x x
3. ♠ x	♡ x x x	◇ A J x x	♣ K x x x x
4. ♠ x x	♡ x x x	◇ A Q x x	♣ K J x x
5. ♠ x x x	♡ K x x	◇ A Q J x	♣ x x x

"Barbara, why would I recommend a heart-raise rather than a no-trump response with the third hand?"

"Every bid must be a compromise or a choice of the least of evils. Partner might pass a one-no-trump response, and two hearts looks safer than a one-no-trump contract."

"Why?"

"The opponents might take five or six spade tricks at no trump. Their long suit is quite likely my short suit."

"Why won't they get these spade tricks at a heart contract?"

"Because my little hearts act as stoppers to prevent the run of the suit. Besides, partner can probably gain an extra trick or two by ruffing spades."

"Isn't it possible that partner has very good spades, something like A K J, and very weak hearts, perhaps Q 4 3 2?"

"Yes, it is possible, but not very likely. I can't afford to worry about remote possibilities. If partner has poor spades *or* good hearts, we belong in hearts. Besides, a raise is more encouraging than a no-trump response, and I like this hand."

"Why would you raise hearts with the last two hands?" I was asked.

"With the fourth hand a heart-raise looks better than a no-trump response because a raise is more encouraging than a no-trump bid. With 10 points, there is a risk of missing game by bidding one no trump. Also, there is still a chance of gaining a trick by ruffing a spade. With the fifth hand, the only reason for raising is to offer partner more encouragement.

"I have hinted several times that the method of computing support points is different from the method for computing basic points. Support points are based primarily on ruffing values— short suits—rather than on long suits. This is the method:

"First, add up the high-card points.

"Next, assuming you have adequate trump support, add 1 point for each doubleton (outside the trump suit), 3 points for each singleton, and 4 points for each void.

"Finally, from this total subtract 1 point for each trump less than four.

"Here are examples: You are planning to support partner's heart bid.

♠ x x x   ♡ Q x x x   ◊ A x   ♣ x x x x

High-Card Points	Distribution Points	Support Points
6	1	7

One distribution point for doubleton.

♠ x x ♡ Q x x x ◇ A x ♣ x x x x x

High-Card Points	Distribution Points	Support Points
6	2	8

One distribution point for each doubleton.

♠ x ♡ Q x x x ◇ A x x ♣ x x x x x

High-Card Points	Distribution Points	Support Points
6	3	9

♠ x ♡ Q x x x x ◇ A x x x x ♣ x x

High-Card Points	Distribution Points	Support Points
6	4	10

♠ x ♡ Q x x ◇ A x x x x ♣ x x x x

High-Card Points	Distribution Points	Support Points
6	2	8

Three points for singleton minus one for only three trumps.

♠ x x ♡ Q x x ◇ A x x x ♣ x x x x

High-Card Points	Distribution Points	Support Points
6	0	6

Add one for doubleton, subtract one for only three trumps.

♠ x x x ♡ Q x x ◇ A x x x ♣ x x x

High-Card Points	Distribution Points	Support Points
6	−1	5

♠ x x x ♡ Q x x x ◇ A x x ♣ x x x

High-Card Points	Distribution Points	Support Points
6	0	6

♠ x x ♡ Q x ◇ A K x x x ♣ K x x x

High-Card Points	Distribution Points	Support Points
12	−1	11

You responded two diamonds and partner rebid two hearts. Until partner rebid hearts, you lacked adequate trump support. You get one distributional point for the doubleton spade (you don't add points for a doubleton in partner's suit) and subtract two for only having two hearts. With eleven points you would raise partner's heart rebid to the three level.

"Alice," I asked, "when partner bids one heart, what do you bid with the following hands?"

(a)
♠ x x   ♡ Q x x x   ◇ K x x x x   ♣ x x   (7)

(b)
♠ x x   ♡ Q J x   ◇ K x x x x   ♣ x x x   (6)

(c)
♠ x x   ♡ J x x x   ◇ A Q x x   ♣ K x x   (11)

(d)
♠ x   ♡ K Q x x   ◇ K x x   ♣ J x x x x   (12)

(e)
♠ x   ♡ K Q x x   ◇ K x x   ♣ Q x x x x   (13)

(f)
♠ x x   ♡ K J x x   ◇ A Q J x x   ♣ x x   (13)

(g)
♠ x   ♡ K x x x x   ◇ A x x x x   ♣ x x   (11)

(h)
♠ x   ♡ Q 10 x x x   ◇ K J 10 x x   ♣ x x   (10)

"I bid two hearts with first two, three hearts with the next two, four hearts with *(e)* and *(f)*, three hearts with *(g)*, and two hearts with *(h)*."

"You followed the rules correctly, but there is an exception to the rule for the last two hands. Despite having just 10 or 11 points, you should bid four hearts. With five trumps and a singleton, it pays to overbid. There are two reasons. If partner has a minimum hand with fitting cards, he may be able to make game.

With ♠ x x x ♡ A K x x x ◇ A x ♣ J x x, for example, he will be cold for four hearts opposite the last 10-point dummy, and he would pass a raise to two or three. Of course, he could have a much better hand without a good play for game—

♠ K Q x ♡ A K x x x ◇ x x x ♣ Q x—

but since you can't tell, it pays in the long run to gamble and bid game. The other reason why it pays to overbid with hands like these is that if partner has a minimum hand, the opponents can make a lot their way. The length in partner's suit cuts down on his defensive values. It is better to play four hearts, down one, than to let the opponents play the hand. Suppose all four hands are as follows:

NORTH

♠ x
♡ Q 10 x x x
◇ K J 10 x x
♣ x x

	WEST		**EAST**
	♠ Q x x x		♠ A K 10 9 x
	♡ x		♡ x x
	◇ x x x		◇ A x
	♣ A Q x x x		♣ J 10 x x

SOUTH

♠ J x x
♡ A K x x x
◇ Q x x
♣ K x

"As it happens, North and South cannot make four hearts. Still, they belong in game. They could make it if East rather than West should hold the ace of clubs. However, there is an even more convincing reason for North to bid four hearts. If he were only to bid two hearts, East would bid two spades, which West would raise to four. The way the cards lie, East-West can make six spades. But it would be very dangerous for East to bid four spades by himself. If North bid four hearts, East would probably just pass."

"When do we use the support count?" Henry asked. "Is responder the only player who can use it?"

"No. Any player may use it when he plans to raise his partner's suit. This applies to subsequent rounds of bidding as well as right away. For example, partner bids one club and you respond one diamond with ♠ Q 10 x x ♡ x x ◊ K Q x x x ♣ x x. Partner rebids one spade, and with your 9 support points you raise to two spades. With ♠ Q 10 x x ♡ x x ◊ K Q x x x ♣ K x you would have 12 support points and would raise to three spades. With ♠ K 10 9 x ♡ x x ◊ A J x x x ♣ K x you would have 13 support points and would raise to four spades. Suppose you open one diamond with ♠ K J x x ♡ x x ◊ A K x x x ♣ A J. Partner responds one spade, and you figure up your support points to determine how high to raise him. You have 18 points and should raise to three, urging him to bid four, but allowing him to pass when holding only 6 or 7 points. Can you remember any hands from last week where delayed support was given?"

"Yes," said Henry. "I responded two diamonds to partner's heart-bid with

     ♠ K x x ♡ Q x x ◊ A Q x x x ♣ x x
and
     ♠ K Q x ♡ Q x x ◊ A Q x x x ♣ x x.

When he rebid his hearts, I raised to three with the first hand and to game with the second hand."

"Did you make the right bids? How many support points did you hold?"

"Yes, apparently I made the right bids. The first hand had 11 support points; the second, 13."

"Whenever you have four or more cards in partner's major suit, you must always raise him immediately or make a forcing bid followed by a raise to game. Suppose that partner bids one heart and you hold ♠ K Q x x ♡ K x x x ◊ J x x ♣ x x. You must not bid one spade, but should raise hearts. In this case a raise to two hearts is sufficient. With the jack of diamonds exchanged for the queen, you could raise to three hearts. With

     ♠ K Q x x ♡ K x x x ◊ A J x ♣ x x

it would be all right—in fact, best—to bid one spade and then jump to four hearts next time. However, when the bidding goes:

OPENER	RESPONDER	*or*	OPENER	RESPONDER
1 ♡	1 ♠		1 ♡	2 ♣
2 ♡	3 ♡		2 ◇	3 ♡

opener knows that responder has no more than three hearts. With four hearts, responder would either raise right away or jump all the way to game on the next round.

"Another thing you should remember about raises is that they are not forcing. Whenever you raise partner to two hearts it means that you are not strong enough to bid three; whenever you raise to three hearts you are not strong enough to bid four. This is true whether the raised bid is an opening bid, a response, or a defensive bid. The only time a raise is forcing is when a game-forcing bid has previously been made. For example:

OPENER	RESPONDER
1 ♣	1 ◇
2 ♡	

"Opener's jump-bid shows at least 20 points and is forcing to game. If responder now bids three hearts the heart bid is forcing NOT BECAUSE IT IS A RAISE, but because a game-forcing bid has been made and game has not been reached. A similar situation is the following:

OPENER	RESPONDER
1 ♠	2 ◇
2 NT	3 ♠

If you want to be technical, you might say that the three-spade bid is a preference for spades over no trump rather than a true raise, but whatever you call the bid, it is forcing because the partnership has at least 26 points. The two-no-trump bid, as we shall discover next week, guarantees 15 points, and the two-diamond bid shows at least 11."

QUIZ

1. How many points do the following hands have in support of diamonds?

(a)

♠ K Q x x   ♡ A x   ◇ K x x x x   ♣ x x

(b)

♠ A K x x x   ♡ A x x   ◇ K x x x   ♣ x

(c)

♠ K x   ♡ x x x   ◇ A J x x x x x   ♣ x

(d)

♠ A Q x x x   ♡ Q x x   ◇ Q x   ♣ x x x

(e)

♠ x x   ♡ x x x   ◇ Q J x x   ♣ K x x x

(f)

♠ x x x   ♡ A K x x x x   ◇ J x x   ♣ x

2. If partner had opened the bidding with one diamond, what would you respond with each of the above hands?

3. In the following sequence can you tell how many hearts responder has? Can you tell how many spades he has?

OPENER	RESPONDER
1 ♡	1 ♠
2 ♣	3 ♡

4. What should responder bid over opener's spade-bid with the following hands?

(a)

♠ Q x x x x   ♡ Q x   ◇ A x x   ♣ J x x

(b)

♠ K J x   ♡ x x   ◇ A x x x x   ♣ Q J x

(c)
♠ Q 10 x x   ♡ Q x x   ◊ Q x x   ♣ J x x

(d)
♠ J 10 x x x   ♡ x   ◊ A Q J x   ♣ x x x

(e)
♠ K J x   ♡ K J x   ◊ Q J x x   ♣ K x x

(f)
♠ K J x x   ♡ A x   ◊ Q J x x   ♣ Q 10 x

ANSWERS

1. (a) 14   (d) 8
   (b) 17   (e) 7
   (c) 12   (f) 10

2. (a) One spade.   (d) One spade.
   (b) Two spades.   (e) Two diamonds.
   (c) Three diamonds.   (f) One heart.

3. Responder has three hearts. He would not make a jump-preference with less than three. With four hearts he would have raised hearts immediately or jumped to game on the second round. You cannot tell how many spades responder has.

4. (a) Two spades.   (e) Two no trump.
   (b) Two diamonds.   (f) Four spades or two dia-
   (c) One no trump.   monds, followed by four
   (d) Four spades.   spades next time.

CHAPTER 12

Rebids by Opener

"ALICE, when may opener pass responder's bid?"

"When the response is a limit-bid and opener can tell that the combined point count is not enough for game."

"Give us some examples."

"A single raise, a double raise, and a one-no-trump response."

"Besides having a minimum opening bid, what other characteristics must opener's hand have to justify a pass of one no trump?"

"The hand must be balanced. With an unbalanced hand, opener will rebid in an effort to find a safer spot."

"What are the maximum point counts opener may have to pass each of these responses?"

"Opener must not pass a single raise or a no-trump response with more than 15 points because responder may have as many as 10 points. Opener must not pass a double raise unless he has a bare 13 points because responder may have 12 support points."

"Based on what you have been told, your answer is one hundred per cent correct. Now let me give you additional factors to consider. Suppose that opener bids a suit with a balanced 16 points, and responder bids one no trump with 6 points. Opener thinks responder may have 10 points, so he raises to two no trump. What practical and theoretical problems can you foresee?"

"I don't know. I am not even sure that I understand your question."

"What do you think, Jerry?"

"The theoretical problem is how to get to game with 26 points and stay out with less. Responder may have 6 to 10 points inclusive. Should he go to three no trump with 8? Or does he need a full 10? It looks to me as though the real difficulty is that the no-trump response covers too wide a range."

"Yes, the wide range does cause problems. When raising an opening one-no-trump bid, it was pointed out that in order to get to game whenever you had a combined total of 26 points, you would occasionally get there with 25. The range of the opening no-trump was rather narrow with only a 2-point spread. In this sequence, where the response has a 4-point spread, in order to bid all games with 26 points you must sometimes bid game with 24 points. That is the theoretical problem. Now what is the practical problem?"

"I should think that if you are not going to get to game, you would prefer to play a comparatively safe one-no-trump contract rather than to be in two no trump where bad breaks might defeat you. When responder has 6 points and opener has 16, two no trump would be a very dangerous contract."

"What is the solution?" I asked.

Jerry shook his head, so I called on Henry, who replied, "The obvious solution is for opener not to try for game with 16 points over a minimum response. He may occasionally miss a good game contract that way, but all the other theoretical problems disappear. Also, the partnership will not be set so frequently in partscore contracts."

"Can you think of any other solution?"

"No."

"Barbara, can you?"

"On balanced hands, opener may open one no trump with 16 points. In fact, a no-trump response to a suit-bid followed by a raise to two no trump should be rather rare, because most hands that would justify a raise would be perfect one-no-trump openings. I'll bet it was to avoid these problems that you urged us to open one no trump, whenever the hand meets the requirements, rather than one of a suit."

"That is right. Henry was also right about passing with 16-point hands.

OPENER	RESPONDER		OPENER	RESPONDER
1 ♠	1 NT		1 ♠	2 ♠
2 NT		*and*	3 ♠	

In each case, opener's rebid shows 17-18 points. With 19 points opener would jump to game himself. It is more logical for him to stretch a point than to expect responder to make another bid with 7 points. Barbara, can you think of any other way to avoid missing game when responder has 10 points?"

"Last lesson you told us that a raise was slightly more encouraging than a no-trump response. With 10 points, we were urged to raise partner's major suit rather than respond one no trump. However, I don't yet see why—since opener is supposed to pass either response with 16 points."

"The reason is that after a raise, opener re-evaluates his hand and uses a new point count called the rebid count, which I shall explain to you in a few minutes. This rebid count is sometimes the same as the basic count, but usually it is higher. After a no-trump response, opener still uses the basic count. What this amounts to is that after a raise, opener frequently re-evaluates his hand more optimistically than he was able to previously.

"Alice, you bid one diamond with

♠ K Q x x   ♡ x   ◇ A K x x x   ♣ x x x

and partner responds one no trump. What do you rebid?"

"Two diamonds. Two spades would be a reverse."

"What is a reverse?"

"A reverse is a rebid which may force responder to the three-level to show a preference."

"Explain what you mean without using the terms 'reverse' and 'preference.'"

"Well, whenever I bid two suits, partner is supposed to tell me which he likes better. With the same length in each suit, he takes me back to my first suit. With greater length in the second suit, he chooses it. He can show a preference for my second suit by passing. However, even when partner has a minimum response, he must take me back to my first suit if he prefers it. When that might take the bidding to the three-level, I have to have a very good hand."

"In other words, you bid two diamonds because if you were to bid two spades, partner would have to bid three diamonds with ♠ 10 x ♡ Q J x ◇ x x x ♣ K 10 x x x. With your minny, you want to keep the bidding as low as possible. Suppose that your four-card suit had been clubs instead of spades?"

"In that case I would be glad to bid two clubs and offer partner a choice of contracts. With a minimum hand, partner could pass or bid two diamonds. In either case the bidding would remain at the two-level."

"Suppose you bid one diamond and partner responds one spade. What rebids can you make with a minimum hand?"

"One no trump, two clubs, two diamonds, and two spades."

"Would all of these rebids *guarantee* a minimum hand?"

"No. Two clubs would show a minimum or intermediate hand. The other rebids would all show a minimum."

"You omitted two hearts. Why would two hearts show extra values?"

"Because if partner preferred diamonds, he would have to bid three diamonds."

"Why does a two-heart bid show extra values while a two-spade bid—a higher bid—guarantees a minimum opener?"

"Because partner can pass when I raise him. There would be no reason for him to return to three diamonds with a minimum response."

"If he should bid three diamonds over your raise to two spades, would that show extra values and an interest in game?"

"I should think so."

"How many points do we need for a reverse?" asked Jerry.

"Eighteen or 19," I replied. "You may reverse with somewhat less strength when partner has responded at the two-level. Naturally, with 20 points or more you must bid game or make a forcing bid."

"I gather that a reverse is not forcing," said Henry.

"No, not unless the response has been at the two-level. When responder has shown at least 11 points, it is logical that game must be reached after a reverse. Henry, which of the following two sequences would you expect to be stronger?"

OPENER	RESPONDER	OPENER	RESPONDER
1 ♡	2 ◊	1 ♡	2 ◊
2 ♠		3 ♣	

"The second one," he replied. "The bidding is *already* at the three-level. In the first case, the bidding will probably reach the three-level. Wait! I take that back. In the first case, the bidding must continue to game because there was a reverse after a two-level response. The two sequences look roughly equivalent to me."

"They are equivalent. How do those bidding sequences compare with the following?"

OPENER	RESPONDER
1 ♠	2 ♣
3 ♣	

"In the latter sequence the bidding has again reached the three-level. Consequently, I suppose this bidding should show about the same amount of strength."

"What is bothering you, Barbara?"

"I was just thinking about certain hands the opener might have. If he were to hold ♠ xx ♡ A K x x ◊ K Q x x ♣ x x x, he should bid one heart, the higher of touching suits. When his partner bids two diamonds, what should he bid?"

"What do you think he should bid?"

"Three diamonds. What else? But this is a minimum opening bid."

"Three diamonds is right. What should opener rebid with

♠ x x ♡ A K x x x ◊ K Q x x ♣ x x?"

"Now opener *could bid* two hearts to show a minimum. However, if he is strong enough to bid three diamonds with the other hand, he is surely strong enough to bid three diamonds with this hand. He has one more support point. Besides, I should think responder would want to know about this nice fit.'"

"You have hit the nail on the head, Barbara. Opener can raise responder's suit with a good fit and no extra values. Responder has at least 11 points to respond at the two-level, and hearing about the fit often enables him to re-evaluate his hand upward. Of course, if he is considering bidding game in a minor, he needs a combined total of 29 points. Without a major-suit fit or a hand suited for no trump, he may occasionally pass your raise. It won't happen very often.

"One of the most peculiar ranges is for a non-jump two-no-trump rebid.

OPENER	RESPONDER
1 ♠	2 ♣
2 NT	

This bid shows 15-17 points. Barbara, can you guess why we have this range?"

"The 15-point minimum is logical because responder needs 11 to respond at the two-level. It sounds as though this rebid must be forcing to game. The reason for the maximum of 17 points is that all no-trump bids apparently have a narrow range."

"Most of what you said was right, Barbara. The two-no-trump rebid is forcing, but not quite forcing *to game*. Suppose the responder has ♠ x x ♡ J x ◇ K x ♣ K J 10 x x x x. His hand is worth 11 basic points, but unless the long suit can be established, it may be of little value at no trump. When opener rebids two no trump, responder should bid three clubs as a warning. Opener should then pass with ♠ A K x x x ♡ Q x x ◇ A Q x ♣ x x, but should bid three no trump with

♠ A J x x x   ♡ Q x x   ◇ A x   ♣ A x x.

The difference is that the latter hand fits clubs well, and opener can expect to establish the suit.

"There is another no-trump range that may seem odd to you. It is for a jump to two no trump after a one-level response.

OPENER	RESPONDER
1 ◇	1 ♡
2 NT	

"What would you expect the range to be, Henry?"

Henry said he would expect it to be 17-18 the same as—

OPENER	RESPONDER
1 ◇	1 NT
2 NT	

"The actual range is 18-19," I continued. "Responder assumes 19 points and raises to game with seven points. Can you guess why this range is chosen? Barbara?"

"I am stumped. Of course, I would normally open 17-18-point balanced hands with one no trump. If we were to adopt a range of 18-19 points, this sequence would show 19 points more often than 18, because with 18 points the opener would tend to open one no trump. Still, I can't see why this sequence should be one point stronger than the other one."

"What would you respond to partner's opening diamond-bid with ♠ K J 9 x x ♡ x ◇ x x ♣ 10 x x x x?"

"One spade. I have 7 basic points. Oh, the reason is clear now. A suit-response may be made with fewer than 6 high-card points, even fewer than 6 points in support of no trump. But a one-no-trump response should show at least 6 high-card points."

"Most intermediate rebids by opener, when the response has been at the one-level, show 17-18, possibly 19 points. The reason for the 17-point minimum rather than 16 points has been thoroughly discussed. The reason for a possible 19-point maximum is more difficult to explain.

"When the hands may not fit, there is good reason to be slightly conservative. For example, suppose you hold

♠ x ♡ A K J x x x ◇ K Q x ♣ A x x.

You open one heart and partner bids one spade. Even though you hold 19 basic points, a jump to three hearts is adequate. Give partner a badly fitting hand such as

♠ K Q x x x ♡ x ◇ x x x ♣ x x x x,

and even three hearts will be too high. On the other hand, when he responds one no trump, I think it is a good gamble to bid four hearts. There is less chance of a singleton or void in hearts, less chance that his strength will all be opposite your singleton, and partner should have *at least* 6 high-card points. He would pass a three-heart rebid with

♠ x x x   ♡ Q x   ◊ J x x x   ♣ K x x x,

but you would belong in game. Naturally, if he were to raise to two hearts you would bid four.

"Alice, can you think of any example of a rebid by opener showing an intermediate hand which we have not discussed tonight?"

"Yes. A double raise of responder's suit. For example . . ." Alice drew the following on the board.

OPENER	RESPONDER
1 ♣	1 ♡
3 ♡	

"Put a couple of example hands on the blackboard which justify that bidding," I then said, "and write the number of support points after each hand."

Alice wrote the following.

(a)

♠ x x   ♡ K Q x x   ◊ A x   ♣ A Q x x x (17)

(b)

♠ A x x   ♡ K x x x   ◊ x   ♣ A K J x x (18)

"Suppose that you open one heart and partner responds one spade. What would you rebid with the following hands?"

(a) ♠ A Q x x   ♡ A K x x x   ◊ x x   ♣ A Q   (21)

(b) ♠ K Q x x   ♡ A K J x x x   ◊ K x   ♣ x   (20)

"Four spades," Alice said. "Both hands are too strong for a raise to three, which partner might pass."

"Did you consider jumping in hearts instead of spades with the latter hand?"

"No. Because it is only worth 19 points at hearts and 20 points at spades."

"I didn't think of using the point count like that, but perhaps it is a good idea. The main reason is that spades *must* be a good trump suit while hearts may or may not be. It depends upon whether or not partner has heart support.

"Alice, give us some example hands justifying a jump-rebid in opener's suit after a one-level response."

These were the examples she wrote:

(*a*) ♠ A x   ♡ A K J 10 x x   ◇ K x x   ♣ J x

(*b*) ♠ A J   ♡ K Q J x x x x   ◇ K x   ♣ x x

(*c*) ♠ A x x   ♡ A Q 10 x x   ◇ A x x   ♣ K x

"Your first two examples are excellent," I said. "Opener needs at least a good six-card suit because he doesn't know whether responder has support for it. The second example shows that with a longer suit, opener needs fewer high cards. You tried to illustrate that with a shorter suit he needs more high cards, but in the third example the suit is too weak for a jump-rebid. Opener probably should have bid one no trump orginally, but having failed to do so, he should bid two no trump over a one-spade or one-no-trump response. After opening one heart and getting one spade response, what would you rebid with

♠ A x   ♡ A K Q J x x   ◇ K x   ♠ x x?"

"Four hearts. I have 20 basic points and a good suit."

"Correct. You should have been slightly worried when you bid one heart. Now that partner has bid, you must take no further chances of stopping short of game. If partner has nothing but the ace of diamonds, you are cold for ten tricks. As little as the king of spades will give you a good play for game.

"Now I shall explain the rebid count, which I mentioned a short while ago. Incidentally, this will be the last point count you will have to learn. Basic points are a combination of playing strength—trick-taking ability—and defensive strength. Remember, you were told that while ♠ x ♡ K Q J x x x ◇ Q J x x x ♣ x was at least as good as ♠ x x ♡ A K x x x ◊ K Q x ♣ x x x, if you knew that you would play the hand at hearts; nevertheless, you needed more general strength to open the bidding. The reason for this is that partner or the opponents might buy the bid, and partner should be able to count on you for a certain amount of general strength. However, once partner raises your suit, and you know that you are going to play the hand, the important thing is how many tricks you can take. You are no longer worried about how good your hand is on defense or in support of a suit partner may bid. A new type of count is needed to evaluate your hand.

"To determine the 'rebid count,' take the basic count and add 2 points for each card in excess of five cards in your long suit. Also add 1 point for each singleton and 2 points for each void, provided your suit is at least five cards in length. The answer gives you your 'rebid points.'

"To illustrate, you open the bidding one spade with

♠ A K x x x x ♡ K x ◊ Q J x ♣ x x.

You have 15 basic points. Once partner raises to two spades, add 2 more points for your sixth spade, giving you 17 points. That gives you enough to rebid three spades.

♠ A K x x x x ♡ K x x ◊ Q x x ♣ x

contains only 14 basic points, but you get 17 rebid points, 2 for the sixth spade and 1 for the singleton club. Note that if partner has a maximum raise and a reasonably good fit, there will be a good play for game.

(♠ J x x x ♡ A x x x ◊ K x ♣ x x x,
or
♠ Q x x ♡ A x ◊ K x x x x ♣ J x x.)

After a raise, opener bids three spades with 17 or 18 rebid points, and bids four spades with 19."

"Does opener select one of these different counts depending upon his rebid?" asked Jerry.

"Yes. Suppose he opens one diamond and gets a one-spade response. To rebid one no trump, he should have 13-15 points *for no trump.* To rebid two clubs, he needs 13-19 *basic points.* To rebid two hearts he needs 18-19 *basic points.* To raise to two spades, he needs 13-16 *support points.* If responder had raised his suit, he would compute his rebid points to determine whether or not to bid again."

"I have a question," said Barbara. "Suppose I open the bidding with one diamond, holding

♠ x x   ♡ K J x   ◇ A K x x   ♣ J x x x,

and partner responds one spade. I thought I should rebid no trump to show a minimum balanced hand, but this hand is only worth 12 points for no trump. Should I rebid an unbiddable club suit? I would have 13 basic points at a suit contract."

"What do you think?"

"I think I should rebid one no trump. This hand doesn't look as though it belongs in a suit—at least not from my point of view. I would rather mislead partner about 1 point than to raise the bidding level. At least he would pass with 10 balanced points, while if I bid two clubs he might bid again, hoping I had 18 points."

"The real solution is not to open the hand. Whenever you open the bidding, you should look ahead at least one round. On borderline hands, the question to ask yourself is, which will give partner a more accurate picture of my hand, an opening bid and rebid, or an original pass? Distribution of 4-4-3-2 is supposed to be worth 1 distributional point for opening the bidding, but 4-4-3-2 distribution is not as good as 5-3-3-2 distribution. If you think you can conveniently bid your hand as a suit-hand, open your hand with 12 high-card points. This is particularly true when your strength is concentrated in two suits. With

♠ K Q x x   ♡ x x   ◇ x x x   ♣ A K x x,

bid one club, planning to rebid one spade over partner's response. Change the suits as follows:

♠ x x   ♡ K Q x x   ◇ x x x   ♣ A K x x,

and you have a borderline decision. You should probably open anyway, but if partner responds one spade, you will have to rebid one no trump. This is slightly misleading, but less misleading, in my opinion, than failure to open the bidding. But with

♠ Q x ♡ J x x ◊ A J x x ♣ K J x x,

I definitely prefer a pass. It is very unlikely that you would play the hand in one of your suits. You would have to rebid one no trump, and at no trump or in support of partner's suit, this is a less-than-minimum hand.

"As I said," I continued, "when planning to open the bidding, look ahead one round and anticipate partner's probable responses and your probable rebid. Suppose your hand is

♠ x x ♡ K Q x x ◊ A K x x x ♣ x x.

What would you open, Alice?"

"One diamond, the long suit."

"Yes, that is what I've been telling you. If partner bids one spade or two clubs, what will you rebid?"

"Two diamonds. The hand is not nearly strong enough to reverse."

"Suppose partner has ♠ Q x x x x ♡ A x x x ◊ x x ♣ Q x. Where would you like to play the hand?"

"In hearts. Two hearts looks about right."

"How will you get into hearts?"

"We won't. The bidding will go as follows:

OPENER	RESPONDER
1 ◊	1 ♠
2 ◊	Pass

Responder is too weak to bid over two diamonds."

"Suppose that opener had mis-sorted his hand. Under the impression that he had five hearts and four diamonds, he opened one heart. Responder would raise to two hearts, and he would be in a good contract, wouldn't he?"

"Yes. His mistake would turn out well this time."

"Let's change responder's hand to

♠ Q x x x x   ♡ x x   ◇ A x x x   ♣ Q x.

If opener bid one heart and rebid two diamonds over one spade, things would still turn out all right. I'll admit that sometimes it would work out badly for opener to bid hearts first. Responder might have three cards in each suit and prefer hearts. But in the long run, it is more descriptive to tell partner you have hearts and diamonds rather than just to say, 'I have a long diamond suit.' When the suits are touching suits, and you have a minimum hand, you know that if you bid the lower-ranking suit, you will never be able to show the other suit.

"Make one suit very weak and the other very strong—as, for example, in

♠ K x x x   ♡ A K Q 10 x   ◇ x x x   ♣ x

or

♠ x x   ♡ Q x x x   ◇ A K J x x   ♣ A x—

and you may properly decide to bid and rebid the strong suit and forget about the other suit unless partner can bid it. But usually it will pay to show both suits. This means that it is correct to open the higher ranking of touching suits even when you have one more card in the lower ranking suit."

"What about the rule that we should open our long suits?" asked Alice, looking quite distressed. "It seems to me that all of the rules you gave us are being disregarded, one by one."

"No, the rules I gave you were good rules which should be followed most of the time. In the beginning it would have been too confusing if you were told all of the exceptions."

"Are there other exceptions to the rule of bidding the long suit besides opening the higher ranking of touching suits?" asked Alice.

"Yes, but this exception is the most important one. Needless to say, when you have a strong hand, bid it naturally, long suit first. Thus with ♠ K J x x ♡ A K x x x ◇ Q J x ♣ x, open one spade, but with ♠ K J x x ♡ A K Q x x ◇ A x ♣ x x, bid one heart and plan to bid spades next time. The reverse shows your true distribution plus a good hand—just the message you wish to convey."

"What are the other exceptions?" asked Barbara.

"When you have two suits you would like to show, use a trial-and-error method—mentally, of course. Imagine that you open one suit and decide what your rebid would be over partner's various minimum responses. Then try bidding the other suit and see which opening works out better. For example, you hold ♠ x ♡ K Q 10 x ◇ K J x ♣ A x x x x. Suppose you open one club. If partner responds one diamond or one heart, you will have a very easy rebid. If he responds one no trump, you have a close decision whether to pass or rebid two clubs. Either contract will probably be safe, since partner's no-trump response over one club shows a fairly good hand. But if partner bids one spade, you will have no satisfactory rebid. You should not rebid one no trump with a singleton, even when it is in partner's suit. You would have to rebid two clubs, which could turn out very badly. I might add that partner's most likely response is one spade. Partner usually bids the suit in which you have the fewest cards.

"Let's try opening one heart. Just as before, partner's most likely response is one spade, and you can rebid two clubs, showing both suits. If partner rebids two diamonds, he will prevent you from showing clubs, but you can raise partner's diamonds. It is better to risk not being able to show clubs than not being able to show hearts, because a major suit is more important. Besides, a two-diamond response is much less likely than a one-spade response for two reasons: partner is usually longest in your short suit; and when he has a diamond suit, he cannot bid it unless he has at least 11 points.

"Barbara, what would you open with

♠ K Q x x ♡ K x x ◇ A Q x x ♣ x x?"

"The rule you gave us at first was to bid one diamond. Let's see how that would work. Over a heart-response, I don't know whether I would bid one spade or two hearts, but the main problem seems to be what to rebid over a two-club response. I am slightly too weak to rebid two no trump, and yet no other bid looks at all satisfactory.

"Let's try one spade. I could pass a no-trump response, bid two diamonds over two clubs, raise a two-diamond or two-heart response. So it looks as though one spade is the best opening. Apparently the key to the hand is that I have heart support rather than club support. Change my hearts and clubs, and I would bid one diamond. I could then raise a two-club response, while I could not handle a two-heart response over one spade."

"The last hand should be easy for you to figure out," I said. "What would you bid with ♠ K J x x ♡ A x x ◊ Q x x ♣ K x x?"

"One club. If I were to open one spade, I would be forced to raise partner's response to the three-level with this minimum balanced hand. If I open one club, I can rebid one no trump over a diamond or heart response."

"Why not rebid one spade?"

"If I bid clubs and spades, partner wouldn't expect me to have 4-3-3-3 distribution. I think rebidding one no trump gives him a better description of my hand. Am I right?"

"That is difficult to say. Many experts would rebid one spade, but I prefer a one-no-trump bid myself for the very reasons you gave."

QUIZ

1. The bidding has been

OPENER	RESPONDER
1 ♣	1 ♡

What would opener rebid with the following hands?

(a) ♠ K x x	♡ Q x x	◊ K x x	♣ A K x x
(b) ♠ K x x x	♡ Q x	◊ x x x	♣ A K J x
(c) ♠ A x x x	♡ K x x x	◊ x x	♣ A K x
(d) ♠ A x x x	♡ K x x x	◊ x	♣ A K x x

(e) ♠ A Q x   ♡ Q x   ◊ A K x   ♣ A 10 x x x

(f) ♠ A x   ♡ K Q x x   ◊ A x   ♣ A J 10 x x

(g) ♠ A x   ♡ K x   ◊ x x x   ♣ A K Q 10 x x

(h) ♠ A x   ♡ x x   ◊ A K x x   ♣ A J 10 x x

(i) ♠ A Q x   ♡ J x   ◊ A K x   ♣ A Q 10 x x

(j) ♠ A Q x x   ♡ K J x   ◊ x   ♣ A K Q x x

2. The bidding has been

OPENER	RESPONDER
1 ♡	2 ♣

What should opener rebid?

(a) ♠ A x   ♡ A J 10 x x   ◊ Q J x   ♣ x x x

(b) ♠ A Q   ♡ A J 10 x x   ◊ K J x   ♣ x x x

(c) ♠ A x   ♡ A J 10 x x   ◊ K J x x   ♣ x x

(d) ♠ A x   ♡ A J 10 x x   ◊ x x x   ♣ A Q x

(e) ♠ A x   ♡ A Q J 10 x x   ◊ K x   ♣ J x x

(f) ♠ x x   ♡ A K J x x   ◊ A x   ♣ K Q x x

(g) ♠ x   ♡ A Q x x   ◊ Q x x   ♣ K J x x x

(h) ♠ A Q x   ♡ K Q x x x   ◊ A K x   ♣ x x

3. The bidding has been

OPENER	RESPONDER
1 ♡	2 ♡

What should opener rebid?

(a) ♠ x   ♡ A Q x x x   ◊ K J x x   ♣ Q J x

(b) ♠ x   ♡ A Q x x x   ◊ K J x x   ♣ A Q x

(c) ♠ x x   ♡ A K x x x   ◊ A Q x x x   ♣ x

(d) ♠ A   ♡ A x x x x   ◊ K Q J x   ♣ x x x

(e) ♠ K x   ♡ A Q x x x x   ◇ K x   ♣ Q 10 x

(f) ♠ x x   ♡ A K x x x x   ◇ K J x x x   ♣ —

(g) ♠ x x   ♡ A K x x   ◇ K Q x x x   ♣ K x

4. What opening bid on the following?

(a) ♠ Q x x x   ♡ A J   ◇ Q x x x   ♣ A K x

(b) ♠ Q x x x   ♡ A K Q x x   ◇ K x   ♣ x x

(c) ♠ x x   ♡ A Q x x   ◇ J x x x x   ♣ A J

(d) ♠ J x   ♡ A Q x x   ◇ K J x x   ♣ A Q x

(e) ♠ Q x x x   ♡ Q x x x   ◇ K x   ♣ A K x

(f) ♠ x   ♡ A J 10 x   ◇ K x x   ♣ K 10 9 x x

(g) ♠ x x   ♡ Q x x x   ◇ K Q x   ♣ A Q x x

(h) ♠ A x   ♡ K J 10 x   ◇ K J x   ♣ Q J x x

(i) ♠ K x x   ♡ A Q J 9   ◇ K 10 x   ♣ x x x

(j) ♠ A   ♡ K Q x x   ◇ A Q x   ♣ J 10 9 x x

(k) ♠ x   ♡ A Q J x x   ◇ A Q 10 x x x   ♣ x

(l) ♠ x x   ♡ A Q x x x   ◇ A K x x x   ♣ A

(m) ♠ A x x   ♡ A K x x   ◇ A Q 10 x   ♣ x x

5. What should opener bid in the following sequence?

OPENER	RESPONDER
1 ♡	1 NT
2 NT	3 ♣
?	

(a) ♠ A K x   ♡ A Q x x x   ◇ K J x   ♣ x x

(b) ♠ A K x   ♡ A Q x x x   ◇ x x   ♣ K J x

(c) ♠ x x   ♡ A K Q x x x ◇ A x x   ♣ Q x

ANSWERS

1. (a) 1 NT   (d) 3 ♡   (g) 3 ♣   (i) 3 NT
  (b) 1 ♠   (e) 2 NT   (h) 2 ◊   (j) 2 ♠
  (c) 2 ♡   (f) 4 ♡

2. (a) 2 ♡   (c) 2 ◊   (e) 3 ♡   (g) 3 ♣
  (b) 2 NT   (d) 3 ♣   (f) 4 ♣   (h) 3 NT

3. (a) Pass   (d) 3 ♡ *or* 3 ♣   (f) 4 ♡
  (b) 4 ♡   (e) 3 ♡ *or* 2 NT   (g) 3 ◊
  (c) 3 ◊

4. (a) 1 NT   (f) 1 ♡   (j) 1 ♣
  (b) 1 ♡   (g) 1 ♣   (k) 1 ◊
  (c) 1 ♡   (h) 1 ♡   (l) 1 ♡
  (d) 1 NT   (i) 1 ♡   (m) 1 NT *or* 1 ♡
  (e) 1 ♣

5. (a) Pass. Partner has a long club suit, and you have no fit.

(b) 3 NT. This is a gamble, since the opponents may be able to run the diamond suit. However, it is a good gamble. Your club fit means that you probably have six club-tricks. A likely hand for partner's bidding is ♠ x x ♡ x x ◊ x x x ♣ A Q 10 x x x. If you do not bid game, three clubs should be safer than two no trump.

(c) Pass. Game is out of the question. Quite likely neither three clubs nor three hearts can be made, but you have not been doubled yet. Besides, you have a mild club fit while partner may have a singleton or void in hearts.

CHAPTER 13

Making the Bidding Mesh

"I SUSPECT that you will have several questions about last week's quiz."

"Yes, we do," said Jerry. "First, in question 1(c) you had opener bidding one club. In problem 4(e) your answer was to bid one club. In both cases, opener could bid naturally by opening one spade, and no rebid problems would arise. My question is, why bid a three-card suit when you don't have to?"

"Let me answer your question with a question. Suppose you open one spade and partner responds one no trump. What would you rebid?"

"I would pass, of course. My hand in both cases is minimum and balanced."

"A pass is correct. It would be very dangerous and misleading to rebid two hearts. However, in either case partner might have ♠ x ♡ J 10 x x x ◇ A J x ♣ J x x x. He would not be strong enough to bid two hearts over one spade, but could easily respond one heart over a one-club opening. Besides, even if you get a good chance to bid both suits, would you want to? Both suits are weak, and the hand is balanced. Showing a two-suiter is somewhat of a distortion."

"If you open one club and partner responds one diamond, what should you rebid?" asked Henry.

"One heart, the lower suit, since you do not expect to bid both major suits. It is true that you would be showing two suits, clubs and hearts, this way also, which is somewhat misleading. However, the bidding is still at a low level, and there is a good chance for you to land on your feet."

"In question 4(*i*)," Jerry asked, "what would I rebid if partner were to respond two of a minor?"

"You would have no good rebid. My suggestion would be to rebid two hearts. Normally, this shows a fair five-card suit—at least K J x x x. However, you hope that partner will respond one spade or one no trump so as not to give you this problem. The alternative, opening one club on three small, seems even less desirable."

"Apparently, the next hand is strong enough for a reverse," Jerry said, "but hand (*k*) looks awfully skimpy to me. It only adds up to 17 basic points."

"With 6-5 distribution and strength concentrated in those two suits, you can afford to reverse with close to a minimum opening. You need very little help from partner to make game—if his help is in the right spots."

"Why not bid one diamond on the next two hands so that opener can show his strength next time by reversing?"

"A reverse does not just show strength," I replied. "Equally important is the information it conveys regarding distribution. When you bid diamonds first and later hearts, partner will assume that you have more diamonds than hearts."

"My questions concern rebids over a raise," said Henry. "When the bidding is one heart by me, two hearts by partner, I think I know when to pass and when to jump to game, but when should I bid a new suit or no trump?"

"You bid a new suit for either of two reasons. One reason might be that your opening suit is a four-card suit, and you think there may be a better spot. The other reason is that you want to tell partner where his help will be most appreciated. When you show two suits, partner will pay particular attention to his holding in your second suit, and will tend to devalue his kings, queens and jacks in the unbid suits, since they are quite likely to be opposite a singleton, and thus worthless to you. It is for the latter reason that most experts would bid three clubs with hand 3(*d*). If partner has club strength—rather than spade strength—it will be valuable. Also, if he has a ruffing value for you, you hope that it is in clubs rather than diamonds. You really don't care what partner has in diamonds other than the ace, so that is the reason for not bidding diamonds. You want partner to bid game with ♠ x x x ♡ K x x x ◊ x x x x ♣ A x or ♠ x x x x ♡ K Q x x ◊ x x x x ♣ x, but to return to three hearts with ♠ K x x ♡ 10 x x x ◊ A x ♣ x x x x or

$$\spadesuit \text{ x x x x x} \quad \heartsuit \text{ K Q x x} \quad \diamondsuit \text{ x} \quad \clubsuit \text{ x x x.''}$$

"The new suit must be forcing," said Henry, "or you could never afford to bid a new suit with three small cards."

"Right. Barbara, why would I suggest a two-no-trump rebid as an alternative to three hearts on question 3(e)?"

"It seems odd, because there are not nearly enough points. However, when I try to visualize hands that partner might have, the bid looks reasonable. Suppose partner has

$$\spadesuit \text{ J x x} \quad \heartsuit \text{ K J x} \quad \diamondsuit \text{ A x x x} \quad \clubsuit \text{ J x x,}$$

for example. With a favorable opening hand, such as a low spade from the ace, I would have nine cold tricks."

"In tonight's lesson we will discuss how both hands should bid together, rather than emphasize how either opener or responder should bid. When either player makes a limit-bid, his partner can rather easily place the final contract. At least he can tell whether game is almost certain, probable or improbable. When neither partner has made a limit bid, a more serious problem arises. After

OPENER	RESPONDER	*or*	OPENER	RESPONDER
1 ♣	1 ♡		1 ♡	1 ♠
1 ♠			2 ◊	

for example, opener's rebid may show either a minimum hand or an intermediate hand. The range is 13-18 points, conceivably even 19. For that reason responder, even with a minimum hand, must try to give opener another chance if game is possible, without offering much encouragement. After

OPENER	RESPONDER
1 ♣	1 ♡
1 ♠	

suppose that responder has ♠ x x x ♡ K Q x x ◇ J x x x ♣ x x.
He has already given opener one chance. Since opener has not
made a jump shift or game-bid, and since responder has a tol-
erance for spades, he should pass. Suppose responder has a
slightly better hand: ♠ x x x ♡ K Q x x ◇ Q 10 x x ♣ Q x.
These 9 points may combine with 17 in opener's hand, so responder should bid one no trump. This no-trump rebid shows
about 8 to 10 points. With ♠ K x x x ♡ K Q x x ◇ x x ♣ x x x,
responder should raise to two spades. This bid shows about 8
to 10 points in support of spades. With

♠ x x ♡ K Q x x x ◇ x x x ♣ Q x x,

responder should return to two clubs. As you will remember,
this is called preference. It does not require extra strength to
return partner to his first suit if you have better support for it.

"With equal length in support of both suits you should return
to the first suit, unless you have such a minimum response that
you think game is completely out of the question. Thus with

♠ K Q x x x ♡ J x ◇ Q x ♣ x x x x,

you would respond one spade to partner's opening heart-bid,
and return him to two hearts if he should rebid two diamonds.
With

♠ K Q x x x ♡ x x ◇ x x ♣ x x x x,

the situation looks so hopeless that you should pass two diamonds rather than give partner another chance to get into
trouble.

"With an intermediate hand, responder must take stronger
action than he would with a minimum hand. After

OPENER	RESPONDER
1 ♣	1 ♡
1 ♠	

responder should bid three spades with

♠ Q 10 x x ♡ A J 10 x x ◇ x x ♣ Q x

(11 support points), two no trump with

♠ Q x x ♡ A 10 9 x ◊ K Q x ♣ 10 x x,

or three clubs with

♠ Q x ♡ A J 10 x ◊ x x x ♣ K J x x.

"Barbara, what should responder bid in the following sequence?

OPENER	RESPONDER
1 ♡	1 ♠
2 ◊	?

Responder has ♠ K J x x ♡ Q x x ◊ A J x x ♣ x x."

"Three diamonds."

"Suppose that opener then bids three no trump. Would you pass?"

"Yes."

"Could he hold ♠ Q x ♡ K J 10 x x ◊ K Q x x ♣ A x?"

"Yes, and we would belong in hearts."

"What would you have bid with the responding hand in the same sequence if the hand were changed to

♠ K J x x x ♡ Q x x ◊ A J x ♣ x x?"

"Three hearts, a jump preference. I suppose I should do the same thing even with four diamonds in my hand."

"In either case, if you bid three hearts over two diamonds, will partner expect you to have four hearts?"

"No. He will know that I don't have four hearts, because if I had, I would have raised immediately or jumped to four hearts on the next round."

"Since game in a minor suit is hard to make, the raise of partner's minor suit should deny a good alternative bid. With ♠ K J x x x ♡ Q x ◊ A J x x ♣ x x, a raise to three diamonds would be correct, since there is no other reasonable choice. What would you bid with ♠ A J x x ♡ x x ◊ J x x x ♣ K Q 10?"

"Two no trump. It must be more important to show strength in the unbid suit than it is to show diamond support."

"Many times it is hard to evaluate one's hand, because it is impossible to know what the final contract will be or whether partner has undisclosed support."

I then drew the following on the board.

OPENER	RESPONDER
1 ♠	2 ◇
2 ♡	?

"Responder has ♠ x x ♡ K x x ◇ A Q x x x ♣ K x x. This hand is worth 13 points for no trump if partner fits diamonds, but if there is no diamond fit and no second club stopper, three no trump will be a very dangerous contract. The best bid is two no trump—conservatively counting just the high cards. If opener has ♠ A K x x ♡ Q J x x x ◇ x x ♣ Q x, he will pass, and two no trump is probably as high as you belong. If he has

♠ A K x x x ♡ A 10 9 x x ◇ x x ♣ x,

he will bid three hearts, and you can raise to four. He would pass a jump to three no trump because he would expect you to have a double club stopper, better diamonds, or both—something like

♠ x x ♡ J x ◇ K Q J 10 x x ♣ A Q x

or

♠ x x ♡ K x ◇ A Q J x x ♣ A 10 9 x.

"Suppose the bidding had gone:

OPENER	RESPONDER
1 ♡	1 ♠
2 ◇	?

"Responder holds ♠ A Q 9 x x x ♡ K x ◇ 10 9 x ♣ x x. If opener had raised spades, responder would have jumped straight to game—13 rebid points. If opener had rebid one no trump showing a balanced hand with at least two spades, responder would have jumped to three spades in order to invite game. But when opener shows two suits, he is quite likely to be short in one of the other suits. Because of the possibility of a misfit, responder should bid only two spades. A bid and rebid of a major suit covers a very wide range, since the same bid would be made with

♠ K Q x x x x ♡ x x ◇ x x x ♣ x x.

"Alice, you open one diamond with

♠ K J x ♡ K x x ◇ K Q x x ♣ J 10 x.

Partner responds one spade, you rebid one no trump, and he bids three spades. What would you bid now?"

"Is three spades forcing?"

"No."

"Then I would pass. My hand is a bare minimum."

"Suppose the bidding is the same, but this time you hold

♠ x x ♡ K J x ◇ A Q J x ♣ Q J x x?"

"If I bid, I would bid three no trump. But I think I would pass. The poor spade fit with partner make this hand almost as bad as the last one."

"That is right. However, with 15 points, no matter what other bad features you might have, you should bid either three no trump or four spades. With ♠ x x x ♡ K x ◇ A Q x x x ♣ A x x you would gladly raise to four spades, since you have a potential ruffing value and strength mostly in aces and kings. In a later lesson we shall discuss the finer points of hand evaluation, but we can say now that when your high cards consist mostly of aces and kings, your hand is better than when your points are made up largely of queens and jacks. This is particularly true when the final contract will be a suit rather than no trump. The reason is that aces are almost always valuable. A king is usually worth something. But Q x x or Q J x opposite your singleton or doubleton is probably worth nothing at all.

"A non-jump rebid is not forcing or even encouraging. As we pointed out a long time ago, after one player makes a limit-bid, his partner is usually in a position to decide upon the final contract.

OPENER	RESPONDER
1 ◊	1 ♠
1 NT	?

Responder would bid two spades with

♠ K J x x x x ♡ x x ◊ J x ♣ x x x

or two hearts with

♠ K x x x x ♡ Q J x x x ◊ x x ♣ x.

In both cases, responder would just be looking for a safe spot. Of course, he would pass with a weak *balanced* hand."

"Is a new suit by responder on the second round forcing or not?" asked Jerry. "I am confused now."

"A new suit by responder is forcing unless opener has rebid one no trump, thereby limiting his hand both as to strength and distribution. In order to force over a one-no-trump rebid, responder must jump in a new suit. Jerry, suppose you open one spade and partner bids three spades. What would you rebid with the following two hands?"

♠ K Q x x ♡ A Q x x ◊ Q x ♣ x x x

♠ Q J x x x ♡ A Q x ◊ K x x ♣ x x

"In each case I would pass," he replied. "Partner's hand is limited, and I have a bare opening bid."

"That's right. You need 15 rebid points or possibly a good fourteen to bid again. In the same bidding sequence, what should you bid with ♠ K Q x x ♡ A Q x x x ◊ K x ♣ x x?"

"Four spades."

"Why not four hearts?"

"There is no reason to look further. Partner must have at least four spades."

"How can it do any harm to bid four hearts?"

"It will tell the opponents how to defend the hand. Also, it might mislead partner. He would think I was interested in a slam since, if I were only interested in game, I would not bother to show my hearts."

"Excellent, Jerry! It pleases me when any of you draw conclusions of this sort. Henry, the next question is yours. Partner opens one diamond, you respond one spade, and he bids two clubs. What would you bid with

♠ x x x x x   ♡ K J 10   ◊ K Q x x   ♣ x?"

"Three diamonds."

"Why not two no trump? You have very good strength in the unbid suit, and three no trump will probably be easier to make than five diamonds."

"I guess that's right."

"Don't agree with me so readily. Are you strong enough to bid two no trump?"

"No. I should have 11 or 12 points to bid two no trump on the second round, and I only have 9. But I have 12 points in support of diamonds."

"Consequently, most players, including many experts, would bid three diamonds. However, I prefer a two-diamond bid. Can you guess why?"

"Probably because it takes 29 points to make five diamonds, so you raise the requirements for a jump preference in a minor suit."

"That is one good reason. Another is that partner often bids three no trump over a jump preference in a minor. You only have 9 points for no trump, so when he bids three no trump with something like ♠ x x ♡ A Q ◊ A J x x ♣ K x x x x, he will not have a good play for it. The jump preference in a minor normally shows about 11 or 12 points for no trump—but not much strength in the unbid suit—since no trump is often the final contract. In this case, whether game is bid in diamonds or no trump, opener needs 17 points, and with that good a hand he can bid over two diamonds himself.

"Barbara, what would you bid with

♠ A J x x   ♡ x x   ◊ Q 10 x   ♣ Q x x x?

The previous bidding has been one diamond, by partner, one spade by you, two clubs by partner."

"Two diamonds, I suppose."

"That is an unusual bid. Please explain your reasoning."

"Partner's bid is ambiguous. I don't want to pass and risk missing game when he has an intermediate opening. On the other hand, my hand is a minimum. If I were to raise to three clubs, partner would assume that I had an intermediate hand and might bid three no trump with 14 or 15 points. I don't really prefer diamonds to clubs, but I like them almost as well, and I want to give partner another chance without overstating my hand."

"So you are willing to give partner a preference for a suit you do not prefer!"

"Yes, because there is no other satisfactory bid."

"Tell me how you think the following two hands should be bid, and explain why."

OPENER	RESPONDER
♠ A K x x x x	♠ Q x x
♡ A x x	♡ K x x
◇ K x	◇ Q J x
♣ x x	♣ Q 10 x x

Barbara replied, "The bidding should go

OPENER	RESPONDER
1 ♠	2 ♠
3 ♠	3 NT
Pass	

Responder should bid two spades rather than one no trump, because with 10 points he wants to be encouraging. Opener has 18 rebid points, so he bids three spades. Responder has enough strength to accept the invitation, but from his point of view no trump may be the best spot. Opener should pass because his hand is well-suited for no trump. He has a long suit, which will probably run, and no singleton."

"As it happens, four spades would be slightly safer than three no trump, but if the minor holdings were changed so as to have Q J x opposite two small, three no trump would be much safer. How should the following hands be bid? Write the proper bidding on the blackboard below the hands."

OPENER	RESPONDER
♠ A Q J x	♠ K x x
♡ Q x x	♡ A J x x
◇ x x	◇ x x x
♣ A Q x x	♣ K x x x
1 ♣	1 ♡
1 ♠	3 ♣
3 ♡	3 ♠
4 ♠	Pass

"Explain the bidding," I said.

"The first two bids by both partners are obvious," Barbara replied. "Opener should not pass three clubs with 15 high-card points; yet he cannot logically bid three no trump with two small cards of the unbid suit. He bids three hearts, hoping responder will have five hearts. Besides, this gives responder another chance to bid three no trump, if that is where the hands belong. Since responder's hearts are not very good and he has no stopper in diamonds, he bids three spades to show three-card support."

"How will opener know that responder has three, rather than four, spades?"

"With four spades, responder would have raised spades on the previous round."

"All the bids so far are fairly clear-cut," I said. "Now opener has all the information he can hope to receive and must make a decision. Obviously, three no trump is out of the question when both partners are short in diamonds, and neither has a stopper. The conservative bid would be four clubs. Five clubs is also a possibility, but with two quick diamond losers the rest of the hand would have to be solid. The best chance for game is in four of a major. Why did you select spades rather than hearts, Barbara, with a combined holding of seven cards in each suit?"

"Because the spades were stronger."

"Suppose the two hands were as follows:

OPENER	RESPONDER
♠ A Q x x	♠ K x x
♡ K x x	♡ A Q x x
◇ x x x	◇ x x
♣ A Q x	♣ K J x x

It might be difficult to stay out of a no-trump contract, but if you were to bid four of a major, which major would you prefer?"

"Spades. I would prefer to ruff the third round of diamonds with the three-card suit and keep my four-card length intact."

QUIZ

1. In the following examples, decide who is at fault for reaching the wrong contract.

	OPENER	RESPONDER
(a)	♠ K x x	♠ A J 5 4 3 2
	♡ A K Q x x	♡ x
	◇ x x	◇ x x x
	♣ x x x	♣ A x x
	1 ♡	1 ♠
	2 ♡	2 ♠
	Pass	

	OPENER	RESPONDER
(b)	♠ K x	♠ x x
	♡ A Q x x	♡ K x x
	◇ Q 10 x x	◇ K x x
	♣ K J x	♣ A Q x x x
	1 ♡	2 ♣
	2 ◇	3 ♡
	4 ♡	Pass

	OPENER	RESPONDER
(c)	♠ K x x	♠ J x x x
	♡ A J x x x	♡ 10 x x
	◇ A x x x	◇ K Q x x
	♣ x	♣ J x
	1 ♡	1 ♠
	2 ♠	Pass

	OPENER	RESPONDER
(d)	♠ —	♠ A Q J x x x
	♡ A Q x x x x	♡ x
	◇ K x x	◇ x x x
	♣ Q 10 x x	♣ A x x
	1 ♡	1 ♠
	2 ♡	3 ♠
	3 NT	Pass

	OPENER	RESPONDER
(e)	♠ x	♠ A Q x x x
	♡ A K x x x	♡ Q x
	◇ K Q 10 x	◇ J x
	♣ x x x	♣ x x x x
	1 ♡	1 ♠
	2 ◇	2 ♠
	Pass	

	OPENER	RESPONDER
(f)	♠ x	♠ A 10 x x
	♡ x x	♡ A 10 x
	◇ A K x x	◇ Q x x
	♣ A Q 10 x x x	♣ J x x
	1 ♣	1 ♠
	2 ♣	2 NT
	3 ◇	4 ♣
	Pass	

OPENER		RESPONDER	
(g)	♠ K Q x x x		♠ A x x
	♡ A K x x		♡ Q J x
	◊ x x x		◊ K Q x x
	♣ x		♣ Q x x
	1 ♠		2 NT
	3 ♡		3 NT
	Pass		

OPENER		RESPONDER	
(h)	♠ K x		♠ A J x x x
	♡ A x		♡ K Q x x
	◊ A 10 x		◊ x
	♣ K x x x x		♣ Q x x
	1 ♣		1 ♠
	2 ♣		2 ♡
	2 NT		3 ♣
	3 NT		Pass

OPENER		RESPONDER	
(i)	♠ x		♠ J x x
	♡ A Q x x x		♡ K x
	◊ K x x		◊ A J 10
	♣ K J x x		♣ A x x x x
	1 ♡		2 ♣
	3 ♣		3 NT
	Pass		

2. Following are two groups of five hands. At least one of the hands in each group justifies the bidding shown, while many of the other hands do not. Pick out the right hand for the bidding.

NORTH	SOUTH
1 ♡	2 ◊
2 ♡	3 ♣
3 NT	Pass

Following are five potential North hands:

(a) ♠ J x x   ♡ K Q 10 x x   ◊ A x   ♣ K x x

(b) ♠ A x x   ♡ K Q J 9 x x   ◊ x   ♣ K x x

(c) ♠ Q J x   ♡ K J x x x   ◊ K x x   ♣ K x

(d) ♠ A x   ♡ A K x x x x   ◊ x x x   ♣ x x

(e) ♠ K Q x   ♡ K Q x x x   ◊ A x   ♣ Q x x

Following are five potential South hands:

(a) ♠ K J x   ♡ x   ◊ K J 10 x x   ♣ K 10 x x

(b) ♠ x x   ♡ x   ◊ A Q J x x   ♣ A J 10 x x

(c) ♠ x   ♡ J x x   ◊ A K x x x   ♣ A J x x

(d) ♠ x   ♡ x x   ◊ A J x x x   ♣ K J x x x

(e) ♠ x   ♡ —   ◊ K Q J x x x   ♣ A J 10 9 x x

3.	OPENER	RESPONDER
	1 ◊	3 ♡

We have not discussed responder's bid. What would you guess that it means?

4. What difference would you expect the following sequences by opener to show?

OPENER	RESPONDER	OPENER	RESPONDER
1 ♣	1 ♡	1 ♣	1 ♡
4 ♡		3 ◊	3 NT
		4 ♡	

ANSWERS

1. (a) Opener is at fault. He should raise his partner's suit. It is important to show a fit. After the raise, responder would jump straight to four spades. The two-spade bid may seem slightly con-

servative with 11 basic points, but with a weak six-card suit and an apparent misfit, the responder's pessimism is justified. Change opener's hand to ♠ x x ♡ A K Q x x ◊ K x x ♣ x x x, and three spades would be a dangerous contract. Give opener a singleton or void in spades, and three spades would be hopeless.

(*b*) Opener is again at fault. He knows responder has only three hearts. Holding a four-card heart suit, a good club fit, and a spade stopper, opener has a clear-cut three-no-trump bid over three hearts. Opener might well have rebid two no trump on the previous round.

(*c*) Responder should have bid one no trump, and opener would have rebid two diamonds. If opener is supposed to raise with K x x and a ruffing value, responder must not bid "unbiddable suits." This is particularly true when responder has a mild fit for opener's suit. Over an opening heart-bid, responder should not respond one spade with a weak four-card spade suit and a tripleton heart. With a singleton or void in hearts, the spade response is permissible because badly fitting hands do not play well at no trump.

(*d*) Opener should pass three spades with this terrible misfit.

(*e*) Responder should have bid two hearts, rather than two spades, over two diamonds. When partner shows two suits you should not rebid your own suit unless you are willing to play it opposite a singleton.

(*f*) Responder is at fault. Once opener shows his distribution, responder can tell that the hands fit very well, and he should jump to five clubs. Responder's bidding would be correct with

♠ K Q x x x   ♡ K 10 x   ◊ Q J x   ♣ x x.

(*g*) The two-no-trump bid was forcing to game. Over three hearts responder should have bid three spades to show three-card support.

(*h*) Responder bid perfectly to show a good hand with a singleton diamond. Opener should have bid five clubs instead of three no trump.

(*i*) Over three clubs responder should have bid three diamonds to show where his side strength was, and to warn opener that the spade suit was unprotected. Had he done so, the final contract would have been four hearts or five clubs.

2. Only North hand (*c*) qualifies. Hand (*a*) contains no spade stopper. With hand (*b*), opener should jump to four hearts. The suit is self-sufficient, and there is only one spade stopper. With hand (*d*), opener should rebid three hearts or three diamonds. It is too dangerous to bid three no trump with one spade stopper and no fitting honors in either of partner's suits. Hand (*e*) is much too strong for a two-heart rebid. The hand should be opened one no trump, or at least the rebid should be two no trump.

Of the South hands, only hand (*b*) qualifies. Hand (*a*) is too weak virtually to force partner to game. Responder should rebid two no trump on the second round. Responder would raise to four hearts with hand (*c*). He should pass the two-heart rebid with hand (*d*). With hand (*e*) he would bid two diamonds and three clubs but would not pass three no trump. He would insist on playing the hand in a minor suit.

3. It means that responder has a long, fairly good heart suit but not much else. He should have six tricks in his own hand, playing at hearts. A typical hand would be

♠ x x   ♡ K Q J x x x x   ◇ x x   ♣ J x.

There are two purposes in the jump. It tells partner the hand must almost surely play in hearts, and he doesn't need to worry about lack of heart-support. He can raise to game with four top tricks

(♠ A K x x   ♡ x   ◇ A x x   ♣ A x x x x).

Also, if opener is weak, this bid will make it more difficult for the opponents to enter the auction.

4. The first sequence often shows 2-4-2-5 distribution. The latter sequence shows a singleton-spade and good controls, as well as four hearts and at least 20 support points. The latter sequence more strongly suggests a slam.

CHAPTER 14

Scoring and Pre-emptive Bids

"I THOUGHT the problems you gave us last week were, by far, the most difficult we have had," said Jerry.

"I disagree," said Alice. "There were many rules to apply. We had to remember and use everything we had learned about bidding, but if we applied all the rules, we could tell what to do."

"One hand still puzzles me," said Henry. "In problem 1(i) responder was supposed to rebid three diamonds to show where his strength was. It would have worked out fine this time, but how would opener know that the diamond-bid did not show a suit?"

"He would not know," I replied. "Opener could not tell whether responder had the actual hand—

♠ J x x ♡ K x ◇ A K 10 ♣ A x x x x—

or

♠ J x ♡ K x ◇ A J 10 x ♣ A x x x x.

In either case, he would know that the hand did not belong in no trump. Furthermore, the recommended three-diamond bid could scarcely lead to any difficulty. Opener is not likely to hold four diamonds, since he failed to bid two diamonds. When opener does raise diamonds, it will mean that he is short in spades and has no stopper. Consequently, no trump would have been a horrible contact."

"In this sequence you said that responder should bid where his strength is, even when he does not have a suit," said Barbara. "Is the converse also true? Suppose that responder has

♠ A Q   ♡ x x   ◊ Q 9 x x   ♣ A J x x x.

After a heart-opening and a club-raise, should responder bid
three diamonds or three no trumps?"

"What do you think?"

"Three no trump. That looks like the most likely game contract, and if responder were to rebid three diamonds, opener
might be stymied if he were weak in spades. He might then bid
four clubs, when three no trump is the right contract."

"Your reasoning is sound, and your conclusion is correct.

"In the first lesson on bidding you were told just enough
about scoring to appreciate the necessity of accurate game bidding. Now I shall explain the details. As you remember, the score
sheet looks like this:

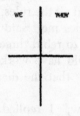

The points for your bid go below the line, and the points for your
overtricks go above the line. Thus, if you bid two no trump and
make three, 70 points go below the line and 30 above the line.
Whenever you get 100 or more below the line, you score a game
—although you do not get any points immediately—and a line is
drawn under your score. This line indicates that you have made
a game and are 'vulnerable.' The term 'vulnerable' means that
you are in danger or subject to being hurt. If you overbid when
vulnerable, the penalties are greater. Nevertheless, it is an advantage to be vulnerable, since there is a sizable bonus for scoring
two games before the opponents do—called 'winning the rubber'—
and you can't score two games without scoring the first one, which
makes you vulnerable. The game bonus is 700 if the other side
is not vulnerable, 500 if both sides are vulnerable. The line is
drawn below both your score and the opponent's score when the

total of 100 points below the line is reached. If the opponents have points below the line, they will have to start all over in their effort to score. Whenever you bid something and fail to make it, the opponents receive 50 points for each trick you are short of your contract if not vulnerable, and 100 points per trick when vulnerable. These scores go above the line and do not count toward game. If the opponents think you are too high, they can increase these penalties by 'doubling.' The penalties for defeating a doubled contract are 100 for the first undertrick and 200 for each subsequent undertrick when not vulnerable; 200 for the first undertrick and 300 for each subsequent undertrick when vulnerable.

"Of course, if there were no risk attached to doubling, the opponents would double every time. The risk in doubling is that when the contract is made, the successful side gets double the trick score below the line, plus 100 points per overtrick, not vulnerable, and 200 points per overtrick, vulnerable. Also, there is a 50-point bonus for making a doubled contract. Consequently, there is some risk in doubling any contract. It is particularly risky to double an undergame contract. Suppose that you bid three diamonds, and you have no points below the line. Even if you make your contract, you will not make game; the most you can get below the line is 60 points. But if the opponents double you, and you make your contract, you will get 120 points below the line, which will give you game. Since a game is worth about 300 points, the double, counting the extra 60 points below the line and the 50 points above the line for making a doubled contract, will have cost the opponents 410 points. If they had set you a trick, the double would have gained them only 50 or 100 points. Consequently, it is very risky to double a part-score contract which will give the opponents a game if they make it, unless you expect to defeat them by at least two tricks. It is not so dangerous to double two diamonds, for example, since even if the opponents make it, they will only get 80 points below the line—not enough for game.

"When the person who is doubled thinks he can make his contract, he—or his partner—may redouble. This doubles the doubled penalty if he is set, and it doubles the trick score—including overtricks, if any—if the contract is made.

"Above the line, a player gets a bonus for possession of certain honor combinations. At a suit-contract this bonus is 100 points for four honors in one hand, such as A Q J 10. For all five honors—A K Q J 10—the bonus is 150 points. At no trump the bonus is 150 for all four aces in one hand. Normally, it is declarer or his partner who scores honors, but in the unusual case that one of the *defenders* has honors, the defenders are entitled to the bonus.

"The best way to make you remember all of this is to play an imaginary rubber and write up the score after each hand. The following rubber is not typical; there is more than the usual amount of 'action,' but it is for the purpose of illustrating the different ways of scoring.

"The first hand we bid two spades and make three. When the result is scored, the score sheet should look like this:

WE	THEY
30	
60	

The second hand the opponents bid three diamonds and make four. One of the opponents had A K Q 10 of diamonds. The score sheet now looks like this:

WE	THEY
	100
30	20
60	60

The 100 points is for honors.

"The third hand, the opponents bid one no trump and make three. This makes a game for them—there would have been no advantage to their bidding three no trump, since they only needed

40 points below the line—and we draw a line below the score to indicate that *someone* is vulnerable and that both sides will have to start all over again to score 100 points for game. We said that the line indicates that someone is vulnerable. If we should forget which side it is, we merely have to look to discover which side has 100 points or more below the line before the new line is drawn.

"The score sheet will now look like this:

```
        WE   |   THEY
             |
             |
             |
             |
             |    60
             |   100
        30   |    20
        60   |    60
             |    40
             |
```

"On the fourth hand we bid six spades, but we do not make it. We are set one trick. If we had made our contract, we would have scored 180 points below the line and 500 above. The slam bonus is 500 points for a small slam when not vulnerable, 750 when vulnerable. The grand slam bonus—for successfully bidding seven—is 1000 points when not vulnerable, 1500 points when vulnerable. You can see one of the *advantages* of being vulnerable! Anyway, we did not make our bid, and the opponents get 50 points. The score sheet now looks like this:

```
        WE   |   THEY
             |
             |
             |
             |
             |    50
             |    60
             |   100
        30   |    20
        60   |    60
             |    40
             |
```

"The fifth hand, the opponents bid three clubs. Partner doesn't think they can make it, so he doubles. The opponents take only seven tricks, and are down two. If we had not doubled, we would have received 200 points. Our doubled gained us 300 points, and we score 500 points above the line. The score now looks like this:

WE	THEY
	50
	60
500	100
30	20
-----	------
60	60
	40

"The sixth hand, the opponents bid six diamonds, which they could have made, but we bid six spades and are defeated four tricks, doubled. While we do not like to lose any points, the hand is a 'victory' for our side because we only lost 700 points. How many points would we have lost, Henry, if the opponents had been allowed to play their slam?"

"Seven hundred for game, 750 for slam and 120 for trick score, or a total of 1570 points."

"Correct. The score sheet now looks like this:

WE	THEY
	700
	50
500	100
30	20
-----	------
60	60
	40

"On the seventh hand, the opponents make a costly mistake. We bid three diamonds and they double. We make our contract with an overtrick. We score 120 below the line, 100 above the line for the overtrick, and 50 as a bonus for making the contract. We draw another line under our score to indicate that a game has been made. The score now looks like this:

WE	THEY
50	700
100	50
500	100
30	20
60	60
	40
120	

"The eighth hand, the opponents bid three spades and we double. The opponents do not think we can set them, so they redouble. We defeat them by one trick and partner has K Q J 10 of spades. Without the redouble, we would have scored 200 points for defeating the contract one trick, doubled. The redouble increases the penalty to 400 points, and we also get 100 points for honors! The score sheet now looks like this:

WE	THEY
100	
400	
500	700
50	50
100	100
30	20
60	60
	40
120	

"The ninth hand is rather tame after all this excitement. The opponents bid four hearts and make five. They now receive their rubber bonus of 500 points. The score now looks like this:

WE	THEY
100	500
400	30
500	700
50	50
100	100
30	20
60	60
	40
120	
	120

"The rubber is now over. We add up the points and get 1360 for us and 1620 for the opponents. We now carry the difference to the new score sheet and start a second rubber. The new score will look like this:

"When we talked about carrying the difference to the new score sheet, we were talking about a 'set' game where the partnerships remain intact throughout the session. If this were a pivot game, we would change partners either by following a prescribed rotation or cutting for partners. On the master score sheet the difference would be entered as follows:

A (PARTNER)	B (OPPONENT)	C (OPPONENT)	YOU
− 3	+ 3	+ 3	− 3

The 3 stands for 300. When the scores are transferred to the master score sheet, they are rounded off to the closest 100 points. Next rubber if you play with B—who was an opponent this

rubber—and win by 710 points, the master score sheet will look
like this:

A	B	C	YOU
— 3	+ 3	+3	— 3
— 10	+ 10	— 4	+ 4

At the end of the evening, if all goes well, the master score sheet
will look like this:

A	B	C	YOU
— 3	+ 3	+3	— 3
— 10	+ 10	— 4	+ 4
— 18	+ 2	+4	+ 12
— 6	— 10	— 8	+ 24
— 4	— 12	— 6	+ 22
— 13	— 21	+3	+ 31

Each round the pluses and minuses must be equal.

"Henry, can you tell us what the objective is in bridge?"

"It is to score as many points as possible."

"That is part of the objective. What should you attempt to do
when the opponents hold the superior cards?"

"Hold our losses to a minimum. Our objective is to score as
many points as possible for ourselves, and to lose as few as possible to the opponents."

"A good example to illustrate the last part of the objective is
the hypothetical hand where the opponents could have made
six diamonds for a score of 1570. By sacrificing at six spades you
saved 870 points. Similarly, when the opponents bid game, it is
better to lose 300 points than to let them score a game. Their
game is worth at least 300 points, in addition to their trick score
of 100 points or so. In fact, if you have to quit in the middle of
a rubber, the opponents are entitled to score 300 points for their
one game even though they don't normally get these points till
they score two games, and their points below the line will be at
least another 100. It is no great tragedy to take a 500-point set
when the opponents can make game, but you never want to take

a larger set against a game contract. Also, you feel a bit foolish when you take a deliberate sacrifice and find that the opponents could not have made their bid. With these factors in mind, you can understand the theory of pre-emptive bidding.

"Barbara, suppose on the first hand of a rubber that you are dealt ♠ x ♡ K Q J 10 x x x ◊ Q x x ♣ x x. If partner has a Yarborough,* how many tricks would you take at a heart-contract?"

"Six."

"How many tricks do you suppose the opponents could take in their best suit?"

"Quite likely all thirteen tricks, perhaps just twelve."

"What would they score for bidding and making a slam; for example, six spades?"

"They would score 980 points counting the 300 points their game is worth."

"What would they score by doubling you in seven hearts?"

"They would get 1300 points, and we would score 100 for honors."

"Consequently, it would be no bargain to play this hand in seven hearts, would it?"

"Not unless the opponents could make a grand slam, and even then we would save very few points."

"But you would be delighted to play three hearts, whether doubled or not, wouldn't you?"

"Of course."

"Let's change the conditions slightly. Instead of a Yarborough, give partner ♠ A x x ♡ A x x ◊ x x x ♣ x x x x. How many tricks can you take at hearts?"

"Eight."

"How many tricks can the opponents take in spades?"

"Probably eleven, perhaps twelve, if one of the opponents has

---

* Technically, a hand with no card above a nine-spot. The term is loosely used to indicate a worthless hand. Thus ♠ J x x ♡ x x ◊ x x x x ♣ 10 x x x would qualify, since neither the jack nor the ten would be of any value to you.

a void in hearts. We can take at most one heart-trick, one spade-trick and one diamond-trick."

"With these hands, you would like to play four hearts whether doubled or not, wouldn't you?"

"Yes. Our net loss after honors would be 200 points, while the opponents can make anywhere from 420 to 980 points, depending upon how well their hands fit."

"Suppose that you open the bidding with three hearts, holding the example hand. How is it possible for such a bid to lose?"

"It is hardly possible. If partner has a good hand, he can raise, and we will make game. If he has a terrible hand, the opponents can make a slam. When partner has a mediocre hand, the opponents can make game, and we will not lose as many points as they would earn by playing the hand themselves."

"Remember how much information you gained after an opening bid, a response, a rebid by opener, and a rebid by responder? Once the opponents open with a three- or four-bid, you have to guess what to do, and your bidding accuracy suffers greatly. Suppose your right-hand opponent bids three hearts. If you bid three spades with ♠ A Q x x x ♡ x x ◇ K Q x x ♣ A x, the person sitting behind you may hold

♠ K J 10 9 x   ♡ x   ◇ A x x   ♣ K J x x

and you will be slaughtered at three spades, doubled. The next time you decide to play safe and pass, partner has to pass also with

♠ K x x x   ♡ x x x   ◇ J 10 x   ♣ K Q x,

and you miss a game."

"It seems to me that three spades is the right bid over three hearts," said Henry. "The chances of making game are greater than the chances of taking a big set."

"You are probably right, Henry. Weaken the hand by taking away the queen of spades, and it is definitely too dangerous to bid. Yet, a game could easily be missed. The point is that the opening three-heart bid forces the opponents to guess what to do, and they are bound to guess wrong some of the time. Let's write an example on the blackboard.

<pre>
                        NORTH
                        ♠ J 10 x
                        ♡ A x
        WEST   ◇ J 10 x x   EAST
     ♠ A K x x x   ♣ A x x x   ♠ Q x x x
     ♡ x x   ♡ x x
     ◇ K x x   SOUTH   ◇ A x x
     ♣ Q J x   ♠ x   ♣ K 10 x x
                        ♡ K Q J 10 x x x
                        ◇ Q x x
                        ♣ x x
</pre>

"How would you expect the bidding to go?"

"Quite likely three hearts, pass, pass, pass. This time West would do well to bid three spades, which his partner would raise to game. But a three-spade bid could result in a disaster."

"What should opener bid with

♠ x   ♡ K Q J 10 x x x   ◇ Q J x x   ♣ x?"

"Four hearts."

"Why?"

"For one thing, partner might pass three hearts when the hands belong in game. He would not even consider a raise with ♠ x x x ♡ x x ◇ K 10 x ♣ A x x x x. For another reason, the higher you bid, the more difficulty the opponents have in getting to the right spot if it is their hand."

"You picked an excellent example, Henry. You and partner can easily make a game in hearts; yet, you have no defense against four spades. It is true that with weak defensive hands you should bid as high as you can with reasonable safety. These bids are called 'pre-emptive bids.' Alice, what are the requirements for a pre-empt?"

"Culbertson gave us the rule of two and three. We could

overbid our hand two tricks when vulnerable and three tricks when not vulnerable."

"That is one rule which is just as good today as it was thirty years ago. The idea is to risk not more than 500 points, which is only slightly greater than the value of the opponents' game. If partner has nothing of value for you, and the opponents double, you will come out about even, provided they can only make a game. When they can make a slam, but fail to reach it, you will gain quite a bit. You also gain when the strength is evenly divided between the opponents' hands and they fail to double or reach their game. Occasionally, when they bid over the pre-empt, they arrive at the wrong contract, and that is when the pre-empt really pays off. Instead of making five diamonds or four spades, the opponents play five clubs and are set."

"You make the pre-empt sound awfully good," said Jerry. "Can't it also work out badly?"

"Of course. Sometimes partner has enough cards to defeat the opponents' game, but they are of little value to you. Thus, when you bid four hearts with

♠ x ♡ K Q J 10 x x x ◇ Q J x x ♣ x,

partner may have

♠ K Q 10 x ♡ x ◇ x x x ♣ K Q x x x.

If partner produced this hand when I opened four hearts, I would consider myself very unlucky. However, if I were to pre-empt with a weak suit—something like K J 8 x x x x—and find partner with a singleton or void, I would figure I got what I deserved. It is dangerous to pre-empt with weak suits. Change the suit to K J 10 9 x x x, and a pre-empt is within reason."

"The requirements for a pre-empt are a good suit and the rule of two and three. What else?" asked Alice.

"You should not have a good defensive hand. Any opening three-bid denies the strength to open with a one-bid. An opening four-bid in a major is permissible with a minimum opening in high cards, provided most of the strength is in the long suit.

♠ A K J x x x x x ♡ x ◇ Q J x ♣ x will not be worth much defensively if an opponent has a void in spades. If you pre-empt with defensive strength, you are likely to find your penalty is a total loss, since the opponents cannot make anything. Also, you should not have good support for a major. The pre-empt makes it difficult for the opponents to find the right contract, but it makes it difficult for partner also. If you were to bid three clubs with ♠ Q 10 x x ♡ K x ◇ — ♣ K J 10 8 x x x, partner would not find the spade fit with ♠ K 9 x x x ♡ A J x ◇ A J x x ♣ x. In fact, you would have a much better chance to get to the right contract—four spades—if you were to pass originally."

"The only examples of pre-empts which you have given us were opening bids," said Barbara. "It looks to me as though the same considerations would apply to other situations."

"They do. When an opponent opens ahead of you, you should bid three or four of a major on the same type of hands with which you would open a pre-empt. Also, you may remember several lessons ago that I recommended raising partner's heart-opening bid to four with ♠ x x ♡ Q 10 x x x ◇ K J 10 x x ♣ x. This was pre-empt and made for the same purpose. When partner is weak, the opponents can probably outbid you, if you bid slowly and scientifically. If partner is strong—or if he fits your hand well—he should make the contract.

"There is one more rule about pre-empts. Once you make a pre-emptive bid, you should not bid again. Suppose you open three diamonds, the next opponent bids three spades, partner bids four diamonds, and right-hand opponent bids four spades—you should not bid five diamonds. Why not, Barbara?"

"Because partner knows what you have but you do not know what he has. Consequently, he should make the decision. Perhaps he was tempted to double three spades, but thought it slightly too risky."

"One more question, Barbara. Partner bids three hearts, with neither side vulnerable. The next player passes and you hold ♠ x x ♡ K x x x ◇ x x x ♣ J x x x. What would you bid?"

"Four hearts."

"Wasn't partner counting on you for three tricks when he bid three?"

"Yes. I don't expect to make four hearts, but I know the opponents can make at least a game, and probably a slam. My raise may make it look to the next player as though I hold some of the strength which is actually in his partner's hand."

QUIZ

1. Now that you know more about scoring, would you prefer to be in six spades or six no trump with the following hands:

♠ A Q x   ♡ A x   ◇ A Q x x   ♣ A x x x

♠ K J 10 x x   ♡ K J x   ◇ K x x   ♣ x x.

2. When you believe that you can make your doubled contract, but are not too sure, when do the percentages favor a redouble? (*a*) When vulnerable or not vulnerable; (*b*) In a two-diamond or three-diamond contract; (*c*) In a three-spade or six-spade contract?

3. When you are positive that you can make a doubled contract, should you always redouble?

4. Partner opens three hearts, not vulnerable, against vulnerable opponents. What should you bid with:

(*a*) ♠ A x x   ♡ x x   ◇ A K x x x   ♣ K x x

(*b*) ♠ K J x   ♡ J x   ◇ K J 10 x x   ♣ K Q x

(*c*) ♠ Q 10 x x   ♡ x x   ◇ A Q x x   ♣ J 10 x

(*d*) ♠ A x   ♡ x   ◇ A K Q J x x x   ♣ x x x

(*e*) ♠ x x x   ♡ A x x x   ◇ Q x x   ♣ x x x

5. Both sides are vulnerable, and you are the dealer. What would you bid with the following hands?

(*a*) ♠ A Q J x x x x   ♡ x   ◇ K Q x   ♣ Q x

(b) ♠ J 10 9 x x x x ♡ A J x ◇ A x ♣ x

(c) ♠ J 10 9 x x x x ♡ A J x ◇ K x ♣ x

(d) ♠ K 10 9 8 x x x x ♡ x ◇ Q J x ♣ J

(e) ♠ x x ♡ K J 10 9 x x x ◇ K Q 10 9 ♣ —

(f) ♠ x ♡ x x ◇ A K Q 10 x x x ♣ x x x

(g) ♠ A Q J x x x ♡ Q 10 9 x x ◇ x ♣ x

(h) ♠ K 10 x x ♡ x ◇ x ♣ K Q J x x x x

ANSWERS

1. Six spades. The honors are worth only 150 points, which is insignificant compared to the bonus for making a slam. A slam is almost a sure thing at spades and requires more luck at no trump.

2. (a) When not vulnerable; the redouble increases the trick-score by the same amount when you make your contract, regardless of vulnerability; but a redouble is more costly vulnerable when you are set.

(b) Two-diamond contract; the redouble would allow you to make game.

(c) Six spades. For going down, the redouble will be equally costly, but if you make your contract the redouble will gain 360 points at six spades, only 180 points at three spades.

3. No. Sometimes the opponents will change their minds and decide to bid again themselves. You may get 300 points instead of 790.

4. (a) Four hearts. Partner was counting on you for three tricks, but you have a good three and a half tricks, and one of your cards may promote one of partner's doubtful cards to a sure winner.

(b) Pass. You are missing too many tricks off the top. When partner pre-empts, he wants aces and kings, not queens and jacks. In both examples give partner

♠ x ♡ K Q 10 9 x x x ◇ Q x x ♣ x x

and see where you belong.

(*c*) Pass. You should probably be down one, and you have enough smattering of defensive strength, so that the opponents should not be able to bid or make game.

(*d*) Three no trump. The best chance for game. Partner might have the ace of hearts.

(*e*) Four hearts. The opponents can make game or slam. It is more difficult for them to bid over four hearts than over three. Some experts might even bid five, six, or seven hearts!

5. (*a*) One spade, a perfectly sound opening-bid.

(*b*) One spade—a minimum one-bid but a pre-empt would be very misleading with so much defensive strength on the side, so little in the long suit.

(*c*) Pass. Too weak a suit, too much on the side for a pre-empt.

(*d*) Three spades.

(*e*) Four hearts.

(*f*) One diamond. Yes, I know you only have 9 points and no side strength. But if you also open three diamonds with

♠ x x ♡ x ◇ K J 10 9 x x x ♣ K J 10,

how will partner know whether or not to bid three no trump with

♠ A x x ♡ A J x x ◇ x x ♣ Q x x x?

(*g*) One spade, least of the evils. With both majors, the best way to show your hand is to start bidding them. It would be very bad to pre-empt, since you would not be able to show both suits.

(*h*) Pass. If you pre-empt in clubs, you are likely to miss a spade-fit.

CHAPTER 15

Overcalls

"JERRY, when the opponents open the bidding ahead of you, would you expect the requirements for your bid to be the same as for an opening bid?"

"I can't see why they should be any different."

"Would your prospects of making game be as good when an opponent had opened the bidding as when he had passed?"

"No. There would be fewer high cards outstanding, and consequently, partner would not be as likely to have a good hand for me."

"That is correct. To simplify matters, let's talk about point count for a moment. Right-hand opponent opens the bidding. Let's say he holds, on an average, 14 high-card points. You hold 14 high-card points also. The most partner can have is 12, and it is quite unlikely that either he or opener's partner has all 12 outstanding points. When you are the opening bidder, partner may have 26 points to go with your 14. When an opponent has opened, it is very unlikely that partner has over 12. Obviously, your chances of game are greatly decreased by an opponent's opening bid."

"I see that quite clearly," said Jerry. "But how should that affect my bidding?"

"Let me digress a moment. Suppose your right-hand opponent opens three hearts and you hold

♠ A Q x x x   ♡ x x   ◇ K Q x x   ♣ A x.

This was a hand we mentioned last week. Henry said he thought you should bid three spades because there was a good chance for game, which would be missed if you were to pass. He was willing to risk a big set because his chances of making good score compensated for this risk. But suppose you knew that your partner had a poor hand or for some reason was not allowed to bid. If there were no chance of making game, it would be foolish to stick your neck out with a three-spade bid, wouldn't it? The point is that any bid you make is a form of gamble, and your expectancy of gain should outweigh your expectancy of loss; otherwise, you must surely lose in the long run."

"Does what you said mean that we need better than a minimum opening bid to compete when an opponent has opened?"

"Not necessarily. However, you need better than a minimum when your hand is balanced. Suppose that your right-hand opponent bids one heart and you hold

♠ K J x   ♡ Q x x   ◇ A J x   ♣ Q J x x.

Your chances of game are very poor, and there is considerable risk in any bid other than a pass. Unlikely as it is, suppose partner has 12 points. In that case, responder will pass, and partner is allowed to bid with 12 points and a balanced hand or somewhat less with an unbalanced hand. We won't discuss his problems just now, but the point is that you won't miss a game by passing if partner has the balance of strength, and you would risk a substantial penalty if you were to bid and find your left-hand opponent with the balance of strength."

"I just noticed another factor myself," said Jerry. "If I were to open, I would bid one club. I can no longer bid one club, and two clubs doesn't seem logical. I would never plan to bid two clubs, even on a subsequent round, if I were the opening bidder. Two clubs would be a horrible contract whenever partner was short in clubs, regardless of his strength.

"Surely this hand would bid one no trump if it bid at all," Jerry continued. "However, it is too weak to open one no trump, and I can see that it would be still more dangerous to bid one no trump with sub-minimum values after an opponent had opened."

"You don't have to find all the outstanding cards in the opponents' hands to run into trouble," I said. "Suppose you bid one no trump and your left-hand opponent has 9 or 10 points. He doubles, because he knows that his side has the balance of strength. Partner turns up with 3 or 4 points, enough to have stopped the opponents from making game, but you are set 300 or 500 points. That is a very bad result."

"What you said frightens me," said Jerry. "It looks to me as though it is quite dangerous to *open* with a balanced 13 or 14 points."

"Remember, the odds are quite different when you open. You know you have a better than average hand, and there is no reason to believe that all the outstanding strength is in the opponents' hands. Besides, even when partner has only a point or two, it is much more difficult for the opponents to penalize you when you open the bidding than it is when you overcall. A bid by you over an opponent's bid is called an 'overcall.'"

I then laid out the following hand.

```
                        NORTH
                        ♠ J x x x
                        ♡ x x x
                        ◇ x x x
        WEST            ♣ x x x            EAST
   ♠ K x x                               ♠ 10 x x
   ♡ J x                                 ♡ A Q 10 x x
   ◇ K 10 x x            SOUTH           ◇ Q x
   ♣ K 9 x x          ♠ A Q x           ♣ A J x
                      ♡ K 9 x
                      ◇ A J x x
                      ♣ Q 10 x
```

"Suppose South is the dealer," I said. "He would bid one no trump, which would be followed by two passes. East knows that his partner has something, because if he had a Yarborough, North would bid game. But North could easily have 5 or 6 points. All that East knows for sure is that he has a weaker hand than South, so he would probably pass.

"Now suppose that East is the dealer. He bids one heart, and South bids one no trump. West can now afford to double, because he knows that the combined strength of his side is greater than the opponents'! Besides, he knows what to lead, his partner's suit."

"Shouldn't South have overcalled one no trump?" asked Henry.

"Yes, he made the right bid. However, even when he bids correctly, it is more dangerous to compete when the opponents have opened. That was the point of this example."

"So the rule is that you need about 3 points more for an overcall than for an opening bid?" asked Alice.

"No. That is only true with balanced hands. With unbalanced hands you may bid with less high-card strength than would be required for an opening bid. Suppose that an opponent opens one heart and you hold ♠ A Q J 9 x ♡ x x ◊ K 10 9 x ♣ x x. The risk of bidding one spade is not great. If partner has nothing at all, you still should take four or five tricks at a spade contract, and the opponents would surely have a game. Besides, there is still hope for game your way. If partner has

♠ K x x x ♡ x x x ◊ A Q x x x ♣ x,

for example, you would have only two heart-losers and a club-loser at a four-spade contract, despite the fact that your side has less than half the high-card strength! Furthermore, it is quite likely that the opponents can make four hearts, and if you do not bid one spade right away, they may steal the hand from you. It is actually 'safer' for you to bid one spade than it is to pass, since you can lose points just as easily by letting the opponents bid unopposed as by taking big 'dives' yourself.

"In order to overcall you need 'playing tricks'—the ability to win tricks whether partner's hand is good or bad. With A Q J 9 x as your trump suit, you can reasonably expect to take four tricks if partner has a singleton. With

♠ K Q J 10 x x ♡ A x ◊ x x x ♣ x x,

you should take six tricks at a spade-contract, whatever partner may have. However, even with overcalls, you should have some defensive strength. So far as being doubled is concerned, you could safely overcall a one-heart opening bid with

or

♠ Q J 10 9 x x   ♡ x   ◇ J 10 9 8   ♣ x x

♠ x x   ♡ x x   ◇ K Q J 10 x x x   ♣ x x,

but what would you accomplish? There is no game in the hand unless partner has a very good hand, and if he has a very good hand, he should be the one to enter the bidding. The trouble with bidding with hands like these is that partner won't be able to cooperate with you in the bidding. He won't know when to bid game or when to double the opponents if they keep bidding. With slightly more playing-tricks and a defenseless hand, you could make a pre-emptive overcall. This might foul up the opponents' bidding without misleading partner. Over the one-heart bid, you could bid three spades vulnerable or four spades not vulnerable with

or

♠ K Q J x x x x   ♡ x   ◇ x   ♣ Q 10 8 x

♠ Q J 10 x x x x x   ♡ —   ◇ Q J x   ♣ x x."

"Apparently we use Culbertson's rule of two and three for overcalls, just as we do for pre-emptive bids," said Alice.

"Yes, that is more or less true. However, with broken five- or six-card suits, it is rather difficult to estimate your playing tricks, and I tend to apply other tests. The requirements for an overcall at the one-level are (1) 8 to 15 high-card points, including at least one ace or king; (2) a good suit, and (3) a good playing hand—preferably with better than 5-3-3-2 distribution; (4) a hand that looks as though it should play in the suit overcalled unless partner has an unusual hand.

"Let us look at a few hands and discuss the desirability of making an overcall with them. In each case the opening bid is one diamond.

♠ x x x x x   ♡ A x   ◇ K J   ♣ J x x x

"Pass. The weakness of the spade suit makes an overcall un-

desirable. Even if partner has a fair hand you may be in trouble
if he is short in spades. Can you think of another disadvantage
in a spade overcall, Jerry?"

"If the opponents buy the contract, which is likely, partner
might lead a spade, thinking I had strength in the suit."

♠ J 10 8 x x   ♡ A x   ◇ x x   ♣ A Q x x

"Bid one spade. The spades are still not very good. However,
the risk of overcalling at the one-level is not great, and if partner
has a good spade fit, the overcall may be necessary for you to
reach game.

♠ J 10 8 x x   ♡ A x   ◇ x x x   ♣ A Q x

"Pass. You still have the same weak spade suit but a poorer
playing hand than the last one. Game is unlikely unless partner
has a better hand than yours, and if so, he should be the one to
take aggressive action.

♠ Q 10 9 x x   ♡ A x   ◇ x x x   ♣ A Q x

"Bid one spade. The 5-3-3-2 distribution is undesirable, but
the good suit combined with good honor-count makes the overcall worthwhile. Obviously, the previous hand was close to being
worth an overcall, and many players would have bid.

♠ 10 x x x x   ♡ A   ◇ A K 10 x x   ♣ Q x

"Barbara, what would you do with this hand? Would you
overcall or not? If so, which suit?"

"I believe I would bid one spade. The suit is not very
good, but if we have a game, it is probably in spades. Unless
I overcall, how would we reach game when partner has

♠ A J x x   ♡ x x x   ◇ Q x x   ♣ x x x
or
♠ K J x x x   ♡ x x x   ◇ x x   ♣ K x x?"

"Aren't you afraid of missing a game in diamonds? Why don't
you bid your stronger suit?"

"Our chance of taking eleven tricks in diamonds is not as good as our chance of taking ten tricks in spades. Even when we can make game in diamonds, how will be be able to tell? It is partner's spade-holding which is crucial. Let's say I bid two diamonds and partner raises. If he has

♠ x x x   ♡ K x x   ◇ Q J x x x   ♣ K x,

we can't make game in anything. If he holds

♠ x x   ♡ K x x   ◇ J x x x x   ♣ A x x,

we can make five diamonds, but getting to game in diamonds would just be a matter of guesswork."

"I am curious to find out how far you will carry this preference for a major suit. Suppose the opening bid is one diamond, and you hold ♠ x x ♡ K J 10 x ◇ x ♣ A Q 10 x x x. What would you bid?"

"I don't know. A heart overcall seems awfully dangerous, but four hearts is probably our best chance for game. All partner needs is five hearts to the ace to give me some sort of play for four hearts. Well, I won't be wishy-washy. I would bid two clubs and hope to bid hearts later. What should I do?"

"I cannot truthfully answer your question because I don't know myself. I have been experimenting with a heart overcall on hands like this. A heart overcall is not dangerous. If you are doubled, which doesn't happen very often, you can run to two clubs. There is little doubt that a heart overcall gives you the best chance to reach game. On the other hand, it makes the bidding easier for the opponents. A two-club bid is, in effect, a mild pre-empt. It prevents the next player from bidding one spade.

"Be reluctant to overcall with a mediocre suit and support for an unbid major. After an overcall, it is difficult to find a fit in another suit. After an opening diamond bid, you can afford to bid one spade with ♠ K Q J 9 x ♡ K J x ◇ K x x ♣ x x. Partner may have a heart suit, but your spades are good enough so that the hand will probably play as well in spades. With

♠ Q 10 x x x   ♡ Q 10 x   ◇ A K   ♣ J x x,

I prefer a pass to a one-spade overcall. Partner needs a fairly good hand for you to make game, and ironically, you have a better chance to reach game in hearts if you pass than if you bid one spade. Holding

♠ K 10 x x x   ♡ Q x x x   ◇ A K   ♣ x x,

you should double. This is a bid we shall discuss next week. The point being emphasized is that an overcall normally shows a hand which should play in overcaller's suit or in one of his suits rather than in a suit which his partner might have.

"The partner of the overcaller should not bid a suit of his own unless he has a very good suit—A Q J 9 x or Q J 10 x x x for example—and an interest in game if the overcaller can raise this new suit. The bid of a new suit is not forcing. With 10 to 12 points and a stopper in the opponents' suit, the partner of the one-level overcaller can bid one no trump; with 13 or 14 points he should bid two no trump (not forcing). Jerry, what is the reason for the higher range than in the case of responses to an opening bid, and why is two no trump not forcing?"

"It must be because of the lower range for an overcall. You said that an overcall at the one-level can be made with as few as 8 high-card points and seldom more than 15. The minimum overcall is at least 2 or 3 points lighter than a minimum opening bid."

"That is correct. Consequently, all responses to overcalls have a slightly higher range. In raising an overcall, count your support points, and raise to the two-level with 8 to 11 points, to the three-level with 12 or 13, and to game with 14 or more. The raise with as few as 8 support-points is designed primarily as a mild pre-empt to make the bidding more difficult for the opponents. However, if the overcaller has an unusual hand—such as

♠ Q x x x x x   ♡ —   ◇ x x   ♣ A K J x x—

after a single raise he can gamble on game, since he needs very little—provided partner's strength is in the right spot. A raise of an overcall may be made with poorer trump support than a raise of an opening bid. If the bidding were

NORTH	EAST	SOUTH	WEST
1 ◇	1 ♠	Pass	?

West should bid two spades with

♠ Q x ♡ A x x ◇ x x x ♣ A J x x x.

He cannot bid no trump without a diamond stopper, and a two-club bid is not desirable with so weak a suit; the overcaller would pass two clubs with

♠ K J 9 x x x ♡ K Q ◇ Q x x ♣ x x.

"Over a two-level overcall, a two-no-trump bid may be made with 10 to 12 points including a stopper in the opponents' suit. With more, a jump to three no trump is in order. A single raise should be made with 9 to 11 support points.

"An overcall at the two-level shows a better hand in both defensive strength and playing-tricks than a one-level overcall. The range in high cards is approximately 11 to 16 points, and you should be within three playing-tricks of your bid, not vulnerable, and within two tricks of your bid, vulnerable. Your suit must be a very strong five-card suit or a fair six-card suit—or longer. Overcalls at the two-level are doubled much more frequently than overcalls at the one-level, so you must be careful about making them. It is very foolish to overcall a one-spade bid with two diamonds holding ♠ x x ♡ A J x ◇ A Q 8 x x ♣ Q x x. Aside from the fact that you have support for partner's possible heart suit, your diamond suit is too weak. You risk being doubled and set badly, and you have little chance to gain anything worthwhile. If partner has 12 or 13 points, which is about what you will need to make game, responder will pass and partner can reopen the bidding. An overcall, especially at the two-level, is not worth the risk unless it will improve your chances of reaching a game contract.

"A single jump-overcall in a major shows a good six-card suit and 12 to 15 high-card points. With only 12 points they should be concentrated and contain mostly aces and kings. With 14 or 15 points the distribution should not be too good, since partner will not raise with less than 8 points. A jump in a minor is an invitation to three no trump. In the following examples, the opening bid is one diamond.

♠ x x   ♡ A K J 9 x x   ◊ x x   ♣ A 10 x

Bid two hearts. This is a typical minimum jump-overcall.

♠ x x   ♡ A K J 9 x x   ◊ J x   ♣ K x x

You should bid just one heart, since the jack of diamonds is probably worthless.

♠ x   ♡ K Q J x x x   ◊ K x   ♣ K J 10 x

Bid two hearts again. In playing strength, this is a maximum; the queen of clubs plus an ace are all of the high cards partner will need for you to make game. However, it is unlikely that he will have these two specific cards and nothing else.

♠ x   ♡ K Q J x x x   ◊ K x   ♣ A J 10 x

If you had opened this hand with one heart and partner had raised to two, you would not consider bidding less than game. Consequently, this hand is too strong for either a one- or two-heart overcall. The proper bid is to double, as will be fully explained next week.

♠ x x   ♡ A x   ◊ x x x   ♣ A K Q 10 x x

Bid three clubs. Partner is invited to bid three no trump with a diamond stopper and a little smattering of side strength."

QUIZ

1. What would you bid over an opponent's opening one-club bid?

(*a*) **♠ Q 10 x   ♡ K x x x x   ◊ A   ♣ A J x x**

(*b*) **♠ Q 10 x   ♡ K Q J 10 x   ◊ x   ♣ A J x x**

(*c*) **♠ A Q J x x x   ♡ x x   ◊ x x   ♣ x x x**

(d) ♠ A Q J x x x   ♡ K x   ◇ x x   ♣ K x x

(e) ♠ A Q J x x x   ♡ K x   ◇ K x   ♣ K x x

(f) ♠ K Q J x   ♡ x x   ◇ A x x x x ♣ x x

(g) ♠ K J 10 x x x   ♡ K J 10 x x x ◇ —   ♣ x

2. What would you bid over an opponent's opening one-heart bid?

(a) ♠ A x   ♡ K x   ◇ A Q 8 x x   ♣ J x x x

(b) ♠ A x   ♡ K x   ◇ A Q 10 9 x   ♣ J 10 x x

(c) ♠ A 10   ♡ K x x   ◇ A Q 8 x x   ♣ K 10 x

(d) ♠ A Q 10 9 ♡ x x   ◇ K J x x x   ♣ x x

(e) ♠ A Q 10 9 ♡ x x   ◇ K J 10 9 x   ♣ K x

(f) ♠ K x   ♡ x   ◇ Q J 10 9 x x x x ♣ Q x

(g) ♠ A K   ♡ x   ◇ K Q 10 9 x x   ♣ K 10 x x

3. Partner has overcalled an opening diamond bid with one heart and right-hand opponent (responder) has passed. What would you bid with the following hands?

(a) ♠ x x   ♡ Q x x x   ◇ x x   ♣ K J x x x

(b) ♠ K x   ♡ Q x x x   ◇ x x   ♣ A J x x x

(c) ♠ x   ♡ Q 10 x x x ◇ x x   ♣ K J 10 x x

(d) ♠ K x x x x ♡ J x   ◇ K Q x   ♣ Q x x

(e) ♠ K x x x x ♡ J x   ◇ K Q 10   ♣ A Q x

(f) ♠ K J 10 x x x ♡ x x   ◇ J x x   ♣ x x

(g) ♠ K J 10 x x x ♡ Q x   ◇ x x x   ♣ A x

(h) ♠ K J 10 x x x ♡ Q x   ◇ K x x   ♣ A x

4. This is your hand: ♠ Q x x x ♡ K x ◇ J x ♣ A J x x x. What is your bid in the following sequences?

	N	E	S	W		N	E	S	W
(a)	1 ♣	1 ◇	P	?	(e)	1 ♡	2 ◇	P	?
(b)	1 ◇	1 ♠	P	?	(f)	1 ◇	1 NT	P	?
(c)	1 ◇	2 ♡	P	?	(g)	1 ◇	1 ♡	P	?
(d)	1 ♣	2 ◇	P	?	(h)	1 ◇	2 ♣	P	?

ANSWERS

1. (*a*) Pass.

(*b*) One heart.

(*c*) One spade. This is a weak hand, but your strength is concentrated in spades, which is an advantage, and the bid is slightly pre-emptive. It prevents responder from bidding one heart or one diamond.

(*d*) Two spades.

(*e*) Double. You are too strong to bid either one or two spades.

(*f*) One spade. Your most likely game is four spades. Also note that a one-spade overcall is more pre-emptive than a one-diamond overcall.

(*g*) One spade. With a freakish hand there is usually more bidding, and you can bid hearts next time.

2. (*a*) Pass. An overcall is too dangerous with so weak a suit.

(*b*) Two diamonds.

(*c*) One no trump. Your best chance for game is in no trump. Two-diamond overcall would be more risky and would have less to gain.

(*d*) One spade. For one thing, you are too weak to bid two diamonds.

(*e*) One spade. Your best chance for game is in spades.

(*f*) Four diamonds if not vulnerable; pass if vulnerable. A double jump is weak.

(*g*) Two diamonds. You have a good hand, but you don't want partner to bid no trump unless he has a heart stopper *and* a diamond fit (or two heart stoppers).

3. (a) Two hearts.
   (b) Three hearts.
   (c) Four hearts (pre-empt).
   (d) One no trump.
   (e) Three no trump.
   (f) Pass. No hope for game.
   (g) One spade.
   (h) Two spades—almost forcing.
4. (a) One no trump.
   (b) Three spades.
   (c) Four hearts.
   (d) Three no trump.
   (e) Two no trump.
   (f) Three no trump.
   (g) Two hearts.
   (h) Three clubs (hoping partner will rebid three no trump).

CHAPTER 16

Take-out Doubles

"Henry, suppose that your right-hand opponent opens one diamond, and you hold ♠ K x x x ♡ A x x x ◇ A ♣ K J x x. What do you think of your prospects for game?"

"They look pretty good to me. Partner doesn't need much strength if he has a long suit."

"Does this hand meet the requirements for an overcall?"

"No, none of the suits are strong enough. However, with such a good hand, my inclination would be to disregard the requirements and bid *something*."

"What would you bid?"

"I don't know. That is the problem. Whatever suit I bid may be the wrong one. I might overcall one heart and find partner with ♠ Q x x x x ♡ x ◇ x x x ♣ Q 10 x x, for example. Is this hand described by a take-out double? You mentioned 'take-out double' a couple of times previously without explaining what it is."

"Yes, this hand is a perfect take-out double. The primary purpose of this double is to make partner bid *his* suit. With this hand, that is just what you want to do."

"When is a double for take-out, and when does it mean you think you can set the opponents?" asked Alice.

"The following rule has a few exceptions, but it is generally reliable. A double is for take-out when

(1) it is a suit bid—rather than no trump—which has been doubled;

(2) the doubled bid is at the one- or two-level;

(3) the double is made at the doubler's first opportunity;

(4) the partner of the doubler has not bid (a pass is not considered a bid for the purpose of this rule).

"A double not meeting all four conditions is for penalties. Let's look at a few examples.

	NORTH	EAST	SOUTH	WEST
(a)	1 ♡	DBL		
(b)	1 ♡	P	2 ◇	DBL
(c)	1 ♡	P	2 ♡	DBL
(d)	P	1 ◇	P	P
	DBL			
(e)	P	1 ◇	P	1 ♡
	DBL			
(f)	1 ♡	2 ◇	P	P
	DBL			

"In each case the double was for take-out. Notice that it does not matter whether the *doubler* has previously bid.

	NORTH	EAST	SOUTH	WEST
(a)	1 ♡	2 ♣	DBL	
(b)	1 NT	2 ◇	DBL	
(c)	4 ♠	DBL		
(d)	1 NT	DBL		

"These doubles were all penalty doubles. In the first two examples, the reason was that partner had bid. In the third case, the reason was that the doubled bid was at the four-level. In the last example, the double was a penalty double because all doubles of no-trump contracts are for penalties."

"Alice can remember rules better than I can," said Jerry. "Unless I understand the reason for a rule, I usually forget. Can you tell us why take-out doubles have to meet all those conditions?"

"Why don't you try to tell us, Jerry?"

"I'll start with the second condition. It seems logical that doubles of high-level bids should be for penalties. You don't want to force partner to bid at the four-level, because you would seldom have a good enough hand to guarantee a play for such a contract opposite a possible Yarborough. Besides, the higher the opponents have bid, the less strength we need to defeat them."

"Very good. Continue."

"I can understand the fourth condition also. The purpose of the take-out double is to make partner bid his suit. Once he has already done so, your double must be for penalty. Even when he has bid no trump, you know his approximate strength and distribution and you can place the contract. There would be little purpose in forcing him to bid again. However, I can't see the reason for the other two conditions."

"Whenever you make a take-out double," I said, "it is because you believe, or at least hope, that your side is stronger than the opponents. Does that seem logical to you?"

"Yes. If I knew that I was out-gunned, I would just keep quiet. If the opponents are going to play the hand, I don't want to tell them where the outstanding strength is."

"Of course, you may be wrong. Partner may have an exceptionally weak hand, but at least you hope that your side has the balance of power when you make a low-level double. If you have the balance of power and the opening hand, how should the opponents fare in a doubled no-trump contract?"

"Not very well."

"Thus, when partner doubles an opening no-trump bid, you will pass and expect to collect a big score when holding

♠ Q x ♡ 10 9 x x ◇ K x x ♣ Q 10 x x.

Naturally, partner needs at least as good a hand as the opening no-trump bidder to double, and you have the balance of power. With

♠ Q x ♡ 10 9 x x ◇ J x x ♣ 10 9 x x,

you are not at all confident, but you would pass, because any bid would be quite dangerous, and partner may be able to set the contract by himself or with the little help which you can furnish. With

♠ x x　♡ J 10 9 x x x　◊ 10 9 x x　♣ x,

you would bid two hearts, not because partner has asked you
to bid, but because you have less strength than he expects.
Besides, your hand should be worth nothing at no trump and
several tricks at hearts. Now let's consider the first condition.

NORTH	EAST	SOUTH	WEST
1 ◊	P	1 ♠	P
2 ◊	DBL		

"Why isn't the double for take-out?"

"I don't know, except that you told us it wasn't."

"Barbara?"

"Because if East wanted his partner to bid, he would have
asked him to bid right away. It would be safer to force West to
bid over one diamond, when his response could be at the one-
level, than to force him to bid at the two- or three-level."

"Suppose the bidding had gone as follows.

NORTH	EAST	SOUTH	WEST
1 ♠	DBL	2 ♠	P
P	DBL		

"Would the second double be for penalties or take-out?"

"For take-out."

"Why?"

"When East doubled the first time, he wanted his partner to
bid. That means he probably was short in spades and had support
for the other three suits. Well, he still has the same hand. He
cannot have acquired any more spades during the bidding."

"Why would he double again? He has already requested his
partner to bid."

"The second double probably shows additional strength. Perhaps if partner bid, East was going to raise the response to the
three-level. Since partner did not bid, he can still afford to ask
partner to bid at the three-level. Or he may figure that partner
has a little strength, though he failed to bid voluntarily, because
opener did not even try for game."

"The ideal hand for a take-out double is 4-4-4-1 distribution with a singleton in the opponents' suit. Since partner is being forced to bid, it is nice to have support for any suit he might bid. Unfortunately, this ideal distribution does not occur frequently enough to wait for it—or to state the matter another way, there are times where the wisest action is to make a take-out double even without good support for all unbid suits. You should have four or more of an unbid major, and preferably no less than three of any unbid major. With an independent suit or a very strong hand, you don't need support for everything that partner may bid. If he bids a suit which you cannot support, you can then bid a suit of your own. Over an opening one-diamond bid, the following hands are suitable for a take-out double.

(a)	♠ J x x	(b)	♠ Q x x x x	(c)	♠ K J x x
	♡ K Q x x		♡ A Q x x		♡ Q 10 x x
	◇ x x		◇ A x		◇ x
	♣ A K x x		♣ K x		♣ A J 10 x

(d)	♠ A Q 10 x	(e)	♠ K x
	♡ A K J x		♡ A K Q x x x
	◇ x x		◇ x x x
	♣ K J x		♣ A J

"It is dangerous to double with the second example hand because partner may respond two clubs. However, a double is still the best bid, because partner will go out of his way to respond with a major suit rather than a minor, even when the major suit is shorter. Also, there is a greater danger in *not* doubling. If you were to overcall one spade, for example, partner might hold ♠ x ♡ J x x x x ◇ x x x ♣ A Q x x, and you would miss a game in hearts. When you overcall rather than double, you warn partner *not* to bid a suit unless it is very strong. In the last example hand, if partner responds one spade or two clubs, you will bid two hearts. To double and then bid a suit over partner's forced response shows a good suit and a good hand—just the message you want to give with this hand. You are too strong to overcall one or two hearts.

"Jerry, if the opening bid had been one heart rather than one diamond, would you have doubled just the same?"

"No, I would not double with any of those hands."

"Why not?"

"With length in the opponents' suit, I would pass. A double asks partner to bid, and I would rather have the opponents play the hand in my long suit than to have partner play the hand in my short suit."

"The partner of a take-out doubler must never pass unless he thinks he can set the contract. At the one-level it is necessary to have a very good trump holding—something like Q J 10 9 x. In fact, when a take-out double is passed, the doubler is supposed to lead a trump to prevent declarer from scoring his small trumps. No matter how weak he may be, the partner of the doubler must bid something rather than pass, permitting the opponents to make a doubled contract.

"With 9 basic points or less, the response to the take-out double should normally be your longest suit—other than the suit bid by the opponents. Tend to bid a major in preference to a minor, even when the minor suit is better or longer. The reason is that a take-out double most strongly implies major-suit support, and finding a major-suit fit is usually the easiest way to game. A one-no-trump response shows about 7 to 10 points with a stopper in the opponents' suit. A two-no-trump response is not forcing, and it shows 11 or 12 points, preferably with a double stopper. A jump in a suit shows 10 or 11 basic points, but is not forcing. The only forcing bid is a bid of the opponents' suit. If the bidding is

OPPONENT	PARTNER	OPPONENT	YOU
1 ◇	DBL	P	2 ◇

partner knows you don't want to play diamonds—if so, you would have passed—and is forced to bid.

"Alice, in each of the following examples your partner has doubled an opening diamond-bid and your right-hand opponent has passed. What would you bid?"

(*a*) ♠ K x x x   ♡ x x x   ◊ x x x   ♣ x x x

(*b*) ♠ K x x   ♡ x x x   ◊ J x x x   ♣ x x x

(*c*) ♠ K x x   ♡ x x   ◊ K J 8 5 3   ♣ J x x

(*d*) ♠ x x x x   ♡ x x   ◊ Q x x   ♣ Q J 10 x

(*e*) ♠ Q x x x   ♡ x x   ◊ x x   ♣ Q x x x x

(*f*) ♠ K Q x x x   ♡ x x   ◊ x x   ♣ A x x x

(*g*) ♠ Q J x x   ♡ x x   ◊ x x x   ♣ A K x x

(*h*) ♠ K Q x x   ♡ K Q x x   ◊ x x   ♣ K x x

(*i*) ♠ J x   ♡ Q 10 x   ◊ K Q 10   ♣ K 10 x x x

"With (*a*) I would bid one spade, my longest suit. With (*b*) my response would be one heart, the cheapest three-card suit. I can't pass or bid one no trump, because I am not strong enough. With (*c*) I would pass, because I like diamonds as well as anything else—"

"No," I interrupted, "with (*c*) you should bid one no trump. In order to convert your partner's take-out double by a 'penalty pass,' your holding in the opponent's suit should be something like K J 10 9 7, so that you could pull the opponents' trumps and not let them score anything but the ace and queen. I am sorry for the interruption, but I didn't want any of you to learn this wrong. Please continue."

"With (*d*) I suppose I should bid one spade. You hinted that we should prefer a major to a minor, even when the minor is stronger. With (*e*) should we still prefer the major?"

"Yes, for two reasons. Partner is more likely to have good major support than good minor support for his double. For example, he might hold ♠ K x x x ♡ A Q x x x ◊ A x ♣ J x. Another reason, the reason which applies to many other situations as well, is that you are more likely to be able to make game in a major than in a minor. Continue, Alice."

"With (*f*) and (*g*) I would bid two spades, since I have so much more than I might have. With (*h*) I would bid two diamonds. A two-heart or two-spade bid might be passed, and this hand is strong enough to make game opposite any hand partner is likely to have."

"How much strength does partner need for a take-out double?"

"I don't know. I assume at least an opening bid."

"That is generally correct. You need enough high-card strength for an opening bid, and either reasonable support for any suit partner may bid or enough extra strength to safely bid a suit of your own if partner bids a suit for which you have no support. What would you bid with the last example hand?"

"Three clubs."

"Do you agree, Henry?"

"No, I'd be more inclined to bid two no trump."

"What about your weakness in spades?"

"Partner can take care of the spades. He is usually strong in the majors when he doubles. What I need to bid no trump is strength in the opponents' suit."

"So far we have considered the simplest situation, when the partner of the opening bidder has not bid. The partner of the take-out doubler must bid unless he has the one hand in a hundred with which he can make a penalty pass. For the sake of convenience, let's call the opening bidder South, the doubler West, responder North, and the partner of the doubler East. When North bids, East is no longer obligated to bid. With a very bad hand he can and should pass. However, he does not need a very good hand for a 'free' bid. Suppose the bidding has been

SOUTH	WEST	NORTH	EAST
1 ◇	DBL	1 ♡	?

With ♠ Q x x ♡ J x x ◇ J x x x ♣ x x x, East is glad that he is no longer required to bid. With

♠ K J x x   ♡ x x x   ◇ x x x   ♣ x x x,

he should also pass. With

♠ K J x x x ♡ x x ◇ x x x ♣ x x x,

or

♠ Q 10 x x ♡K x x ◇ x x ♣ 10 9 x x,

he should bid one spade. A free bid at the two-level requires a slightly better hand. Bid two clubs with

♠ Q x ♡ x x x ◇ x x x ♣ K J x x x

bid one no trump with

♠ Q x ♡ x x x ◇ K J x ♣ J 10 x x x.

Only a stopper in opener's suit is required—presumably West has something in hearts for his double. If the bidding is

SOUTH	WEST	NORTH	EAST
1 ◇	DBL	3 ◇	?

about the worst hand East should bid with is

♠ K J x x x ♡ Q x ◇ x x x ♣ x x x

or

♠ Q 10 x x ♡ K x ◇ x x x ♣ Q 10 x x.

Partner must be conservative about raising; he knows you may have been stretching to avoid being shut out. With

♠ K J x x x ♡ K x ◇ x x x ♣ K 10 x,

you should bid four spades, since partner would pass a three-spade bid with

♠ Q x x x ♡ A J x x ◇ x ♣ A J x x.

"If North redoubles, a pass is not for penalties. It merely denies a long suit and allows the doubler to choose the spot. After

SOUTH	WEST	NORTH	EAST
1 ♣	DBL	RDBL	?

West should bid one spade with

With
    ♠ J 10 x x x ♡ x ◊ J x x x ♣ x x x.

he should pass. Holding
    ♠ x x x ♡ J x x x ◊ Q x x x ♣ x x,

he should pass. Holding
    ♠ Q x x x ♡ K x x x ◊ K x x ♣ x x,

he suspects that someone does not have his values. He should pass. But if partner bids one heart or one spade, he should raise to two on the next round.

"Not playing a pass for penalties after a redouble must be a change from the Culbertson system," said Alice. "I distinctly remember that Culbertson said a pass meant you would have passed without the redouble. Otherwise, the opponents could bluff you out."

"Your memory is correct. At one time Culbertson played the pass over a redouble for penalties. However, he later changed his own system in this regard. One reason is that in the early 1930's 'bluff' bidding was quite popular. Later it went out of style, and it wasn't worth devising a system to compete against it. Players seldom redouble with bad hands, because their partner, as well as the opponents, will be misled. Tell me another reason why the pass should not be for penalties, Barbara."

"I was just thinking how seldom you would get the appropriate hand for a penalty pass. You told us, about one time out of a hundred. When that happened, how often would the next hand have redoubled? This combination sounds like one hand out of a thousand!"

"Later you will discover that the person sitting behind the bidder passes for penalties fairly frequently. Thus in either

NORTH	EAST	SOUTH	WEST		WEST	NORTH	EAST	SOUTH
1 ◊	P	P	DBL	*or*	1 ◊	2 ♣	P	P
P	?				DBL	P	?	

East may pass for penalties with K J 8 x of trumps, for example. He doesn't need solid trumps. In situations such as these where the partner of the take-out doubler is *behind* the bidder, he says he wants to defend when he passes, *even after a redouble.* Let's forget about redoubles for a while and get back to the less unusual situations. After a take-out double and a forced response, East may have nothing at all, and West must be very conservative about raising. After doubling and getting a one-spade response, West should not raise with

♠ K 10 x ♡ A Q x x ◇ x x ♣ A K x x

or

♠ Q x x x ♡ A x x x ◇ x x ♣ A K x.

Even if South rebids, for example:

SOUTH	WEST	NORTH	EAST
1 ◇	DBL	P	1 ♠
2 ◇	?		

West must not raise with either hand. There are two dangers in raising; East may have a Yarborough and may be doubled; and East may bid more because he thinks West has a better hand. The former hand—♠ K 10 x ♡ A Q x x ◇ x x ♣ A K x x —is good enough to raise if partner responds one heart. A single raise shows four trumps and 16 to 18 support points. A raise to three hearts would show 19 to 20 support points—

♠ K Q x ♡ A Q x x ◇ x x ♣ A K x x

or

♠ A K 10 x x ♡ K J x x ◇ x ♣ K Q J.

"Barbara, suppose the opening bid is one diamond. Partner doubles and the next hand bids one spade. What would you bid with ♠ Q 10 8 x ♡ x x x ◇ x x ♣ A J x x?"

"Two clubs. I am strong enough, and I can't bid no trump without a diamond stopper."

"How well would you expect the opponents to do in spades?"

"Not very well if partner has spade strength, as his double indicates. I should double one spade for penalties, shouldn't I?"

"Yes, you should. Since you *wanted* to bid one spade, you should double. Otherwise, the opponents might tend to bid spades when they don't have them, just to keep you from getting to the right contract. Besides, a double, showing spade strength, best describes your hand. If partner does not have the spade strength he has implied, he will pull the double—perhaps by jumping to two no trump with

♠ x x   ♡ A K x   ◇ K Q x   ♣ K Q 10 9 x."

QUIZ

1. Are the final doubles in the following sequences for penalties or take-out, and why?

	SOUTH	WEST	NORTH	EAST
(a)	1 ♠	P	2 ♠	DBL
(b)	1 NT	P	P	DBL
(c)	1 ♡	P	1 NT	DBL
(d)	1 ♡	DBL	1 ♠	DBL
(e)	1 ♡	DBL	3 ♡	P
	P	DBL		
(f)	1 ◇	DBL	P	1 ♠
	DBL			
(g)	1 ◇	DBL	RDBL	1 ♠
	DBL			
(h)	1 NT	P	P	2 ◇
	DBL			

2. The bidding has been

SOUTH	WEST	NORTH	EAST
1 ◇	DBL	P	?

What should East bid with the following hands?

(a)	♠ J x x	♡ x x x	◇ x x x x	♣ x x x
(b)	♠ K x x	♡ K x x	◇ J 10 x x	♣ x x x
(c)	♠ A J x x	♡ Q x x x x	◇ x x	♣ x x
(d)	♠ x x x	♡ K x	◇ x x	♣ A J 10 x x x
(e)	♠ A x x x	♡ x x	◇ x x	♣ J x x x x

(f) ♠ K J x   ♡ x x   ◊ K Q 10   ♣ A J 9 x x

(g) ♠ Q x x x   ♡ x x x   ◊ x   ♣ A J x x x

(h) ♠ Q x x   ♡ A x   ◊ x x   ♣ A J 10 x x x

(i) ♠ K x x   ♡ x x x   ◊ J 10 x x   ♣ x x x

(j) ♠ K x   ♡ x x   ◊ Q J 10 9 6 4   ♣ J x x

(k) ♠ Q 10 x   ♡ A 9 x x x   ◊ x x   ♣ A Q 10

(l) ♠ K x x x   ♡ K x x x   ◊ A x   ♣ x x x

3. The bidding has gone:

SOUTH	WEST	NORTH	EAST
1 ◊	DBL	3 ◊	?

What should East bid with the following hands?

(a) ♠ J 10 x x   (b) ♠ Q x x x
    ♡ Q x x   ♡ K x x x
    ◊ x x   ◊ x x x
    ♣ A J x x   ♣ A x

(c) ♠ x x   (d) ♠ J 10 x x x
    ♡ K x x   ♡ x x x
    ◊ x x   ◊ x
    ♣ A J 9 x x x ♣ J x x x

4. The bidding has gone:

SOUTH	WEST	NORTH	EAST
1 ◊	DBL	P	1 ♠
P	2 ♠	P	?

What should East bid with the following hands?

(a) ♠ Q x x x x   (b) ♠ A x x x
    ♡ K x x   ♡ x x x
    ◊ x x x   ◊ Q J x
    ♣ Q x   ♣ x x x

(c) ♠ Q x x x x
   ♡ K J x x
   ◊ x
   ♣ Q x x

(d) ♠ J 10 x x
   ♡ Q x x x
   ◊ x x x
   ♣ A x

5. The bidding has gone:

SOUTH	WEST	NORTH	EAST
1 ◊	DBL	P	2 ♣
P	2 ♡	P	?

What should East bid with the following hands?

(a) ♠ K x
   ♡ x x x
   ◊ x x x
   ♣ K 10 9 x x

(b) ♠ K x x
   ♡ x x
   ◊ J x x
   ♣ A x x x x

(c) ♠ K x
   ♡ J 10 x
   ◊ x x x
   ♣ A 10 9 x x

ANSWERS

1. (a) Take-out double.

(b) Penalty double.

(c) Penalty double, theoretically. East will usually have a hand quite similar to when the bidding has gone one heart, pass, two hearts, double. In other words, he implies spade strength and a shortage in hearts. West will tend to pass the double with good hearts (Q 10 x x, for example, behind the opener) and to bid a suit without heart strength. Otherwise, declarer might make his contract with five or six solid heart tricks and an outside ace.

(d) Penalty double. Partner's double is equivalent to a bid. If you wanted to make him bid, you would bid two spades.

(e) Theoretically a penalty double because of the level. Partner must use his judgment, knowing that your first double was a take-out double, and you can't have very many hearts.

(f) Take-out double.

(g) Penalty double. Partner's redouble is equivalent to a bid. In fact, the reason he redoubled was that he hoped either you or he would be able to double whatever the opponents might bid.

(*h*) Penalty double. This appears to be an exception to the rule. Once partner has bid no trump, he can't have a shortage in diamonds. Besides, with a balanced hand and known strength, he would not insist upon your bidding, once you have failed to do so. He probably has such good diamonds, he expects to defeat the contract by himself. A probable hand:

♠ A x   ♡ K J x   ◇ A Q J 10   ♣ Q x x x.

2. (*a*) One heart.

(*b*) One no trump.

(*c*) One spade! East has a fairly good hand and he hopes to bid twice. However, if he bids hearts first, the bidding might continue:

SOUTH	WEST	NORTH	EAST
1 ◇	DBL	P	1 ♡
3 ◇	P	P	?

after which East would be too weak to show the spades (a reverse) and perhaps force the bidding to the four-level if partner preferred hearts.

(*d*) Three clubs.

(*e*) One spade.

(*f*) Three no trump.

(*g*) One spade.

(*h*) Two diamonds—too strong for three clubs. Plan to bid clubs next round.

(*i*) One heart

(*j*) Pass.

(*k*) Two diamonds. Failure to cue-bid would limit your hand.

(*l*) Two diamonds—a slight stretch. Actually, the way most experts play, when you force the doubler to show his suit, and you raise, he can pass with a bare minimum hand. If you play that way, the cue-bid is not an overbid.

3. (*a*) Three spades (barely).

(*b*) Four diamonds. This is an overbid, but it looks as though partner is short in diamonds, and the hands fit well. The alternatives are worse. If you bid three of the wrong major, you may do worse than if you were to be in four of the right major.

(*c*) Four clubs.

(*d*) Pass. A free bid here could be misleading. Partner needs an exceptionally strong hand for you to make game.

4. (*a*) Four spades. Partner has 16-18 support points, and the hands should fit well. If part of your strength were in diamonds, you would be more conservative.

(*b*) Pass. Your diamond strength will probably be opposite partner's singleton or doubleton.

(*c*) Four spades. You belong in game, and spades should be as good a contract as any.

(*d*) Three hearts. You have just enough to try for game. Partner can best judge what to do if you show your second suit.

5. (*a*) Three hearts. If partner had opened the bidding, you would want to keep the bidding open with this hand. Your first bid promised nothing.

(*b*) Three hearts. Same reason. Partner's hearts should be good.

(*c*) Four hearts. If you raise to three as a chance-giving bid, when you have this much you should go all the way.

CHAPTER 17

Competitive Bidding

"In the last two lessons we have been considering problems of defensive bidding—that is, the problems of the side which does not open the bidding. In this lesson we shall again identify ourselves with the side which opens the bidding, but shall consider the special problems created by the defender's bidding.

"Jerry, when an opponent overcalls, how would you expect responder's bidding to be affected?"

"You have told us to respond with as few as 6 points because opener might have 20. When the opponents keep the bidding open, opener will have another chance to bid with a powerful hand. Consequently, I should think that responder would only bid when he really wants to."

"When should responder *want* to bid?"

"I don't know. Responder would need 9 or 10 points to offer any assurance that his side has a preponderance of strength, since opener may have only 11 high-card points plus distribution. But should responder assume that opener has a bare minimum hand?"

"No, it does not pay to be so pessimistic. Nor is it necessarily right to keep quiet when the strength is evenly divided or when the opponents have a slight superiority of strength. Suppose the full hand is as follows:

NORTH
♠ A x x x
♡ x x
◇ K x x
♣ A Q x x

WEST
♠ J 10 x
♡ K 10 x x
◇ J 9 x x
♣ K x

EAST
♠ x x
♡ A Q J x x
◇ A x
♣ J 10 x x

SOUTH
♠ K Q x x
♡ x x
◇ Q 10 x x
♣ x x x

"North-South can make two spades; East-West can make two hearts. The strength is as evenly divided as possible. North will open one club and East will overcall one heart. Suppose that South passes. West will raise to two hearts. What can North do? Should he stick his neck out with his minimum hand? It would be much safer for South to bid one spade on the first round than for North to take action when South passes."

"In the example," said Jerry, "opener fit responder's suit. What happens when the hands don't fit?"

"Nothing disastrous," I replied. "Let's give North a real minny without a spade fit and see how the bidding would go.

NORTH
♠ A x
♡ x x
◇ K x x
♣ K J 10 x x x

WEST
♠ J 10 9 x x
♡ K 10 x x
◇ J x x
♣ A

EAST
♠ x x
♡ A Q J x x
◇ A x x
♣ Q x x

SOUTH
♠ K Q x x
♡ x x
◇ Q 10 x x
♣ x x x

```
                          NORTH
                          ♠ x x
                          ♡ K 10 x x
        WEST              ◇ K x x              EAST
    ♠ A J 10 9 x          ♣ A K x x        ♠ x x
    ♡ x x                                  ♡ A Q J x x
    ◇ J x x               SOUTH            ◇ A x x
    ♣ J 10 x              ♠ K Q x x        ♣ Q x x
                          ♡ x x
                          ◇ Q 10 x x
                          ♣ x x x
```

"In the first example, the bidding starts one club, one heart, one spade. West would probably bid three hearts. North would be glad to pass, and the result would be the same as if South had stayed out of the bidding altogether. If West should pass the one-spade response, North would make his normal rebid of two clubs. West would surely raise hearts rather than let North play two clubs. The point is that North-South were never in danger.

"In the second example, if South should pass, West and North would also pass. East can make one heart; possibly two hearts. If South responds one spade, North will rebid one no trump. He may or may not make one no trump, depending upon the diamond- and heart-spots and how the play goes. Whether North makes his contract or is down one, it is much better for him to play the hand than to let his opponents make part-score.

"As you can see from these examples, a fairly light response will gain when opener fits the suit and seldom does any harm when the hands do not fit."

"Was I wrong then? Should responder completely disregard the overcall?" Jerry asked.

"No, you were entirely right in your first statement. He doesn't have to keep the bidding open on minimum values, and a bid by responder shows he *wants* to bid. But he should usually want to bid with 8 points, or even 7 points, when the strength is concentrated. Thus, after a club-opening and a heart overcall, responder should bid one spade with

♠ K Q x x ♡ x x x ◇ x x x x ♣ Q x

or

♠ A Q J x ♡ x x ◇ x x x x ♣ x x x.

He should pass with

♠ Q x x x ♡ Q x x x ◇ Q x ♣ J x x."

"What does responder bid when the overcall prevents him from making the bid he would have made otherwise?" asked Jerry.

"Responder has four choices. He can pass; he can make the bid he intended to make, except at a higher level; he can make a different bid; or he can double the opponents. We shall discuss the latter alternative in a few minutes. Responder's choice will depend both upon his general strength and how he anticipates the bidding will continue. Let's look at some examples. In each case the opening bid has been one club, and there has been a one-heart overcall. Henry, what would you bid with

♠ J x x ♡ J x x ◇ K Q x x ♣ J x x?"

"I would like to keep the bidding open with 8 points, but obviously I am not strong enough to bid *two* diamonds. Nor do I want to bid one no trump without a heart stopper. I suppose I would pass."

"What would you bid with

♠ J x x x ♡ x x ◇ K Q x x x ♣ Q x?"

"I would bid one diamond without the overcall, because my spades are weak, and I don't want to play spades unless partner can bid them. However, I would rather bid one spade than pass with 8 high-card points."

"What would you bid with

♠ J x x x ♡ A x ◇ K Q x x x ♣ Q x?"

"Since I am strong enough, I would bid normally, that is, I would bid two diamonds, my longest suit."

"You are just barely strong enough. A skip-level response, like a two-diamond response over one club, may force partner to rebid at the three-level. Furthermore, he expects you to bid again. Consequently, such a response should show at least 12 points, either basic points or support points for partner's suit, which you intend to support later.

"What would you bid with

♠ x x x   ♡ A x   ♢ K Q x x x   ♣ J x x?"

"Judging by what you just said, this hand is slightly too weak to bid two diamonds. A pass is out of the question, so I suppose my choice is between one no trump and two clubs."

"Right. Either bid would be acceptable, although I slightly prefer two clubs.

"An overcall," I continued, "may compel you to raise partner with less than normal trump support and more than normal side strength. However, a major raise should be made whenever you have a normal raise. You would raise one heart to two hearts with ♠ x x   ♡ K x x x x   ♢ x x   ♣ Q J x x or

♠ x x x   ♡ K x x   ♢ x x   ♣ A x x x x,

and you should raise even though an opponent overcalls one spade or two diamonds. With

♠ x x   ♡ K J x x   ♢ x x   ♣ A J x x x

you would have raised to three hearts without the overcall. The overcall should not change your decision. With

♠ x x x   ♡ K x x   ♢ x x x   ♣ Q J x x,

you would not have raised hearts—you would have responded one no trump—and you still should not raise hearts after an overcall. A minor 'free raise'—called 'free' because you don't have to bid just to keep the bidding open for partner—should show the same sort of hand as a major free raise, except that it should guarantee at least 6 high-card points. After

NORTH	EAST	SOUTH	WEST
1 ♢	1 ♠	?	

do not bid two diamonds with

♠ x x x   ♡ x   ♢ K J x x x   ♣ x x x x,

even though you would have raised without the overcall. The reason for this change in requirements is difficult to explain.

"Do you remember the advice to make a free raise to two clubs with ♠ x x x ♡ A x ◇ K Q x x x ♣ J x x? In case of competitive bidding, opener won't know what to do if the free raise has a range of 4 to 10 or 11 high-card points. With only 4 points and distributional support—such as

$$♠ x x x \quad ♡ x \quad ◇ K J x x x \quad ♣ x x x x—$$

in order to be able to outbid the opponents with your minor suits, partner needs a very strong hand—probably 19 or 20 points. With a strong hand like that, he will do more bidding, and you can support enthusiastically after warning him by your original pass of your lack of defensive strength."

"You haven't told us about a free no-trump response," said Alice. "What are the requirements?"

"As Henry indicated earlier, it shows a stopper in the opponents' suit and about 9 or 10 points—similar to a no-trump response to one club. The reason for raising the requirements is that you don't want to play one no trump with half or less than half the high-card strength when the opponents have a long suit which will be led. With the head start from the opening lead, they usually establish and cash the setting tricks before you can establish and cash your seven tricks. A non-jump two-no-trump bid—

PARTNER	OPPONENT	YOU
1 ♠	2 ◇	2 NT

shows 11 or 12 points and is not forcing. Also, as we shall soon see, it almost invariably shows a good fit for partner's suit; otherwise, you would double.

"In the last lesson you learned that

PARTNER	OPPONENT	YOU
1 ♡	1 ♠ or 2 ◇	DBL

is a penalty double. You are asking partner to pass so that you can set the opponents. What sort of hand do you need for this double? The requirements depend upon the level of the opponent's overcall. At the two-level, you need (1) three-plus defensive tricks—three probable tricks with a little something left over; (2) at least a king or 4 points outside the suit overcalled; (3) a sliding scale of high-card points depending upon your trump holding; a minimum of 8 points with two sure trump tricks, 9 points with two potential trump tricks—like Q 9 x x— 10 points with one trump trick, 11 points with no trump trick; (4) a poor fit for partner's suit unless you are very strong in the opponents' suit. At the one-level the second requirement is the same, but you need four defensive tricks, and you always need a good trump holding with at least two potential trump tricks."

"How are 'defensive tricks' counted?" asked Alice. "Will we learn a new point count?"

"No, you won't learn a new point count. You will just estimate the tricks you will take, which you are all capable of doing at this time. Any ace is one trick. A king is a trick unless it heads a five-card suit or longer—or three-card suit, if it is the one partner bid. Trump tricks are figured as though the honors are favorably placed. Q J x x is two tricks—after the ace and king are gone, the queen and jack will be high. K J 10 x is three tricks. The queen may come up on the left, but you are gambling that it is on your right or in partner's hand. K Q x of a side suit may be counted as two tricks, which you will usually take whether partner or the overcaller has the ace. For queens, a singleton in partner's suit, honors in long side suits, you just have to use your judgment.

"Let us consider some examples. You hold

$$\spadesuit \text{ Q x x x } \heartsuit \text{ x x } \diamondsuit \text{ K J 8 x } \clubsuit \text{ K x x}$$

and the bidding has been

PARTNER	OPPONENT	YOU
1 ♡	2 ♢	?

The second, third and fourth requirements for a double are surely met. What about winners? You have two 'sure' trump

winners. In fact, I would count two and a half. If partner has
as much as the nine-spot, and if the A Q 10 are on your right,
you will take three tricks. Or you may get a heart ruff. The king
of clubs is a probable winner. That makes three and a half, and
the queen of spades is at least a plus value. Perhaps it would
be more accurate to rate the king of clubs four fifths and the
queen of spades two fifths, but we don't want to be bothered
with odd fractions, or to try for an accuracy which does not
exist. Anyway, we have three and a half plus winners when all
we needed was three plus. This is a recommended double. Take
away the queen of spades and you should pass. You have enough
winners but not enough high cards. (However, this is a borderline decision and many fine players would double anyway.)

"You hold ♠ A x x ♡ x x ◇ K Q 10 9 ♣ A x x x, and the
bidding is the same. This hand obviously meets all the requirements. Some players would bid three no trump because they
are too lazy to defend. This is a foolish bid for two reasons. In
the first place, you ought to slaughter the opponents at two
diamonds, doubled, and get more points than you could ever
hope for by bidding game. In the second place, game is not
certain; it is merely probable. The diamonds are stopped well
enough, but there may be a weak spot in the hand, probably in
spades. You would hate to lose not only the penalty you have
coming, but your game besides.

"Barbara, would you double a two-diamond overcall with
♠ K J x x x ♡ x x ◇ K 10 x x ♣ K x?"

"Yes."

"Is there any danger in doubling—I mean, besides the usual
danger that the opponents may have a freak hand with a seven-
or eight-card suit?"

"The danger I see is that partner may have a good spade
fit. We might set the opponents one or two tricks when we could
make a game in spades."

"With that thought in mind, would you still double?"

"I believe so. Partner may not have a spade fit. He is unlikely
to have four spades when he opens with one heart. Even if he

does have the sort of hand with which I could make four spades, we may set the opponents enough to compensate for our game. If I fail to double, the opportunity will be gone forever, and we may play a part-score or a game-contract, down one, instead of scoring 300 points."

"Would you double with

♠ K x x x   ♡ x x   ◇ 10 x x x   ♣ A Q x?"

"I would certainly be tempted to, even though it doesn't meet the requirements. The alternative is to pass with 9 points."

"The requirements should not be followed too rigidly. I would optimistically call 10 x x x of diamonds a trump trick, figuring either that partner will have a diamond honor or that the ten will be promoted by heart leads. These are such good 9 points, I would pretend that they were 10. Change the hand to ♠ Q J x x   ♡ J x   ◇ 10 x x x   ♣ K Q x, and a pass would be correct. Would you double with

♠ A J x x   ♡ x   ◇ 8 x x   ♣ A Q x x x?"

"I don't think so. I don't like my diamond holding, and I have a good enough hand to bid three clubs. If my only alternative were a pass, I would double."

"Would vulnerability affect your decision?"

"It would be tempting to double if the opponents are vulnerable and we are not. However, under those conditions the overcall ought to be stronger. And if partner has a singleton or void in diamonds, the opponents may take eight tricks in the trump suit."

"Perhaps an overcall under these conditions of vulnerability should be stronger than otherwise," I said, "but you will miss a lot of good doubles if you always assume the opponents can make what they bid. Even the best players occasionally stick their necks out. As for partner's having a singleton or void in diamonds, you will soon learn that he is not compelled to pass your double. My recommendation is to double with this hand unless we are vulnerable and the opponents are not. It looks like a misfit hand with game our way not at all certain, and if partner passes the double, we should do quite well.

"Would you double a two-diamond overcall with

♠ J x   ♡ x x   ◇ K Q 10 9 x x   ♣ x x x?"

"You said not to double without defensive strength on the side."

"Why would I say that? Can't you defeat two diamonds?"

"The trouble is that either my partner or the other opponent will surely bid something else. The overcaller and I should have twelve diamonds between us. My hand is worth absolutely nothing at any contract except diamonds. It would be very embarrassing if I double two diamonds, the next hand bids two spades, and partner doubles that."

Then I asked, "Would you double with

♠ x x   ♡ K x x   ◇ K x x x   ♣ K J x x?"

"Not if partner opens with one heart. One of the requirements for a double is a lack of fit for partner or very strong trumps. I have neither.

"The fit for partner increases your offensive prospects and decreases your defensive prospects. Naturally, you would double if partner had bid one spade.

"Alice," I continued, "suppose that partner has bid one diamond and your right-hand opponent has overcalled one spade. Would you double with ♠ K Q 10 x   ♡ x x x   ◇ x x x   ♣ A x x?"

"Yes. This hand meets all the requirements including four defensive tricks."

"Would you double with

♠ K 7 x x   ♡ A Q x   ◇ x x   ♣ K x x x?"

"No, the spades are not good enough."

"Why do you need good spades?"

"You told us we did. Besides, if the opponent has A Q J 10 x x of spades, for example, we can't defeat him very badly, regardless of the rest of his hand. My spades should be strong enough so that I can be sure he doesn't have that holding."

"The opening bidder is expected to have three defensive tricks to leave in the double. With less than that, he should not pass. With a close decision, he should pass the double, holding two trumps, or take it out, holding a singleton. I believe it is safe to say he should never leave in the double with a void.

"The bidding has gone

SOUTH	WEST	NORTH	EAST
1 ♡	2 ♣	DBL	P
?			

with a holding of ♠ x x ♡ A K Q 10 x x ◊ K x x ♣ x x. Bid two hearts. Most of your strength is concentrated in hearts, and if either opponent has a singleton heart, your hand will not be worth much defensively.

"On ♠ Q x x ♡ A K Q 10 x ◊ K x x ♣ x x, you pass. With a shorter heart suit, there is more likelihood of cashing at least two heart tricks. The queen of spades could also be an important card.

"Now take ♠ Q x x ♡ A K Q 10 x ◊ K x x x ♣ x. This is an extremely close decision. My inclination would be to pass. After all, two clubs, doubled, is not game when made. If the singleton club were even the jack or ten, I would be delighted to pass. There would then be a likelihood of promoting a trump trick in partner's hand—in case he doubled with Q 9 x x, for example.

"Jerry, would you pass partner's double or bid two diamonds with ♠ Q x ♡ A K Q 10 x ◊ K x x x x ♣ x?"

"Bid two diamonds."

"Why?"

"The king of diamonds is less likely to take a trick defensively when five-long than when four-long. Also, with 5-5-2-1 distribution our offensive chances are better.

"What would you bid with

♠ A x ♡ A K Q 10 x ◊ K 10 9 x x ♣ x?"

"Pass. Now I have enough defensive strength."

"Yes, you have enough defensive strength, but your offensive

strength is quite good also. Remember, partner guarantees values
outside of clubs by his double. If he has

♠ x x x   ♡ J x   ◊ A Q x x   ♣ Q 10 x x,

for example, you probably defeat two clubs by one trick, while
you are cold for six diamonds. Rather than bid two diamonds,
which suggests that you are too weak to leave in the double,
bid three diamonds.

"When there is an overcall and responder does not bid, opener
still has a chance to rebid. Whether he does so or not depends
upon whether there is still a good chance for game, and whether
opener risks a big penalty by bidding again. Suppose opener
holds ♠ K Q 8 x x ♡ A x x ◊ A x x ♣ x x and the bidding
has been

NORTH	EAST	SOUTH	WEST
1 ♠	2 ♣	P	P
P			

"What would you bid, Henry?"

"I would pass."

"Why?"

"Opener has only about one point over minimum, and he has
no safe bid. Responder can scarcely have more than 9 points,
nor more than 6 with trump support. Any sort of bid risks a big
set, and can gain, at most, a part-score."

"Would you rebid two spades with

♠ K Q J 10 x   ♡ A x x   ◊ A x x   ♣ x x?"

"Yes."

"Why?"

"Because, although game is almost as remote as last time, a
rebid of two spades is comparatively safe. Neither opponent will
have good enough spades to double, and I can take six tricks by
myself."

"In the same sequence—one spade, two clubs, pass, pass—
would you rebid with ♠ A K x x ♡ K Q x x x ◊ Q x ♣ x x?"
I then asked.

"I believe so," he replied, "because there may still be a game.

Responder could easily have ♠ x x ♡ A x x x ◊ K 10 x x ♣ x x x
or ♠ x ♡ 10 x x x x ◊ x x x x ♣ A Q x."

"With ♠ A K x x x ♡ K Q x x ◊ K x x ♣ x, again it is advisable to reopen the bidding. The best is a double, allowing partner to pass if he has club strength, and to bid his best suit or support spades otherwise.

"This has been a long lesson and it is getting late, but I would like for us to consider one more situation because it is so common. What should the responder do after a take-out double? Suppose the bidding has been

PARTNER	OPPONENT	RESPONDER
1 ♡	DBL	?

If responder has a good hand—11 points or 10 points well-placed —he should redouble. Failure to redouble denies a good hand.*
A redouble *suggests* that he wants to penalize the opponents if possible, and it definitely guarantees that he will do *something* if the bid comes back around to him. If the bidding continues

OPENER	OPPONENT	RESPONDER	OPPONENT
1 ♡	DBL	RDBL	2 ♣

opener should double with four clubs or three good clubs. If unable to double, he should pass unless his hand is unsuitable for leaving in the double even if responder is able to double. Thus, opener would double with

♠ A x ♡ A K x x x ◊ x x ♣ J x x x;

he should pass with all balanced hands such as

♠ A x ♡ A K x x x ◊ J x x ♣ x x x

or

♠ K Q x ♡ K Q x x ◊ A J x x ♣ x x;

he may bid two hearts or two diamonds with

---

* One possible exception is when responder plans to double any bid the opponents make. With ♠ K Q 10 x ♡x ◊ K Q x x ♣ Q 10 x x, it is *permissible* to pass. However, you won't go far wrong if you *always* redouble with 11 points or more.

♠ x x ♡ A K Q x x x ◇ K x x ♣ x x

or

♠ x ♡ K Q x x x ◇ A K x x x ♣ x x.

"Of course, responder may not want to double the opponents. With ♠ A x x ♡ K Q x x ◇ K x x x ♣ x x, he will bid four hearts after the redouble; with

♠ A x x ♡ K J x x ◇ Q x x x ♣ J x,

he will bid three hearts after the redouble. An immediate three- or four-heart bid is pre-emptive and would show less defensive strength—fewer than 10 high-card points. Incidentally, after responder redoubles, a new suit by him is forcing for one round—in effect the redouble 'cancels' the double.

"Responder may pass the double, planning to take later action, when slightly too weak to redouble. Holding

♠ A x x x ♡ K x x x ◇ x x ♣ Q x x,

he should pass and plan to bid three hearts on the next round. An immediate three-heart bid is usually made on a poorer defensive hand, such as

♠ x x x ♡ Q J x x ◇ K J x x x ♣ x.

"Or with ♠ A x x x ♡ K x x ◇ x x ♣ Q x x x, he may pass, planning to bid two hearts on the next round. Since he has 9 points, it is unlikely that the opponents will bid to the three-level.

"With ♠ K Q 10 9 x x ♡ x x ◇ K J x ♣ x x, responder may pass the first time, planning to bid two spades later.

"Probably the most important rule of all—and the one that even good players sometimes fail to follow—is that with a mediocre hand, responder should try to show his strength right away while he safely can. He should raise partner's heart-bid to two with ♠ x x ♡ K x x x ◇ K x x x x ♣ x x or

♠ Q x x ♡ K x x x ◇ J x x x ♣ x x.

He should bid one no trump with

or

♠ Q x x   ♡ K x   ◇ Q x x   ♣ x x x x x

♠ K x x x   ♡ J x   ◇ A x x   ♣ x x x x.

This enables opener to compete or keep quiet, depending upon his hand. If responder does not bid right away with hands like these, he usually does not get another chance to bid—without sticking his neck out."

"Why not respond one spade with the latter hand?" asked Jerry.

"Because a new suit-bid is not forcing, responder having limited his hand by failing to redouble, and responder doesn't want to play spades with K x x x opposite two small. A suit-bid shows a suit good enough for an overcall, for example K Q 10 x or Q J x x x, and about 6 to 9 points."

QUIZ

1.

NORTH	EAST	SOUTH	WEST
1 ♡	2 ◇	?	

(a)	♠ A x x	♡ x x x	◇ Q J 9 8	♣ Q x x
(b)	♠ A x x	♡ x x x x	◇ K J 10 8	♣ Q x
(c)	♠ A x x x	♡ Q J	◇ 8 x x	♣ K x x x
(d)	♠ A x x x	♡ x x	◇ K 10 x	♣ A x x x
(e)	♠ A x x x	♡ x x x	◇ K 10 x	♣ A x x
(f)	♠ K x x x	♡ 10 x x x	◇ K 10 x	♣ K x

2.

NORTH	EAST	SOUTH	WEST
1 ♡	2 ◇	DBL	P
?			

(a)	♠ A x	♡ A Q J 9 x x	◇ x	♣ Q 10 9 x
(b)	♠ A x x	♡ K Q x x x	◇ x	♣ K J x x

(c) ♠ A Q x x x ♡ A Q x x x x ◇ x ♣ x

(d) ♠ A x x ♡ K Q 10 x x ◇ — ♣ A Q x x x

(e) ♠ A J x x ♡ K Q 10 x x ◇ — ♣ A Q J x

(f) ♠ K x ♡ A K Q J x x x ◇ x x ♣ Q x

ANSWERS

1. (a) Double.

(b) Double. Your diamonds are strong enough for a double despite the fit for partner's heart suit.

(c) Two hearts! I know this is unorthodox, but it is probably best. Either a double or pass could work out as well or better.

(d) Double.

(e) Two no trump. The heart fit makes this a poorer defensive, better offensive, hand. Partner may pass with a bare minimum.

(f) Two hearts.

2. (a) Borderline between bidding two and three hearts. Remember, partner usually has at least 9 points, not all in diamonds.

(b) Pass. No convenient place to run, and your hand is pretty close to a good leave-in. Besides, two diamonds, doubled, is not game.

(c) Two spades.

(d) Three clubs. Do not pass with a void.

(e) Three diamonds—obviously showing a powerful hand. There may easily be a slam.

(f) Three no trump—probably the safest contract. Partner may have ♠ Q 10 x x ♡ x ◇ Q J x x ♣ K J x x. Even if there are not four tricks off the top, there is a danger of a diamond-ruff at four hearts.

CHAPTER 18

Reopening Bids

"How many high-card points do the four players have together on each hand, Alice?"

"Forty."

"When one side has 25 or more, the other side usually stays out of the bidding altogether, or else makes one bid and keeps quiet thereafter. When each side has about half the high cards, the bidding is frequently quite competitive. It pays to compete when the strength is equally divided, because it is almost as serious a loss to let the opponents make a part-score when you could have made a part-score as it is to miss a game. Occasionally, even though partner never bids, you can tell by listening to the opponents' bidding that they have only about half the high cards, which automatically places your partner with the remaining strength. For example, suppose that you hold

♠ K Q 10 9 x x   ♡ x x x   ◇ x x   ♣ x x.

The bidding has been

OPPONENT	YOU	OPPONENT	PARTNER
1 ♡	P	2 ♡	P
P	?		

Let's see what you can figure out. Alice, what is the greatest number of rebid points which opener can have?"

"Sixteen, because with 17 he would bid again."

"Correct. Let's assume that he has the maximum of 16 rebid points. How many high-card points could he hold?"

"Fifteen at the most."

"Right again. The only way he could have as many high-card points as rebid points is for him to hold 4-3-3-3 distribution, and with that distribution and 16 points he would open one no trump. Consequently, opener should have 10 to 15 high-card points. How many support points does responder have?"

"He could have 10."

"How many high-card points?"

"He could have 10."

"Yes, it is possible, but more likely responder has 6 to 9 high-card points. Consequently, the opponents should have between 16 and 24 high-card points, leaving your side with 16 to 24 points. Since you have 5 points, partner should have 11 to 19 points."

"If partner had 19 points, wouldn't he have bid over two hearts?" asked Henry.

"Yes, he almost surely would have done so. Consequently, partner is much more likely to have 13 or 14 points than 17 or 18. Anyway, knowing that partner has some strength rather than a Yarborough makes it safe for you to bid two spades. Your spades are good enough so that you don't particularly care what partner's spade holding is. Quite likely the reason he failed to double two hearts was that he was short in spades—and of course, he didn't know that you had a good six-card suit. Partner's hand:

♠ J x   ♡ J x   ◇ A K x x   ♣ K J x x x."

"I can see that with these two hands it is better for us to play two spades than to let the opponents play two hearts," said Jerry. "If they bid three hearts, we have a chance to set them. But why be so fancy? Why couldn't the hand with the long spades bid one spade the first time, instead of having to figure out what partner has in order to bid *two* spades?"

"The reason is that an overcall should show more defensive strength. If you overcall one spade with 5 points and find partner with 13, he will either bid too much or double the opponents. If you pass the first time, and only enter the auction when partner is marked with strength by the opponent's bidding, partner will not be misled. He heard your original pass and will know that you do not have a normal overcall."

"Often I have known responders to pass 6- or 7-point hands. Their explanation is, 'I know partner could have 20 or 21 points, but that is very unlikely. He is more likely to have 13 or 14 and my response may get us too high.' The fallacy in such reasoning is this: If the cards lie so unfavorably for us that we can't make one no trump or two of our best suit, then the opponents can surely make something their way. It is better to be down one —surely undoubled—than to let the opponents play the hand and make a part-score. Very often you *can* make something your way, but cowardice permits the opponents to outbid you. For example:

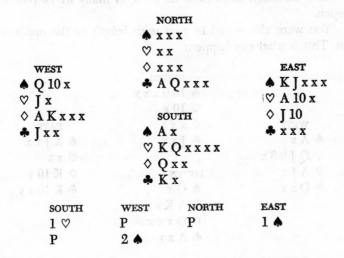

```
                    NORTH
                 ♠ x x x
                 ♡ x x
   WEST          ◇ x x x          EAST
 ♠ Q 10 x        ♣ A Q x x x    ♠ K J x x x
 ♡ J x                          ♡ A 10 x
 ◇ A K x x x      SOUTH          ◇ J 10
 ♣ J x x        ♠ A x           ♣ x x x
                 ♡ K Q x x x x
                 ◇ Q x x
                 ♣ K x
```

SOUTH	WEST	NORTH	EAST
1 ♡	P	P	1 ♠
P	2 ♠		

If North had responded one no trump, South would have rebid two hearts. Neither East nor West could risk a bid at the two-level. But North decided to pass, whereupon East bid one spade and West raised to two spades. This contract could not be defeated, and since South did not know about his partner's strength, he failed to put up the best defense. Consequently, East made three spades."

"East's one-spade bid looks rather risky to me," said Jerry. "You told us we needed more for an overcall."

"We were talking about immediate overcalls when responder

might have been strong. When responder passes, a 'reopening' bid can be made on a weaker hand. The opponents cannot have 26 high-card points between them—unless there is something wrong with their bidding!—and partner must have a few high-card points. In urging you not to overcall, especially at the two-level, with balanced 13- or 14-point hands, I said that if responder passed, partner would reopen with 12 points. That is true. He will bid with as few as 8 or 9 points when he has a good suit, and he will make a reopening double with 10 points and support for the other three suits. In other words, only when he has a balanced hand does he need as many as 12 points to reopen.

"You were also urged to pass with length in the opponent's suit. This is what can happen:

	NORTH	
	♠ 10 9 x x x	
	♡ 10 x	
	◇ x x x	
	♣ J x x	
WEST		EAST
♠ A x		♠ K J x x
♡ Q J 9 8 x		♡ x x
◇ A J x		◇ K 10 x
♣ Q x x		♣ K 10 x x
	SOUTH	
	♠ Q x	
	♡ A K x x	
	◇ Q x x x	
	♣ A x x	

SOUTH	WEST	NORTH	EAST
1 ♡	P	P	DBL
P	P	P	

"West should lead trumps, and declarer can only take his two high trumps and the ace of clubs. If West had doubled—as many inexperienced players would do—the chance for a 'killing' would disappear. East would bid two spades, and presumably a contract of three no trump would be reached. When East had a good hand, a pass by West worked out best. Now exchange the North and East hands so that we have:

NORTH
- ♠ K J x x
- ♡ x x
- ◇ K 10 x
- ♣ K 10 x x

WEST
- ♠ A x
- ♡ Q J 9 8 x
- ◇ A J x
- ♣ Q x x

EAST
- ♠ 10 9 x x x
- ♡ 10 x
- ◇ x x x
- ♣ J x x

SOUTH
- ♠ Q x
- ♡ A K x x
- ◇ Q x x x
- ♣ A x x

"A double by West would now result in a catastrophe. The final contract would probably be one no trump by West, doubled, down three tricks. This would be a very serious loss because North-South have no game. If they should reach three no trump, it would be defeated by a heart lead. If North were declarer, West would double for a heart lead. This is an advanced bid which will be briefly explained in the next lesson.

"Henry, in each of the following problems, the bidding has been the same:

SOUTH	WEST	NORTH	EAST
1 ♡	P	P	?

Tell me what you would bid in East's position. The first hand is ♠ K Q x x x ♡ x x x ◇ K x x ♣ J x."

"One spade. This looks like a near-minimum."

"How about ♠ K Q 10 x x ♡ x x x ◇ A K x ♣ x x?"

"I would bid one spade again. I don't have to have less than a normal overcall to bid in this position, do I?"

"No, but why didn't you double?"

"For the same reason I wouldn't double in second position. I don't want partner to bid two clubs."

"What would you bid with

♠ K Q 10 x x   ♡ x x x   ◇ A K x   ♣ K x?"

"Double. I believe that I am strong enough to bid two spades if partner responds two of a minor. This hand is so much better than the first one we were supposed to reopen with, I feel that I have to bid it more strongly. It is unlikely that partner can pass for penalties when I have three hearts, but if he *can* leave in the double, I will be delighted."

"How would you bid ♠ K Q 10 x x x ♡ x x ◇ A K x ♣ x x?"

"Two spades, just as I would in second position."

"How about ♠ x x ♡ Q J 9 x ◇ A K x x ♣ x x x?"

"Pass. For one thing, there is no satisfactory bid. If I double, partner will probably bid spades, and this is a very poor hand in support of spades. Besides, I don't expect partner to have a good hand."

"Why not?"

"The only time partner is apt to pass with a good hand is when he has length in the opponent's suit. He is hardly likely to be long in hearts when I have four of them myself."

"What would you bid with

♠ J x x   ♡ K J x   ◇ A Q x x   ♣ Q 10 x?"

"Double, I imagine. You said to reopen with 10 points and support for whatever partner might bid, or 12 points with a balanced hand. The extra points must compensate for the lack of distributional support."

"In this case, if your side can make game, what game would you expect it to be?"

"Three no trump looks most likely from my point of view."

"Your best bid is one no trump. That is also where you would like to play the hand when partner has a smattering of strength."

"Yes, I would like to bid one no trump, but what would I do with a real no-trump bid? I mean a 16- to 18-point hand."

"You have shown a very good grasp of the problem, Henry. It really is a problem to cover the entire range. Obviously, you can't make the same bid with 18 points that you make with 12. The way I handle the situation is to play a 12- to 16-point range for a reopening one-no-trump bid. With 17 to 18 points, I double and bid no trump the next time—even though this may result in reaching two no trump with 17 points opposite a possible Yarborough. With 19 to 20 points I reopen with two no trump. The 12- to 16-point range is a wide one, and there is danger in bidding two no trump by oneself with 17 points, but no one has found a better solution to this problem. What would you bid with

♠ x   ♡ x x x   ◇ A K 10 9 x   ♣ Q x x x?"

"Two diamonds."

"Can partner have a good hand with good spades?"

"No. He would either double or overcall."

"For that reason I recommend a pass. The four hands may be

```
                        NORTH
                        ♠ Q x x x x
                        ♡ x
        WEST            ◇ J x x              EAST
        ♠ J 10 x        ♣ x x x x            ♠ x
        ♡ K Q x                              ♡ x x x
        ◇ Q x x x       SOUTH                ◇ A K 10 9 x
        ♣ K J x         ♠ A K x x            ♣ Q x x x
                        ♡ A J 10 x x x
                        ◇ x
                        ♣ A x
```

Over your two-diamond bid, South would bid two spades and North would raise to four. This won't happen very often, but it is dangerous to reopen. If either side can make game, almost surely it is the opponents. Even more dangerous is to reopen when the opening bid is one spade and you are short of hearts.

"You know from the lesson on scoring and pre-emptive bidding that it is better to take a 300-point set than to let the opponents make a game. Of course, whenever you pre-empt, you don't know that you will take a set at all. The theory of a pre-empt is that when you have a long suit and little in the way of defensive values, you should bid more than you can make by yourself. If partner has a good hand, you will make your bid. If he has a mediocre hand, you will be down a trick or two, but the opponents may fail to double, or they may get to the wrong contract. If partner has a bad hand, the opponents can make at least a game and probably a slam. When you pre-empt, you are not taking a deliberate set; you must merely consider the possibility of being set. A different situation arises when the bidding indicates that the opponents have an almost certain game or slam, and you know that any bid you make will be set.

"Barbara, what would you bid in the following examples? In each case the opening bid was one heart, partner overcalled one spade, responder bid four hearts. Your first hand is

♠ J 10 x x x   ♡ x x x   ◇ x   ♣ Q J 10 x."

"Four spades."

"Do you expect to make four spades?"

"No, but we won't be set more than a trick or two, and we might possibly make it. With the opponents bidding hearts so vigorously, I suspect that partner has a singleton or a void."

"That is correct. When he holds

♠ A K x x x   ♡ x   ◇ K 10 x x   ♣ x x x

or

♠ K Q x x x x   ♡ x   ◇ K x x   ♣ K x x,

he will be down a trick or two, but the opponents can easily make four hearts. When partner has

♠ A Q x x x   ♡ x   ◇ Q x x x   ♣ K x x

or

♠ A K x x x   ♡ x   ◇ A x x x x   ♣ x x,

he may make four spades. There is also a chance that the opponents may bid five hearts and go down. With this type of hand it definitely pays to bid four spades, even though the odds are against your making it. What would you bid with

♠ J 10 x x x   ♡ x x   ◇ x x   ♣ A J x x?"

"I don't know. There is now slightly less chance of our making four spades, and slightly more chance of defeating four hearts. However, I think I would bid four spades anyway."

"Four spades is what might be called an 'insurance bid.' You are willing to pay a small premium to avoid a big loss. If you can defeat the opponents, you are unlikely to be down more than one yourself. If you are down one when you could have defeated the opponents one trick, no great tragedy results. When you sell out and let the opponents make four hearts instead of making four spades or taking a one-trick set, then you lose a lot of points. What would you bid with

♠ J x x x   ♡ x x   ◇ J x x   ♣ A K x x

or

♠ Q 10 x   ♡ x x   ◇ Q x x   ♣ A K x x x?"

"I think I would pass. Our chance of making four spades looks pretty slim, and we can probably defeat the opponents."

"Now I shall change the bidding.

SOUTH	WEST	NORTH	EAST
1 ♡	1 ♠	2 ♡	2 ♠
4 ♡	?		

"What would you do with the following hands?"

(a) ♠ K Q x x x x   ♡ x   ◇ A J 10 x x   ♣ x

(b) ♠ K Q x x x x   ♡ x   ◇ Q J x x   ♣ K x

(c) ♠ K x x x x   ♡ x   ◇ Q J x x x   ♣ K x

(d) ♠ J x x x   ♡ x   ◇ A Q J 9 x   ♣ x x

"With the first hand I would bid four spades, hoping to make it. With the second, I would also bid four spades. We probably won't make it, but nothing bad can happen. With the last two hands, I would pass. Four spades we might make, or it might be a good sacrifice, but if partner's hand doesn't fit mine or if the trumps break badly, it could be a disaster. We might lose control of the hand and be set four or five tricks."

"There is another matter which I would like to discuss with

you. It could have been made part of last week's lesson, but that was a long lesson and the subject matter fits in equally well here. Suppose you open with a one-spade bid and partner raises to two. When your sole objective is to reach game, you need 17 rebid points to bid again. But suppose that an opponent overcalls three clubs. Should the overcall affect your bidding, Alice?"

"Yes. I don't bid over two spades unless I want to suggest a game when the opponents are quiet—even when I expect to make three spades. But after the overcall I should bid again when I think we can make three spades—or even when I think I will be down one, provided I also think the opponents can make three clubs."

"If you are vulnerable, I don't think you should bid three spades unless you expect to make it," said Jerry. "Down one, doubled and vulnerable, is 200 points, which is more than the value of the opponents' part-score."

"You are not being very realistic," Henry said. "The opponents can't tell when to double. It is extremely dangerous for them to double for a one-trick set, because they will give you a game if they are mistaken. It looks to me as though you could compete with very little risk, especially when you have a good trump suit. The opponents hate to double without strength in trumps."

"Yes, but when you bid again in this spot, how can partner tell whether you have a good hand and are trying for game or whether you are just competing?" asked Barbara. "Perhaps you were going to make another bid even if the opponents had passed."

"Barbara has discovered the main problem," I said. "Let's see what suggestions she has to solve it."

"In the first place," Barbara said, "I can't see any excuse for opener to bid again with a bare minimum hand. He ought to have *something* extra. If he passes with a bare minimum, responder can compete without risk of a misunderstanding. Naturally, if opener passes he won't bid four when responder competes."

"Why not?" I asked.

"That would be highly inconsistent. Why should opener be

afraid to bid three spades—then suddenly decide to bid four when his partner scrapes up another bid? If opener is interested in game, he must bid over the overcall."

"All right, opener must not bid again with a bare minimum. How good a hand does he need?"

"I should think at least 15 rebid points, possibly 16. Then responder could afford to bid again with an absolute maximum raise. If responder can assume that a competitive rebid shows 15½ to 17 points instead of 17 to 18, he can still afford to raise with 10 points or even 9 points if it looks as though the hands will fit nicely. Sometimes you can tell better how the hands will fit when the opponents bid than you can when they pass."

"What do you mean?"

"Suppose I have Q x x of clubs, with my left-hand opponent bidding clubs. I would figure that queen of clubs was not going to be worth much if we play the hand. However, if I had a singleton club, I wouldn't expect partner to have much wasted club strength, so I would feel optimistic about my hand."

"You are anticipating the material we shall discuss next week. You are quite right, of course. Since you stated that the competitive rebid would show 15½ to 17 points, I assume that you would just gamble and jump to game with 18 points. Is that right?"

"In this case I wouldn't have to gamble. Our suit is spades and the opponent's suit is clubs. I could bid three diamonds or three hearts as a game-try, and save three spades as a competitive bid. But if the bidding were one spade, pass, two spades, three hearts, I believe I would gamble on four spades with 18 points."

"Let's get back to responder. When the bidding goes one spade, pass, two spades, three clubs, pass, pass, should responder always bid again?"

"No."

"When should he bid?"

"Any time he has a good trump holding—like Q 10 x x or any five trumps. As Dad said, when we have a strong trump holding, the opponents are unlikely to double. Also, when he has a maximum raise with three trumps he may take some action."

"Like what?"

"With

♠ Q x x　♡ K J x x x　◊ K x x　♣ x x,

responder should bid three hearts to offer a choice of contracts. With

♠ A x x　♡ A x x x　◊ x x　♣ 10 9 x x,

he should double."

"What should he bid with

♠ Q x x　♡ A x x x　◊ Q 10 x　♣ x x x?"

I asked her.

"Pass, probably. If we can make three spades, we can probably defeat three clubs. We might lose a few points by passing, but we won't risk a disaster."

"What do you mean by a disaster?"

"If the trumps are stacked and we take a 300- or 500-point set at three spades, doubled, that would be a disaster. It would also be a minor disaster if the opponents make three clubs when we can make three spades, but I've already decided that is very unlikely."

CHAPTER 19

The Facts of Life

"THERE comes a time in the life of any child when his parents must quit trying to shelter him, and must tell him the unpleasant —and pleasant—facts of life, so that he will be able to make his own way in the world. I believe you have reached that stage in your 'bridge life.'

"The first unpleasant fact is that not everyone plays as I have told you how to play. For example, some players make an opening no-trump bid with 12 to 14 points instead of 16 to 18. Others refuse to open a four-card major suit. There are many more variations, and it is beyond the scope of these lessons to discuss them. With only one exception, I have taught you basic bridge—the kind you would expect to play if you should wander into a bridge club and play with absolute strangers. This exception is what is called 'limit raises.' I have said that, in the sequence

OPENER	RESPONDER
1 ♠	3 ♠

responder's bid is not forcing. This is the way I play and the way many of the top experts play. It is also logical and easy to explain—a raise to three shows more than a raise to two, less than a raise to four. I am convinced that limit raises are far superior to forcing raises for beginners, average players and experts. But a majority of American players treat the double raise as forcing. So it is good to discuss this when you sit down opposite a strange partner.

"The next unpleasant fact is that the point counts you have

learned are not as accurate as you may have been led to believe. No one has been able to suggest anything better, but there are still several situations where you must use your judgment rather than count points.

"In the first place, aces and kings are slightly undervalued in relation to queens and jacks. Perhaps a more accurate point count would be: ace 4.3; king 3.1; queen 2.0; jack .9—or something like that. We don't want to be bothered with decimals and fractions, so we shall continue to use whole numbers. Nevertheless, whenever you have a borderline decision, you should be aggressive with strength mostly in aces and kings, conservative with strength largely in the form of queens and jacks.

"In the second place, the way your strength is concentrated is important. If you have J x x of hearts and partner has x x x of hearts, your jack is worth absolutely nothing. If either you or partner has other honors in the suit, your jack will probably be of value. J x x opposite Q x x or Q x constitutes a sure stopper at no trump, and you can establish a trick by force if the ace and king are in the same opponent's hand. When you hold J x x, you don't know whether partner will hold an honor in the suit or not; consequently, you do not know whether your jack will be of value or not. When you have Q J x, you know the jack will be a good card. Similarly, Q x x opposite x x or x x x is of very dubious value. When the queen is accompanied by the ace or king, it has an excellent chance of taking a trick. Dealer should pass with ♠ J x ♡ K Q x x ◇ K Q x x ♣ J x x, but should bid one heart with ♠ x x ♡ A Q J x ◇ K Q x x ♣ x x x. Does the latter hand look better to you?"

They all agreed.

"There is more to this matter of how honors are concentrated," I continued. "It is better to have honors in your long suits than to have honors in your short suits. There are several reasons for this. Suppose that you have the ace-queen alone of spades, and partner has the king-jack alone of spades. Together you have 10 points, but you can only take two tricks. If either of you had more length, you would be able to take more tricks—A Q x opposite K J or A Q opposite K J x x, for instance. Once partner bids the suit, your honors are worth full value. Until partner shows length in the suit, you should place a conservative value on such combinations. Or suppose you have a singleton king. If partner has the ace or the queen—plus one or more small cards—the king will be of *some* value. But if partner has only small cards in the suit, the king will be worthless. On the other hand, if you were to hold K x (x x), your king would be more valuable opposite high cards in partner's hand than opposite low cards, but even when partner cards are low, the guarded king may still take a trick if the ace is favorably located."

"I remember several lessons ago that you told us to raise partner's opening no-trump bid to game with

♠ x x   ♡ x x   ◇ A K x x x x   ♣ x x x,"

said Jerry, "but only to two with

♠ A K   ♡ x x   ◇ x x x x x x   ♣ x x x.

In that case, you said that it was easier to establish a suit that had strength in it."

"Yes, that is another reason for preferring strength in your long suit. The value of honors varies with the bidding. Suppose the bidding has been

PARTNER	OPPONENT	YOU	OPPONENT
1 ♡	1 ♠	2 ♡	P
3 ♡	P	?	

with a holding of ♠ K x ♡ J 10 x x ◇ Q J x x ♣ x x x. You have a close decision, but you should bid game, since the king of spades is probably behind the ace. If the bidding has gone

PARTNER	OPPONENT	YOU	OPPONENT
1 ♡	P	2 ♡	2 ♠
3 ♣	P	?	

you should definitely bid three hearts rather than four. Now the king of spades is quite likely to be worthless."

I then drew the following on the board.

PARTNER	YOU
1 ♡	1 ♠
2 ◇	2 NT
3 ◇	?

(a) ♠ K Q J 9   ♡ x x   ◇ J x x   ♣ K Q 10 x

(b) ♠ A x x x   ♡ Q 10   ◇ Q x x   ♣ A 9 8 x

"These hands show two extremes," I continued. "Hand (a), despite the 12 points and a ten-spot, is a terrible hand. Partner will have ten or eleven cards in the red suits, and you have only a jack to help him. Your black-suit holdings may be completely worthless to him, and they surely are not worth much. Hand (b) is ideal; every honor is of value. Let's give partner a typical hand for the bidding, to illustrate what I mean. Suppose that partner has ♠ x ♡ K J x x x x ◇ A K x x x ♣ x. Opposite dummy (a) this hand will have to struggle to make even three diamonds. There is at least one probable loser in each suit. Opposite dummy (b) this hand will have a good play for a slam in either of the red suits.

PARTNER	YOU
1 ◇	1 ♡
1 ♠	2 ◇
2 ♡	?

(a) ♠ J x   ♡ K J x x x   ◇ J x x x   ♣ Q x

(b) ♠ x x   ♡ K J x x x   ◇ K 10 x x   ♣ x x

"Would you rather have the 7-point hand or the 8-point hand, Jerry?"

"I prefer this particular 7-point hand."

"Why?"

"By bidding two suits and supporting my suit, partner has shown a pretty good hand with a probable singleton in clubs. Obviously, it is desirable to have points outside of clubs."

"The second hand is strong enough for a three-heart bid. The first hand should be passed.

"In the fourth place, the points awarded for distribution are not completely accurate to start with, and they become quite inaccurate as the bidding progresses. For example, in a previous lesson you were advised not to open 4-4-3-2 hands containing 12 points unless your strength was concentrated in two suits. It was permissible to open with ♠ K x ♡ A J x x x ◊ Q x x ♣ Q 10 x, which is supposedly worth the same number of basic points as ♠ K x ♡ A J x x ◊ Q x x x ♣ Q 10 x. The fact is that the fifth card of your long suit is worth slightly more than the fourth card of a side suit. That is particularly true in the case of a weak responding hand. Over partner's one-diamond bid, you should bid one spade with ♠ A J x x x ♡ x x ◊ x x x ♣ x x x, but you should pass with ♠ A J x x ♡ x x ◊ x x x ♣ x x x x. The latter hand is too weak for you to expect to be able to establish and use the four-card club suit.

"Usually, you prefer an unbalanced hand to a balanced hand. If anyone were to ask which opening bid were better, you would surely choose ♠ x ♡ A J x x x ◊ K Q x x ♣ K x x—15 basic points—over ♠ x x x ♡ A J x x ◊ K Q x ♣ K x x—13 basic points. But if partner were to keep bidding spades over your opening bid you would prefer the latter hand."

"Now that these inaccuracies have been pointed out," said Jerry, "what should we do about them?"

"Whenever you have a close decision, take all of these factors into consideration. Suppose that partner bids one heart and you hold the following hands:

$$\spadesuit \text{x x} \quad \heartsuit \text{Q x x x} \quad \diamondsuit \text{A x x} \quad \clubsuit \text{x x x x}$$

Bid two hearts. This is clear-cut.

$$\spadesuit \text{x x} \quad \heartsuit \text{Q x x x} \quad \diamondsuit \text{A x x} \quad \clubsuit \text{A x x x}$$

Bid three hearts. This is also clear-cut.

$$\spadesuit \text{x x} \quad \heartsuit \text{Q 10 x x} \quad \diamondsuit \text{A x x} \quad \clubsuit \text{K 9 8 x}$$

This time you have a close choice between bidding two and three hearts. Every card you have is a 'working' card—no wasted strength, like an unsupported jack, and your honors are not in your short suit. Even the ten of hearts may help. Consequently, you should bid three hearts.

"♠ Q x ♡ J x x x ◊ K J x ♣ Q J x x. This time you apparently have 11 support points as compared to 10 in the last example. While the decision is close, I prefer a single raise. Not only is your strength made up largely of queens and jacks; you have an unsupported queen in your short suit. If partner has A x x or x x x of spades, the queen is unlikely to do him any good. He can ruff the third round anyway. Only if partner has the king or ace-jack is the queen going to be of value. This is still another reason why it is better to have honors in long suits than in short suits.

"This time the bidding has been

OPENER	RESPONDER
1 ♡	2 ♡
3 ◊	?

and you hold ♠ x x ♡ x x x x x ◊ Q x x ♣ A x x. Despite possession of only 7 support points, you should bid four hearts, showing a maximum raise. Your hand is very strong opposite a two-suiter in hearts and diamonds. Five small of partner's suit is usually better than J x x x, even though it counts a point less. With ♠ Q x x ♡ x x x x x ◊ x x x ♣ A x or

♠ Q J x ♡ J x x x x ◊ x x x ♣ K J,

you should just return to three hearts.

"Let's give partner a hand consistent with his bidding:

♠ A x ♡ A K x x x ◊ K J x x ♣ x x.

Notice that partner has almost a cinch for four hearts opposite the first responding hand, a very poor play for four hearts opposite the latter responding hands.

"Proper evaluation is the key to competitive bidding. Suppose that the bidding has gone:

SOUTH	WEST	NORTH	EAST
1 ♡	1 ♠	3 ♡	3 ♠
4 ♡	4 ♠	?	

"Henry, what would you bid with the following hand?"

♠ K x x   ♡ J x x x   ◇ A x x   ♣ K x x

"I would double. The king of spades is probably worth a trick defensively, but will not be worth anything to partner if he plays the hand, since partner surely has no more than a singleton spade. This is a good defensive hand, and the opponents should be severely defeated whether or not we can make five hearts."

"What would you bid with

♠ x x   ♡ Q x x x   ◇ K J x x x   ♣ K x?"

"I don't know. This looks like a borderline case. My hand looks valuable to partner with no wasted strength in spades. However, we should set the opponents. I would feel stupid to bid five hearts and be defeated when we could have picked up 300 points."

"Is your choice between bidding five hearts and doubling?"

"Yes. I don't think the opponents can make four spades, and I don't want to let them play it undoubled."

"Won't partner realize that the opponents are beyond their depth? He still has another chance to bid."

"I never thought of that. Perhaps I should pass to imply that I don't care whether he doubles or bids five hearts, just so long as he doesn't pass. Is there any chance that he would pass if I pass?"

"No. Your pass would be forcing because the bidding clearly shows that your side has the balance of strength. What would you bid with ♠ x x x ♡ K x x x x ◇ K Q x x ♣ x?"

"This time I would bid five hearts myself, rather than pass the buck. This is a very poor hand defensively. My five-card heart length will prevent partner from taking more than one heart trick. Besides, this is a very good hand for hearts. Partner almost surely has a singleton or void in spades, and our hands should fit quite well."

"Jerry, suppose the bidding has gone as follows:

NORTH	EAST	SOUTH	WEST
Pass	Pass	1 ♡	Pass
2 ♣	Pass	?	

What would you rebid with

♠ K x x   ♡ A 10 x x x   ◇ Q x   ♣ Q J x?"

"Two hearts, I guess, although I don't like it. Perhaps I should not have opened this hand."

"Why would you rebid two hearts?"

"It is the weakest rebid I can make."

"Why do you rebid at all?"

"Because partner's bid is forcing."

"Why is it forcing?"

"Because I don't know how strong he is or what kind of hand he has."

"You know that he has failed to open the bidding. Doesn't that fact limit his hand?"

"Yes. It is extremely unlikely that we have enough combined strength for game."

"If you play a part-score contract, two clubs should be as safe as any other contract, shouldn't it?"

"Yes."

"Then why not pass?"

"I thought the two-club bid was forcing. But I can see now why it should not be forcing after partner has passed."

"You should seldom pass partner's response, even though it is not completely forcing. When you have more than 13 points you should rebid again; also, when you have a safe, convenient rebid. It was not safe to rebid two hearts with A 10 x x x, since partner might have to pass with a singleton or two small. It would be safe to rebid two hearts, regardless of outside strength, with A Q J x x. If the bidding is

SOUTH	NORTH
Pass	1 ◇
1 ♠	?

North should bid two spades with

♠ Q 10 x x   ♡ x x   ◇ A Q x x x   ♣ K x.

While a game is remote, it is still possible; South's hand may improve upon hearing about trump support.

"For example, he may hold

♠ K J x x x   ♡ x x x   ◇ K x x   ♣ A x.

Another reason for bidding again is that if you only make one spade, the opponents can probably make about three hearts or clubs, and they may reopen the bidding if you pass.

"Jerry, what would it mean for you to pass originally and jump to two no trump over partner's opening bid?"

"I would not have 13 to 15 points after failing to open the bidding. I imagine the bid would show 11 to 12 points—the sort of hand where I would normally bid a suit originally and two no trump on the second round."

"That's right. Now, Barbara, I have a defensive problem for you.

NORTH
♠ x x
♡ x x x
◇ K Q J x x
♣ 9 x x

WEST
♠ Q J 10 x x
♡ J x x
◇ x x
♣ K Q x

EAST
♠ x x x
♡ Q 10 x x
◇ A x x
♣ 10 x x

SOUTH
♠ A K x
♡ A K x
◇ 10 x x
♣ A J x x

"West's opening lead against three no trump is the queen of spades. South wins and leads the ten of diamonds. How must East defend in order to defeat the contract?"

"He must refuse to win the first two rounds of diamonds."

"Suppose the whole hand is as follows:

NORTH
♠ x x
♡ x x x
◇ K Q J x x
♣ 9 x x

WEST
♠ Q J 10 x x
♡ K 9 x
◇ x x x
♣ Q J

EAST
♠ x x x
♡ Q 10 x x
◇ A x x
♣ 10 x x

SOUTH
♠ A K x
♡ A J x
◇ 10 x
♣ A K x x x

"Now, how must East defend?"

"He has to win the second diamond. Otherwise, South will establish his club suit after having been allowed to win two diamond tricks."

"How can East tell that he should hold off till the third round of diamonds in one case, but should win the second round in another?"

"Perhaps the bidding will furnish a clue."

"In both cases the bidding is the same—one club, one diamond, two no trump, three no trump."

"The only remaining possibility is that West has some way of signaling to East."

"What is the most useful message West can give?"

"West can tell East how many diamonds he has. That way East can hold up his ace until South has no more."

"How would you suggest that West tell how many diamonds he has?"

"Since his diamonds are worthless, he can play low-high with a certain number and high-low with a different number. I shouldn't think the method would matter much, so long as both players agree upon the same method."

"The standard procedure is to play low-high, the normal order, with an odd number of the suit, and to high-low with an even number. In the first example, East will know, because of the high-low, that West had two or four diamonds—and the bidding indicates that it is two. Consequently, he will withhold his ace till the third round. In the second example, East will know that West has three diamonds from his failure to high-low. Consequently, there is no purpose in refusing to play the ace on the second round. The most common situation for the distributional signal is when there is a long suit in dummy, but it may occasionally be made in other situations.

"I have another problem for you, Barbara.

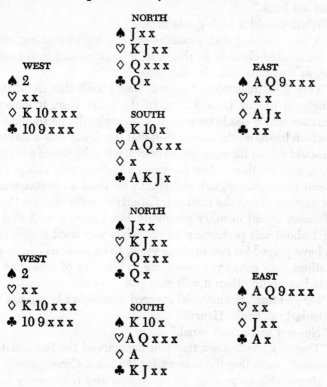

NORTH
♠ J x x
♡ K J x x
◊ Q x x x
♣ Q x

WEST
♠ 2
♡ x x
◊ K 10 x x x
♣ 10 9 x x x

EAST
♠ A Q 9 x x x
♡ x x
◊ A J x
♣ x x

SOUTH
♠ K 10 x
♡ A Q x x x
◊ x
♣ A K J x

NORTH
♠ J x x
♡ K J x x
◊ Q x x x
♣ Q x

WEST
♠ 2
♡ x x
◊ K 10 x x x
♣ 10 9 x x x

EAST
♠ A Q 9 x x x
♡ x x
◊ J x x
♣ A x

SOUTH
♠ K 10 x
♡ A Q x x x
◊ A
♣ K J x x

The bidding is the same for both examples' hands:

SOUTH	WEST	NORTH	EAST
1 ♡	Pass	2 ♡	2 ♠
4 ♡	Pass	Pass	Pass

In both cases, West leads his deuce of spades. East wins the ace and gives partner a ruff, declarer playing small. In the first example, West should return a diamond in order to get a second ruff. In the second example, West should return a club. Should West's proper return be a matter of guesswork?"

"No," Barbara replied. "There should be some convention to tell him which suit to return. If East can read the deuce as a singleton, he can return a high or a low spade to say what suit he wants led back."

"What should a high spade mean?"

"A high-ranking suit, probably—or the higher-ranking suit of the reasonable choices. In this case, a heart return could not be right, so that possibility is eliminated."

"Very good reasoning, Barbara! East knows that the deuce is a singleton or low from K x x. In the latter case, it makes no difference which spade he returns. Consequently, he should make his return based on the assumption that the deuce was a singleton. He should return the nine, or the queen, when he wants a diamond return, and the three when he wants a club return. This is called the suit preference signal, and it may be used whenever you expect partner to ruff the card led. Experts occasionally use the suit preference signal in other situations, but I recommend that you forget about suit preference except when you want a ruff, or till you have played for two or three years. Even then, its use in other situations may cause you more loss in the way of confusion and misunderstanding than it will gain you.

"Do you think the material covered in tonight's lesson has been particularly difficult, Henry?"

"No—not more than usual."

"That is an indication that you understand the basic material quite well, including the reasons for the rules. Consequently, you are almost able to predict the exceptions and refinements before I mention them to you. There is just one more matter to be discussed this evening. That is, doubles which influence the opening lead.

"When both sides have been bidding vigorously, a double of

the opponents' simply means that you think you can set them. If you have bid a suit, and the opponents reach three no trump, you expect to set the contract, provided your suit is led. Partner would probably lead your suit even without the double, so your double can hardly be called 'lead directing.'

"On the other hand, when the opponents bid a game or slam without serious competition from your side, they are seldom defeated by more than a trick or two. Also, a double, warning the declarer of bad breaks, may enable him to make a contract that he would not make otherwise. A double has little to gain unless it increases the chances of defeating the contract. A double under these conditions has a special meaning. If the opponents reach a slam after your overcall, the double says *not* to lead your suit or a trump. For example:

SOUTH	WEST	NORTH	EAST
1 ♡	Pass	2 ◇	2 ♠
3 ♡	Pass	6 ♡	DBL
Pass	Pass	Pass	

West must not lead a spade or a heart. He has to look at his hand and use his judgment in deciding between a club lead and a diamond lead.

"If you have not entered the bidding, the double asks for an *unusual* lead. Usually the doubler has a void and can ruff if his partner leads the right suit.

SOUTH	WEST	NORTH	EAST
1 ◇	Pass	1 ♡	Pass
1 ♠	Pass	4 ♠	Pass
5 ♠	Pass	6 ♠	DBL
Pass	Pass	Pass	

"On this bidding, a club—the unbid suit—would be the normal lead. The double says not to lead a club or a trump. If West has ♠ x x ♡ J x x x x ◇ x x ♣ Q J 10, he should lead a heart. East probably has a void in hearts. If West has

♠ x x   ♡ J x x   ◇ J 10 x x x x   ♣ Q x,

he must guess whether to lead a heart, hoping partner has the ace-queen, or a diamond, hoping partner is void. My inclination would be to lead the diamond. If partner has heart tricks, he may get them later. Besides, he would not be too anxious to double with heart strength, since he has no way of knowing how many hearts declarer has—also, he knows that he may get his heart tricks even without a heart lead.

"A double of three no trump—when the doubler's side has not entered the bidding—requests partner to lead dummy's first bid suit. The opening leader may disregard this request, but only for good reason. The double prevents games from being stolen in cases like the following:

```
                         NORTH
                         ♠ J x x x
                         ♡ x x
      WEST               ◇ A Q x x          EAST
      ♠ x x              ♣ A Q x            ♠ A K Q 10 x
      ♡ K J x x x                           ♡ 10 x x
      ◇ x x              SOUTH              ◇ x x
      ♣ J 10 x x         ♠ x x              ♣ 9 x x
                         ♡ A Q x
                         ◇ K J 10 x x
                         ♣ K x x
```

```
                         NORTH
                         ♠ Q 9 x x
                         ♡ K x x
      WEST               ◇ K x              EAST
      ♠ x x              ♣ A J x x          ♠ K J 10 8 x
      ♡ 10 x x x x                          ♡ A x
      ◇ x x              SOUTH              ◇ Q J x x
      ♣ K 10 8 x         ♠ A x              ♣ 9 x
                         ♡ Q J x
                         ◇ A 10 9 x x
                         ♣ Q x x
```

SOUTH	WEST	NORTH	EAST
1 ◇	Pass	1 ♠	Pass
1 NT	Pass	3 NT	DBL

"In the first example, without the double, West would lead a heart, allowing declarer to take the first ten tricks. In the second case, the double is quite risky. Responder might have 16 points and redouble. But the double pays off this time since the spade lead, followed by a spade continuation, sets the contract. With passive defense, declarer could easily establish nine tricks."

QUIZ

1.

NORTH	SOUTH
1 ♡	2 ♣
2 ◇	2 NT
3 ♣	?

What should South bid with the following hands?

(a) ♠ K Q 10 x   ♡ x x   ◇ J x x   ♣ A J x x

(b) ♠ K x x   ♡ x x   ◇ Q x x   ♣ A J 10 x x

(c) ♠ Q 10 x   ♡ J x x   ◇ K x x   ♣ A J 10 x

(d) ♠ Q 10 x   ♡ J x   ◇ K x x x   ♣ A J 10 x

(e) ♠ A x x   ♡ J x   ◇ Q x x   ♣ K 10 9 x x

2. 1 ♡   DBL   4 ♡   4 ♠
    ?

(a) ♠ K x x   ♡ A Q x x x   ◇ K J x   ♣ J x

(b) ♠ K J 9   ♡ A x x x x   ◇ K Q 10   ♣ x x

(c) ♠ J x x x   ♡ A J 10 x x   ◇ A   ♣ A Q x

(d) ♠ 10 x x   ♡ A 10 x x x   ◇ x   ♣ A Q J x

3. Your hand (West) is ♠ J x x x x ♡ x x ◇ x x ♣ Q 10 x x.
What do you lead on the following bidding?

(*a*)

SOUTH	WEST	NORTH	EAST
1 ♡	Pass	1 ♠	Pass
2 ◇	Pass	4 ♡	Pass
5 ♡	Pass	6 ♡	Pass
Pass	Pass		

(*b*)

SOUTH	WEST	NORTH	EAST
1 ♡	Pass	1 ♠	Pass
2 ◇	Pass	4 ♡	Pass
5 ♡	Pass	6 ♡	DBL
Pass	Pass	Pass	

(*c*)

SOUTH	WEST	NORTH	EAST
1 ◇	Pass	2 ◇	2 ♠
6 ◇	Pass	Pass	DBL

(*d*)

SOUTH	WEST	NORTH	EAST
1 ♡	Pass	2 ◇	Pass
2 NT	Pass	3 NT	Pass
Pass	Pass		

(*e*)

SOUTH	WEST	NORTH	EAST
1 ♡	Pass	2 ◇	Pass
2 NT	Pass	3 NT	DBL
Pass	Pass	Pass	

4.

```
                    NORTH
                ♠ K 5 3
                ♡ 6 4
                ◇ K Q 10 8 4
                ♣ K 6 5
                                   EAST
                                ♠ 7
                                ♡ K J 8 5 2
                                ◇ A J 6
                                ♣ A 7 6 4
```

SOUTH	WEST	NORTH	EAST
1 ♠	Pass	2 ◇	DBL
2 ♠	Pass	3 ♠	Pass
4 ♠	Pass	Pass	Pass

Your partner leads the jack of clubs. Dummy plays low and you
encourage with the seven-spot. Declarer wins with the queen
and leads the three of diamonds. Partner plays the deuce and
dummy plays the queen. What do you play, and why?

ANSWERS

1. It might be helpful to show a couple of typical North hands:

♠ x ♡ A K x x x ◊ A 10 9 x ♣ K x x

and

♠ x ♡ A Q x x x ◊ K 10 9 x ♣ K Q x.

(*a*) Three no trump. The spades are well stopped.

(*b*) Three no trump. You only have a single stopper, but perhaps the club suit will run and you can take nine tricks. It should not surprise you if you are defeated. Partner's bid is forcing, and he may have a stronger hand than either example hand.

(*c*) Three hearts. To bid no trump in the face of partner's warning of a singleton spade would be quite foolhardy.

(*d*) Three diamonds. Surely the most reasonable alternative.

(*e*) Four clubs. With only 10 points, you expect to make five clubs if partner can raise; the hands fit well.

2. (*a*) Pass. There is too good a chance to defeat four spades for you to sacrifice; your chances are not good enough to double, however. Partner is not obligated to bid if you pass, because the bidding does not indicate that your side has the balance of strength. Partner's four-heart bid is pre-emptive; with a good hand, he would have redoubled.

(*b*) Double. The opponents may make it, but the odds are in your favor.

(*c*) Six hearts. This is a gamble, but partner needs very little strength for a slam if he has a void in spades. If he has a singleton, he may have the king of clubs.

(*d*) Five hearts. You may make five hearts, and you are unlikely to defeat four spades.

3. (*a*) A low club.

(*b*) A spade.

(*c*) A heart. Declarer has a two-suiter for his bidding, and his second suit is probably clubs.

(*d*) Probably a spade. You will need a miracle, whatever you lead.

(*e*) A diamond.

Following are the hands which would justify the bidding. You can see for yourself how the recommended lead would work.

(*a*) ♠ A Q 9 x   (*b*) ♠ A Q 10 9 x x   (*c*) ♠ K x
     ♡ J 9 x x   ♡ Q 9 x x   ♡ x x x x
     ◊ Q 10 x   ◊ K x   ◊ K J x x x
     ♣ A x   ♣ x   ♣ x x

     ♠ K x   ♠ K x   ♠ A
     ♡ K Q 10 x x   ♡ A K 10 9 x   ♡ Q x
     ◊ A K J x   ◊ A Q x x   ◊ A Q 10 9 x
     ♣ x x   ♣ J x   ♣ A K x x x

           (*d*) ♠ K x   (*e*) ♠ A Q x
                ♡ x x   ♡ x x
                ◊ A Q J x x   ◊ K 10 x x
                ♣ J x x x   ♣ J 10 x x

                ♠ A Q   ♠ K x x
                ♡ A J 10 x x   ♡ A K Q x x
                ◊ x x x   ◊ x x
                ♣ A x x   ♣ K x x

4. The six of diamonds. Partner should have three diamonds when he plays the deuce. The duck will destroy a necessary entry for declarer. The whole hand is as follows:

                        NORTH
                       ♠ K 5 3
                       ♡ 6 4
        WEST   ◊ K Q 10 8 4   EAST
       ♠ 10 6 4   ♣ K 6 5   ♠ 7
       ♡ Q 10 9 3   ♡ K J 8 5 2
       ◊ 9 7 2   SOUTH   ◊ A J 6
       ♣ J 10 9   ♠ A Q J 9 8 2   ♣ A 7 4 3
                       ♡ A 7
                       ◊ 5 3
                       ♣ Q 8 2

CHAPTER 20

Slam Bidding With Balanced Hands

"HENRY, suppose that you can make eleven or twelve tricks, depending upon whether a certain finesse works. Should you bid a slam?"

"In the long run, it won't matter."

"Why not?"

"Because I gain just about the same number of points by bidding and making a slam as I lose by bidding an unmakeable slam. At least that is what Culbertson said."

"Is this true regardless of vulnerability?" Jerry asked.

"I think so. Is that right, Marshall?"

"Yes. It is easy to demonstrate when both sides are vulnerable, because you gain 750 points by bidding a slam and lose 750 points when you bid six spades, for example, and make only five. You lose the 650 points you would have made, plus another 100 points as a penalty. In other situations, there is an invisible value for scoring a game or for already being vulnerable which complicates matters, but the odds are still approximately the same. What odds do you need for a grand slam?"

"Two to one in favor of making it."

"Right again. If all that you need to make seven is to get a 3-2 suit break, it is theoretically proper to bid it. However, when you need trumps to split 3-2, and a side suit to split no worse than 4-1, the odds are not good enough. Accurate grand-slam bidding is very difficult, and my advice to you is to forget about grand slams till you have had much more experience. Barbara, does knowing the odds on bidding small slams suggest a workable test to apply?"

"During the bidding, if I think a slam will either be a lay-down or may require a finesse, I should bid it. If I think the slam will require at least a finesse and perhaps a little additional luck, I should stop at game."

"That is the test I use," I said. "It may be difficult to apply during tonight's lesson on balanced hands, but you will use it frequently next week. When both hands are balanced, you need a combined total of 34 points for a good small slam, although you should not mind getting there occasionally with 33. Suppose that partner opens one no trump and you hold

♠ A Q x ♡ K J x ◊ K 10 x x ♣ K J x.

You have 17 points plus a ten-spot in your long suit, and partner has *at least* 16. There is no purpose in dilly-dallying. Just bid six no trump. Change the hand to

♠ A Q x ♡ K J x ◊ Q x x x ♣ K J x.

Now if partner has 16 points, you will have just 32, not enough for a good slam. On the other hand, he may have 18 points or even 17 plus some tens and nines or a five-card suit, in which case you would like to be in six. What would you bid, Alice?"

"Five no trump, I imagine. Partner could either pass or bid six."

"You have the right idea, but it is better to bid just four no trump. If partner passes, four no trump should still be quite safe. It is undesirable to play five no trump, since you may occasionally be set with bad breaks, and there is no reward for your bravery when you make it.

"It is easy to add up points when partner bids no trump, either right away or later. Alice, you hold

♠ K Q x x ♡ x x ◊ A J x ♣ K Q x x.

Partner opens one diamond and rebids two no trump over your one-spade response. What do you bid, and why?"

"I bid six no trump. Partner is showing about 19 points, and I have 15."

"You open one heart with

♠ x x ♡ K Q 10 x x ◇ A K x ♣ A Q x

and partner responds two no trump. What is your hand worth at no trump?"

"Nineteen points. The good five-card suit is worth at least one point."

"So what would you bid?"

"Four no trump."

"Obviously, responder should bid six with 15 points and should pass with 13. What should he bid with 14?"

"I don't know."

"Barbara, what do you think?"

"It depends upon how his points are made up."

"Let me give you some example hands. What should responder bid with ♠ A K J x ♡ x x ◇ Q J x ♣ K x x x?"

"He should pass. The worthless doubleton in hearts is a bad feature, and there is no particularly good feature to compensate for it."

"What about ♠ A Q x ♡ A x x ◇ J x x ♣ K 10 x x?"

"This hand is worth bidding a slam. There is an extra ten, and it is in a long suit. There is a good fit for hearts, and the points are made up mostly of aces and kings. The only bad feature is the unsupported jack of diamonds, and I believe I have enough values to go to six, even without that jack."

"What should responder bid with

♠ A K x ♡ J x x ◇ Q x x ♣ K J x x?"

"He should again bid six. The jack of hearts is more important than any other jack, and the other jack is in my long suit."

"When both hands are balanced, you are mostly concerned with how many points are in the two hands. When one hand has a long suit, a slam can be made with fewer combined points, provided partner has a fit and mostly aces and kings on the side. When partner opens one no trump, you were advised to raise to four with ♠ A Q x ♡ K J x ◇ Q x x x ♣ K J x. Holding ♠ A Q x ♡ K J x ◇ Q x x x x ♣ K x or

♠ A Q x ♡ K x ◇ Q x x x x x ♣ K x,

you should respond three diamonds before bidding four no trump. That way partner will pass, even holding certain 18-point hands without a diamond fit, and will bid six with 17 or even 16 points if he has the right sort of hand. He cannot evaluate his hand properly until you show him your suit.

"With ♠ K J x ♡ A Q 10 x ◇ A x ♣ Q J 10 x, he would bid six if you were to raise directly to four no trump, but he will pass if he knows you have a five- or six-card diamond suit for part of your values. Similarly, he would bid six no trump with ♠ K x x ♡ A Q x x ◇ A K x ♣ J 10 x, or six diamonds with ♠ x x ♡ A x x x ◇ A K x x ♣ A J x, if you show your diamond suit before bidding four no trump.

"Sometimes responder has the sort of hand that will be worth more if a suit fit can be found—for example,

♠ K Q x x ♡ x x ◇ A Q 10 x ♣ A J x.

Over an opening no-trump bid, he should bid two clubs. If opener rebids two spades, responder may raise to six spades, since the heart-ruff should produce an extra trick. (Point-wise, this hand contains 17—I'd revalue and call it 18—support points for spades.) If opener does not rebid two spades, responder can still raise to four no trump.

"Slam bidding would be very easy if both hands were always balanced. Let us now consider the situation where one hand is balanced and the other is not. Barbara, suppose that partner opens one no trump and you hold

♠ x ♡ K Q 10 x x x ◇ A J x x x ♣ x.

Which do you think would be more practical—for you to seek information from partner and place the contract, or for you to describe your hand and let him place the contract?"

"The latter. Partner has already described his strength and distribution. The important thing for me is to know whether his strength is mostly in my two suits or in the other two suits. I don't see how partner can tell me that, or how he even knows what I want to know, unless I describe my hand to him."

"How will you describe your hand?"

"I'll jump to three hearts and plan to bid diamonds next time."

"Will that tell partner that you have 6-5-1-1 distribution?"

"No, not necessarily. But partner still should be able to tell whether his hand will be useful."

"How should the bidding go if partner holds

♠ K Q 10   ♡ J x x   ◇ K Q x   ♣ K Q x x?"

"He will bid three no trump over my three-heart bid and four hearts over four diamonds. Then I would give up on slam."

"Suppose partner holds

♠ A J x x   ♡ J x x   ◇ K Q x   ♣ A J x."

"He would probably rebid three no trump, but when I bid four diamonds, he would realize that he had a good hand for me. I don't know just what he would bid. Five hearts?"

"Yes, that looks to me like the right bid. What should he bid with ♠ A J x ♡ A x ◇ K Q x x ♣ Q x x x?"

"Six diamonds. This is a gamble, but if I were just to bid five diamonds, partner wouldn't know my hand is good."

"Suppose you don't feel like gambling. How could you say to partner, 'I have a good hand for you and good diamond support, but I am not sure whether we belong in five or six'?"

"I could bid four spades or five clubs."

"Which would you choose?"

"Four spades. I might as well show where my side strength is."

"Why not show your club *length* rather than your spade *strength*?"

"Because my club length will not be of any value to partner, while my spade strength probably will be."

"Would a four-spade or five-club bid guarantee good support for diamonds?"

"Not necessarily. I might have good support for hearts. Partner will assume I have diamond support unless I return him to hearts later."

"Then why didn't you bid four spades or five clubs over four diamonds a while ago, with

♠ A J x x ♡ J x x ◇ K Q x ♣ A J x?"

"I didn't know about the bid then. Besides, which should I bid when I have the ace of both? If I bid clubs, partner may worry about the ace of spades; if I bid spades, he may worry about the ace of clubs. Since I can't show both, which should I show?"

"Your original suggestion to bid five hearts is best," I said. "Since you cannot show both side-suit controls, it was proper to show neither. Suppose that partner shows a red two-suiter and you have ♠ A 10 x ♡ A x x ◇ K Q x ♣ A x x x for your opening no-trump bid. What would you do?"

"I'd go wild with this hand. Can I just bid seven?"

"It would be slightly risky to bid seven. Partner might have ♠ — ♡ Q J x x x x x ◇ A J 10 x x ♣ x, in which case seven would depend upon a finesse. Even an expert partnership might have difficulty in reaching seven scientifically with these hands. My advice to you is to forget about grand slams and just bid six. And it would be very easy to bid six after responder has shown his two suits.

"Sometimes responder has a hand that is too weak to take really aggressive action. Suppose he holds

♠ x ♡ K Q 10 x x x ◇ A J x x ♣ x x.

A slam is possible if opener has just the right sort of hand. But even if opener raises three hearts to four—which is more encouraging than a three-no-trump rebid—responder still can't afford to bid beyond the game level. Five hearts will not necessarily be safe, and furthermore, opener may accept the invitation when a slam will not make. So responder intends to pass a raise to four hearts, or to bid four hearts—or perhaps four diamonds, if he is feeling reckless—over a three-no-trump rebid.

"Suppose opener has

♠ J x x ♡ A x x x ◇ K Q ♣ A K 10 x.

This is very strong for a raise to four hearts, and the best bid is four clubs, which says, 'Partner, I could have raised you to four hearts—obviously I don't want to play clubs!—but I am a little strong for that bid. So I'll show you where some of my strength is. If you were even *thinking* about a slam, I want to offer some encouragement.'

"If responder had ♠ x x ♡ A J x x x ◊ K J x x ♣ x x, and was merely giving opener a choice between four hearts and three no trump, he would now bid four hearts, ending the auction. With the example hand, responder thinks a slam might be there if opener's cards are located properly, so he goes along with the slam try by bidding four diamonds. Opener bids five diamonds, another encouraging bid—also implying that he doesn't have control of the spade suit. Responder can then bid six hearts, because he has a singleton spade."

"Wow!" said Jerry. "You went over that awfully fast."

"The main principle is of wide application. Suppose that both partners know that the hand should play in a certain suit. If either partner knows what the limit of the two hands is—in other words, if he knows what the final contract should be—he just bids it. For example:

OPENER	RESPONDER
1 ♠	3 ♠
?	

"If opener has ♠ A Q x x ♡ K Q x x ◊ Q x x ♣ x x, he should pass. With ♠ A Q x x ♡ K Q x x x ◊ K x ♣ x x, he bids four spades. With ♠ A Q x x x ♡ A Q x x x ◊ K x ♣ x, he bids four hearts, not in an effort to find a heart contract since a nine-card spade fit has already been discovered, but to suggest a slam.

OPENER	RESPONDER
1 NT	3 ♡
?	

"Opener should bid three no trump with

♠ A Q x ♡ x x ◇ K J x ♣ A Q x x x

or

♠ K J x ♡ Q x x ◇ K Q x ♣ A J 10 x.

He should bid four hearts with

♠ A Q x ♡ K x x ◇ A x x ♣ A x x x

or

♠ K J x ♡ Q x x x ◇ Q x ♣ A K J x.

But when he has a maximum raise with good controls—

♠ A x x ♡ K x x x ◇ A Q x x ♣ A x—

he should bid something other than four hearts to show interest in bidding more. What should he bid, Jerry?"

"Four diamonds, since diamonds are where most of opener's strength lies."

"How should the following be bid, Alice? Write the bidding on the blackboard and then explain it to us."

OPENER: ♠ A Q x x ♡ A x ◇ K Q x ♣ A K J x
RESPONDER: ♠ K x x x x ♡ K x x ◇ x x ♣ Q x x

OPENER	RESPONDER
2 NT	3 ♠
4 ♣	4 ♠
5 ♠	6 ♠

"The four-club bid shows that opener has a very powerful raise. The rest of the bidding is natural. Since spades are agreed upon by implication, perhaps opener should bid five hearts to show the ace instead of five spades."

"What do you think about that, Jerry?" I asked.

"Then responder might worry about diamonds. I believe the five-spade bid was right."

"Does anyone have any comments or questions?" I asked.

"Perhaps I am being unduly pessimistic, but it looks risky for opener to bid over four spades," said Barbara. "Responder may have just 4 or 5 points and no interest in slam."

"Can you think of a hand where five spades would be in jeopardy?" I asked.

"Yes. Responder may hold

♠ K J x x x ♡ J x ◊ x x x x ♣ x x,

for example. The two hands will make five spades more often than not, but I wouldn't want to be in five."

"Yet you would hate to miss a slam if responder has

♠ K x x x x ♡ K x x ◊ x x ♣ Q x x.

What is your solution?"

"Opener already showed a powerful raise and an interest in slam when he bid four clubs. It isn't necessary for him to tell the same story twice. Responder ought to bid six spades, or at least five, directly over the four-club bid."

QUIZ

1.

OPENER	RESPONDER
1 ♡	2 NT
3 ◊	3 ♡
4 ♣	?

What should responder bid with each of the following hands?

(a) ♠ K Q x ♡ Q x x ◊ Q J x ♣ A x x x

(b) ♠ A x x ♡ Q x x ◊ Q J x ♣ A x x x

(c) ♠ J x x ♡ K x x ◊ K Q x ♣ A 10 x x

2.

OPENER	RESPONDER
1 ♡	2 NT
?	

(a) ♠ K x ♡ K Q x x ◊ A K J x ♣ K x x

(b) ♠ K x ♡ K J x x x x ◊ A K x ♣ K x

(c) ♠ x ♡ A Q 10 x x x x ◊ A J x ♣ K x

3. OPENER   RESPONDER
        1 ♣   1 ◊
        2 NT   ?

(*a*) ♠ x x   ♡ K x x   ◊ A Q 10 x x   ♣ A 10 x

(*b*) ♠ x x   ♡ K x x   ◊ A K J 10 x x ♣ x x

(*c*) ♠ K x   ♡ Q J x   ◊ A J 9 x x x x ♣ J x

(*d*) ♠ x x   ♡ A x   ◊ K x x x x   ♣ A x x x

ANSWERS

1. (*a*) Four hearts. Partner's bidding, besides indicating an interest in a slam, shows a singleton or void in spades. Your king-queen will be wasted.

(*b*) Bid four spades. If partner has a singleton spade, the hands should fit well. If he has a void, the ace will be wasted. Your intention is to show a slam interest and the ace of spades, then leave the final decision to partner.

(*c*) Bid six clubs. This hand is a perfect fit. It is conceivable that partner has 1-5-4-3 distribution (not four clubs), in which case he will return to six hearts.

2. (*a*) Bid four no trump.

(*b*) Bid three hearts, to be followed by four no trump. Partner can evaluate his hand better when you show a long heart suit. He will then pass four no trump with

or
                ♠ A Q x   ♡ 10 x   ◊ Q J x x   ♣ A J 10 x

                ♠ Q J x   ♡ Q x x   ◊ Q J x   ♣ A Q J x,

but would bid six with

or
                ♠ A J x   ♡ A Q x   ◊ x x x x   ♣ Q 10 x

                ♠ A 10 x   ♡ Q x x   ◊ Q J x   ♣ A x x x.

(*c*) Bid four hearts. Three hearts would be forcing, so four hearts is a *mild* slam try, which shows a long heart suit and an unbalanced hand. About eighty per cent of the time, partner will pass four hearts but he will bid six with

♠ A x x   ♡ K x x   ◊ K x x x   ♣ A x x,

because he knows his aces and kings will be valuable.

3. (*a*) Bid six no trump.

(*b*) Bid four no trump. You have a long suit, but it is so good that you don't care particularly whether partner fits it or not. Even when he has two small diamonds, there may be a good slam; for example, he may hold

♠ A K x   ♡ A J x x   ◊ x x   ♣ A K x x,

in which case you will make six if either of two finesses works.

(*c*) Bid three diamonds, followed by four no trump. With a long, broken suit it is important to show it. Partner will pass with ♠ A J x x ♡ A K x ◊ x x ♣ A K x x or bid six with ♠ A J x ♡ A K x ◊ Q 10 x ♣ A 10 x x.

(*d*) Bid three clubs, followed by four no trump. When partner has a good club suit, you will usually belong in a club slam (♠ A K x ♡ K x x ◊ A x ♣ K J 10 x x). When his club suit is weak, four no trump will be high enough

(♠ A Q x   ♡ K Q x   ◊ A J x   ♣ K x x x).

CHAPTER 21

Slam Bidding With Unbalanced Hands

"BARBARA and I tried an experiment," said Jerry. "We removed the twos, threes and fours from the deck and dealt ourselves hands to bid. Removing the low cards gave us lots of slam hands. We bid slams just the same way we bid games. Our objective was to bid a slam with 33 or 34 points, and to stop at game with less. We counted rebid points and support points the same as we did for bidding games. It worked pretty well."

"Do you remember any hands that you would like to give as examples?"

"Yes. Here is the first hand.

OPENER	RESPONDER
♠ K x	♠ A Q x x
♡ A 10 9 x x	♡ K Q x x
◇ K Q x x	◇ A J x
♣ K x	♣ x x
1 ♡	2 ♠
3 ◇	3 ♡
6 ♡	

"The two-spade bid, followed by heart support, showed 17 or more support points, and opener has 17 basic points or 17 rebid points. Would you and Eddie Kantar have bid any differently?"

"Not on the first two rounds," I replied. "Instead of jumping to six hearts, opener would have investigated further. Responder could have had an even better hand, since three hearts in this sequence is not a limit bid. If responder has the missing aces and the king-queen of trumps, or five trumps to the king, opener would bid seven hearts."

"Can you really find out about all those cards?" asked Barbara. "Would you be able to bid seven if responder had ♠ A x x x ♡ K x x x x ◊ A x ♣ A x and to stop at six with ♠ A Q x x x ♡ K J x x ◊ A x ♣ A x?"

"Yes, we would. Already you can see that more is required for accurate slam bidding than just counting points. However, the way you and Jerry bid these hands is the way I recommend that you bid them. Remember my advice to forget about bidding grand slams till you are more experienced. Let's see another example, Jerry."

Jerry drew the following on the board.

OPENER	RESPONDER
♠ A Q x x	♠ K x x x x x
♡ K x	♡ Q J x
◊ A Q J x x	◊ x x
♣ x x	♣ A Q
1 ◊	1 ♠
3 ♠	6 ♠

"Opener's three-spade bid shows 17 to 18 support points. Responder has 16 rebid points after his suit has been raised. Consequently, the total must be at least 33 points, and probably more."

"Do you consider this a good slam contract?" I asked.

"Not particularly, since it depends upon a finesse."

"If the diamond finesse works, are you sure of making a slam?"

"Not positive. Someone might get a heart-ruff or even a diamond-ruff, but these possibilities seem rather remote."

"Still, the odds must be very slight against your making a slam. Don't be so discouraged, Jerry. I wish that were the worst slam I had ever reached. But suppose you were the opener and you knew that partner did not have the ace of hearts or the king of diamonds. Applying the test Barbara mentioned last week, you should stop at game, because you know that you would need at least a finesse and perhaps something more. Let's change the responding hand slightly so that the two hands are as follows.

OPENER	RESPONDER
♠ A Q x x	♠ K x x x x x
♡ K x	♡ A Q
◊ A Q J x x	◊ x x
♣ x x	♣ Q J x

Now six spades would be a terrible contract. Even if the opponents got off to the wrong lead and failed to cash their two club tricks, you would still need a diamond finesse and no worse than a 4-2 suit break. Yet, using the methods you two used, you would get to the same contract, six spades, wouldn't you?"

"Yes," Jerry admitted sheepishly. "I guess our method wasn't very good after all."

"The method is all right as a starting point; whenever the total point count approaches 33 points, you can consider a slam. In fact, you may consider a slam with quite a bit less strength, when it is well placed.

OPENER	RESPONDER
♠ A Q x x	♠ K x x x x
♡ x x x	♡ A x
◊ A Q J x x	◊ K x x
♣ x	♣ x x x

"These two hands will provide an excellent play for six spades, with a combined total of 27 points, counting distribution! Adding another 10 points, the king-queen of hearts and the king-queen of clubs, would scarcely improve declarer's chances. Let's look at Jerry's example again.

OPENER	RESPONDER
♠ A Q x x	♠ K x x x x x
♡ K x	♡ Q J x
◊ A Q J x x	◊ x x
♣ x x	♣ A Q

"For all practical purposes, this slam depends upon the diamond finesse. When the diamond finesse works, the slam will make, even when responder has

♠ K x x x x x   ♡ Q x x   ◇ x x   ♣ A x.

In other words, the jack of hearts and queen of clubs are completely wasted cards."

"Why would a method which works so well for game hands be so inaccurate at the slam level?" Jerry asked.

"In order to make a slam, not only do you need enough playing strength to take twelve tricks; you can't afford to lose two tricks. The point count is fairly reliable in telling you when you have enough tricks, but it doesn't tell you how many tricks the opponents can take. Let's suppose you have 28 high-card points and 5 distributional points. That gives you a total of 33 points, and it means that you probably have twelve potential tricks. But the combined point count in itself does not assure you that the opponents cannot take the first two tricks. The typical slam with unbalanced hands contains two good suits and just enough in aces, kings, and shortages in the remaining two suits to prevent the opponents from taking two tricks. The key to successful slam bidding is proper evaluation.

"Henry, partner opens one diamond and raises your spade-response to three. Which hand would you rather have,

♠ Q J x x   ♡ Q x   ◇ x x x   ♣ A Q J x

or

♠ K Q x x x   ♡ x x   ◇ K Q x   ♣ x x x?"

"The latter, because every card will be useful. In the first hand, the queen of hearts and the queen-jack of clubs may be worthless."

"What would you bid with each hand?"

"With the first hand, I would just bid four spades. With the second, I would bid four diamonds. Partner should realize that my four-diamond bid shows an interest in a slam, since I could hardly expect five diamonds to be safer than four spades."

"Henry, how can you even hope for a slam with 11 points when partner can have no more than 19?" Alice asked.

"Perhaps I am optimistic, but I think I can make a slam if partner has the right sort of hand."

"All right," I said, "suppose you bid four diamonds. Which hand should opener be more pleased to hold,

♠ A x x x   ♡ x   ◇ A J 10 x x   ♣ A J x

or

♠ A J 10 x   ♡ K J x   ◇ A J 10 x   ♣ A x?"

"He should prefer the former hand."

"Why?"

"Perhaps I am influenced by seeing the responding hand that goes with it. But the fifth diamond is very valuable, and there is little wasted strength on the side—just enough to prevent the opponents from taking two fast tricks. With the latter hand, the opponents may be able to take two heart-tricks with a lead through the king-jack. Ironically, the singleton, worth 3 support points, is stronger than the king-jack, which is supposed to be worth 4."

"Your analysis is entirely correct. Yet, I have often known players to bid a slam over a try by partner with hands like the second one, and they are utterly dumbfounded when the slam doesn't make. They say, 'You made a slam try, partner, and I had 19 points, the most I could possibly have. What more did you expect?' The fact is that they did not evaluate their hand properly for slam purposes."

"Can you give us some concrete rules?" asked Alice.

"Yes, there are two tests that I use to determine whether to look for a slam. The first is the rule of the ace and the king. Let me explain the logic behind it. As you know, 26 points normally provide a good play for game, and 33 points are enough for a slam, at least when the hands are unbalanced. If you have 26 points plus an ace and a king, your total is 33 points. Consequently, when you and partner have an ace and a king more than you need to bid game, you usually belong in a slam."

"It sounds to me as though we are, in effect, going right back to the point count," said Barbara.

"Yes. It may sound that way, but you will see that we apply the extra-king test very loosely. The basic rule is that when I have an ace or the equivalent more than I need to bid game, I should consider a slam. Then, provided partner's bidding has not ruled out the possibility of his having extra values or sufficient controls, I can make a slam try. If partner has an extra king or the equivalent—and very often this equivalent is just a good fit or no wasted cards—he can accept my invitation. Let's consider some examples. Partner opens the bidding with one heart, and you hold ♠ x x ♡ K Q x x ◇ A Q x x x ♣ x x. With 13 support points, you will insist upon reaching game. Strengthen your hand by an ace, making it ♠ A x ♡ K Q x x ◇ A Q x x x ♣ x x, and you should make a slam try. The proper way to do so is to jump to three diamonds and support hearts on the next round.

"Now suppose that partner bids one club, you respond one heart, and he raises to three hearts. Alice, would you make a slam try with ♠ x x x ♡ K Q x x ◇ A x x ♣ J x x?"

"No. If the ace of diamonds were changed to a small card, I would pass partner's three-heart bid. I don't have an ace more than I need to bid game."

"Right. Suppose that your hand were

♠ Q x x ♡ K Q x x ◇ A J x ♣ J x x."

"I suppose I should make a slam try, according to your new rule, since I would bid game without the ace of diamonds."

"Your common sense told you to settle for game, and your common sense was right. Partner cannot have more than 19 support points, and there is no possibility of an extraordinary fit, because if partner has a good club suit and a distributional hand, part of your strength will be wasted. Suppose partner raises your one-heart response to four, and you hold

♠ A x x ♡ A J x x x ◇ x x x ♣ x x.

Would you make a slam try?"

"I don't know. I might or might not have kept the bidding open without the ace of spades. But aces should be nice at a slam."

"While it is close," I said, "I recommend a further effort in the form of a four-spade bid. None of your strength will be wasted. Partner should not go to six if he has a balanced hand such as ♠ K x x ♡ K Q x x ◊ A x ♣ A K J x, but he may if he is distributional—for example, with

$$♠ x x \quad ♡ K Q x x \quad ◊ x \quad ♣ A K Q J x x.\text{"}$$

"Where is the extra king?" Jerry asked. "This hand has only 19 support points instead of 20. Besides, I see two losers."

"The extra-king value is in having powerful distributional support controls and no wasted values. Declarer's spade losers will be discarded on the club suit.

"Suppose that partner bids one heart and jumps to three hearts over your spade-response. What would you bid, Alice, with ♠ A x x x x ♡ K x x ◊ A Q x ♣ x x?"

"Six hearts. I have an ace and a king more than I need to raise to game."

"Very good. The rule of the ace and king is valuable on the ordinary sort of hands. When the hands become more distributional, there is a better method—one easier to use. You arbitrarily place cards in partner's hand, consistent with the bidding. Culbertson used to call this 'plastic evaluation,' because partner's high cards are fitted, like molten plastic, around your own hand. If it is hard for you to place the cards where you will not have a good play for a slam, just bid the slam yourself. If it is hard to place the cards where you will have a good play for a slam, forget about a slam. If you can think of some hands where a slam will be a lay-down and others where you don't want to be in a slam, try to describe your hand to partner so that he can evaluate his own hand.

"For example: You open the bidding with one spade, holding ♠ A Q J x x ♡ A Q x x x ◊ A x ♣ x, and partner raises to three spades. It is difficult to imagine any hand partner might have where a slam would depend upon more than the heart finesse, and it probably will be a lay-down. An expert would investigate grand slam possibilities, but my recommendation to you is just to bid six spades. With the same bidding sequence, change your hand to ♠ A Q J x x ♡ A Q x x x ◇ K x ♣ x. Applying our old rule, you easily have an ace more than you need to bid game. Applying our new form of evaluation, if partner has

♠ K x x x   ♡ K x   ◇ A x x x   ♣ x x x,

you will have virtually a lay-down slam. If he has

♠ K x x x   ♡ x x x   ◇ A x x x   ♣ K x

or

♠ K x x x   ♡ x x x   ◇ Q J x x   ♣ A x,

you will have no play whatsoever for a slam. So the proper bid is four hearts, showing the second suit. Responder would sign off with three small hearts and probably wasted strength elsewhere; he will bid five diamonds to show the ace when he has the fitting of hearts, and you will gladly bid six."

"Why does a five-diamond bid show the ace?" asked Alice.

"Opener would not be interested in diamond length or even diamond strength other than the ace when he is distributional. Usually after one player has made a slam try and a suit has been agreed upon, new-suit bids by his partner show aces.

"Now for another example: The bidding has gone

YOU	PARTNER
1 ♣	1 ♠
3 ♠	4 ◇
?	

"Your hand is ♠ A J x x ♡ K J x ◇ x ♣ A Q J x x. Bid just four spades. Partner needs the king-queen of spades—or six to the king—the queen of hearts, the ace of diamonds—which he has just shown—and the king of clubs for a lay-down slam. With all those values, he will continue bidding despite your discouragement. You are certain to have wasted values in hearts. You hold the same hand, but this time partner bids four hearts instead of four diamonds. The hand is somewhat better now, but even so, to have a good slam, he will need good spades, the ace of hearts and the king of clubs, which is too much to hope for—unless he bids again over your sign-off.

"Barbara, what would you bid in the following sequence?

OPENER	RESPONDER
1 ♣	1 ♠
3 ♠	4 ♡
?	

Your hand is ♠ A Q x x ♡ K x x ◇ x ♣ A Q J x x."

"I should think my proper bid would be six spades. Partner surely has one black king with his ace of hearts, in which case I would have a finesse for a slam. When he has both black kings or the ace of diamonds the slam will be a lay-down."

"What would you bid in the same sequence if your hand were changed to ♠ A K 10 x ♡ x x ◇ x x ♣ A K Q 10 x?"

"Five spades. Wouldn't this tell partner I thought we had enough strength for a slam but I was worried about diamonds, 'the unbid suit'?"

"Yes, it would. Generally speaking, you should try to make your slam tries below the game level so as to avoid five-heart and five-spade contracts. This time you can't help yourself, and five spades should surely be safe.

"In making and accepting slam tries, make a distinction between below-game and above-game bids.

OPENER	RESPONDER
♠ A Q x x x	♠ K x x x
♡ x	♡ A J x x
◇ A Q x x	◇ x x
♣ A J x	♣ Q 10 x

1 ♠	3 ♠
4 ◇	4 ♡
5 ♣	6 ♠

Responder's four-heart bid did not guarantee extra values. An ace should always be shown on the way to game after partner makes a slam try—unless you have some good reason for going out of your way to discourage partner. Opener has already made his slam try, and if he bids four spades, responder can still continue to bid with the right sort of hand. However, opener felt that he was strong enough for a second slam try beyond the game-level. Responder's hand does not look particularly good to him, but it is not particularly bad, either. After all, he has a doubleton diamond. So he accepts the second slam try even though he definitely would have passed if opener had rebid four spades over four hearts.

OPENER	RESPONDER
♠ A Q x x x	♠ K x x x
♡ x	♡ A x x x
◇ A Q x x	◇ K J x
♣ K J x	♣ x x
1 ♠	3 ♠
4 ◇	4 ♡
4 ♠	5 ◇
6 ♠	Pass

In this last example, responder takes the initiative because he has an excellent diamond fit and no wasted values.

"I'll give you your quiz questions in the usual way. It has been—"

"Surely that isn't all," Barbara interrupted. "What about the Blackwood Convention to find out about aces? And the convention you and Eddie use to find out about trump strength? And asking bids? Well, I suppose you consider some of these bids too complicated for us to use. But Blackwood is simple."

"What makes you think so?"

"I already know the responses, but I thought you would tell us when to use it; also when four no trump is Blackwood."

"I use Blackwood myself on occasion, mostly to find out about grand slams—which you are advised to forget about—and for perhaps one small slam out of ten. Using Blackwood is a lot like driving a car. An eleven-year-old boy can learn within a short time to turn corners as skillfully as you, but he won't have the judgment to know when to slow down and when to be alert for danger. Knowing when and when not to use Blackwood requires a great deal of judgment and experience; deciding when four no trump is Blackwood is a serious problem even for experts. I am firmly convinced that the average slam bidding efficiency in this country would improve within a short time if the Blackwood convention were prohibited. You will probably learn it from your friends and use it, but I won't bear the responsibility for leading you astray."

QUIZ

1. (*a*) The bidding has been

OPENER	RESPONDER
1 ◊	1 ♠
3 ♠	?

Rate the following responder's hands in the order of their slam potential.

♠ Q J 10 x x	♡ Q J x x	◊ x	♣ A K Q
♠ Q x x x	♡ K J x	◊ Q J x x	♣ K x
♠ K x x x x	♡ x x	◊ K x	♣ A x x
♠ K Q x x x x	♡ x x	◊ x x	♣ A Q x
♠ K x x x x	♡ x x x	◊ A J x	♣ x

(*b*) If the bidding continues

OPENER	RESPONDER
1 ◊	1 ♠
3 ♠	4 ♣

Rate the following opening hands.

♠ Q J x x	♡ K Q x	◊ A K J x x	♣ x
♠ K Q x x	♡ x	◊ A K Q J x	♣ x x x
♠ A Q J x	♡ x x x	◊ A Q J x x	♣ x

♠ A J 10 x	♡ K x	◇ A J x x x	♣ Q x
♠ Q J x x x	♡ Q x	◇ A Q J x x x	♣ —
♠ A K x x	♡ K x	◇ A J x x x	♣ x x

2. In the following bidding sequences, decide whether the South hand is worth a slam bid, worth a slam try, or not worth even a try. Also, if a slam try is called for, decide what would be the correct bid.

(a)

NORTH	EAST	SOUTH	WEST
1 ♡	Pass	1 ♠	Pass
4 ♠	Pass	?	

♠ A J x x x
♡ x x
◇ A x x
♣ x x x

(b)

NORTH	EAST	SOUTH	WEST
1 ♡	Pass	1 ♠	Pass
4 ♠	Pass	?	

♠ A J x x x
♡ Q x
◇ A x x
♣ x x x

(c)

WEST	NORTH	EAST	SOUTH
1 ♡	DBL	Pass	1 ♠
Pass	4 ♠	Pass	?

♠ Q x x x x
♡ x x x x
◇ A J x
♣ x

(d)

SOUTH	WEST	NORTH	EAST
1 ♡	Pass	4 ♡	Pass
?			

♠ A Q x
♡ K J x x
◇ K Q x x x
♣ x

(e)

NORTH	EAST	SOUTH	WEST
1 ◇	Pass	1 ♠	2 ♡
3 ♣	Pass	?	

♠ A x x x x
♡ x
◇ K x x x
♣ K x x

(f)

NORTH	EAST	SOUTH	WEST
1 ♠	Pass	2 ♠	Pass
4 ◇	Pass	?	

♠ A x x
♡ x x x x
◇ K 10 x x
♣ x x

(g)

NORTH	EAST	SOUTH	WEST
1 ◇	Pass	1 ♡	Pass
2 ♠	Pass	3 ♡	Pass
4 ♡	Pass	?	

♠ x x x
♡ K Q 10 x x
◇ K x
♣ x x x

(h)

NORTH	EAST	SOUTH	WEST
3 ♡	Pass	?	

♠ K Q x
♡ Q x x
◇ A K Q J x
♣ K J

(i)

SOUTH	WEST	NORTH	EAST
1 ♡	Pass	3 ♣	Pass
3 ♡	Pass	4 ♡	Pass
?			

♠ A x   ♡ K Q x x x x   ◇ x x x   ♣ K x

ANSWERS

1. (a)

(1)	♠ K x x x x x	♡ x x	◇ K x	♣ A x x
(2)	♠ K x x x x x	♡ x x x	◇ A J x	♣ x
(3)	♠ K Q x x x x	♡ x x	◇ x x	♣ A Q x
(4)	♠ Q J 10 x x	♡ Q J x x	◇ x	♣ A K Q
(5)	♠ Q x x x	♡ K J x	◇ Q J x x	♣ K x

(b)

(1)	♠ K Q x x	♡ x	◇ A K Q J x	♣ x x x
(2)	♠ A Q J x	♡ x x x	◇ A Q J x x	♣ x
(3)	♠ A K x x	♡ K x	◇ A J x x x	♣ x x
(4)	♠ A J 10 x	♡ K x	◇ A J x x x	♣ Q x
(5)	♠ Q J x x	♡ K Q x	◇ A K J x x	♣ x

2. (*a*) 5 ◊   (*b*) 6 ♠   (*c*) 6 ♠   (*d*) Pass   (*e*) 6 ◊
    (*f*) 6 ◊   (*g*) 6 ♡   (*h*) 4 ♡   (*i*) 6 ♡

Typical hands to justify bidding are as follows:

(*a*)

♠ K Q x x   ♡ A K J x x x   ◊ K x   ♣ x

(*b*)

♠ K 10 x x   ♡ A K J x x   ◊ K x   ♣ A x

(*c*)

♠ A K x x x   ♡ x   ◊ K x   ♣ A K J 10 x

(*d*)

♠ x x   ♡ A Q 10 x x x   ◊ x   ♣ Q x x x

(*e*)

♠ x   ♡ x x   ◊ A Q 10 x x   ♣ A Q J x x

(*f*)

♠ K Q 10 x x   ♡ —   ◊ A Q x x x   ♣ A x x

(*g*)

♠ A J x x   ♡ A x x   ◊ A Q J x x x   ♣ —

(*h*)

♠ x   ♡ A J 10 9 x x x   ◊ x x   ♣ Q 10 x

(*i*)

♠ x x x   ♡ A J x x   ◊ A x   ♣ A Q J x